5

# A HISTORY OF THE
# HOARE BANKING DYNASTY

## VICTORIA HUTCHINGS

CONSTABLE · LONDON

Constable & Robinson Ltd
3 The Lanchesters
162 Fulham Palace Road
London W6 9ER
www.constablerobinson.com

First published in the UK in 2005 by Constable, an imprint of Constable & Robinson Ltd

A copy of the British Library Cataloguing in Publication data is available from the British Library

ISBN 1-84119-965-6

Printed and bound in Italy

# CONTENTS

To the Customers of Hoare's Bank –

the other half of the story

# PREFACE

My father wrote the first history of our Bank and called it 'Hoare's Bank. A Record'. This was to use the word 'Record' in the senses both of recording events and achieving a record. After entering the Bank in 1923 he became increasingly fascinated by our longevity, and absolutely determined for us to continue.

Family banks were being sold left, right and centre at the time, notably Coutts in 1920 and Childs in 1924. There were enthusiasms for sale within our Partnership, especially from Arthur who had no children of his own and expensive habits such as shooting and yachting. Recording our history was part of my father's campaign to ensure that our Bank was not to be put up for sale.

With this motivation for writing the book it was not surprising that anything which did not redound to our credit received no mention, and in particular the very unsatisfactory events which occurred in the second half of the nineteenth century. Apart from anything else my father's own grandfather had lost all his money, and personal memories were too painful.

For this reason I have particularly enjoyed Tory's account of these times, and especially her part about Hoare's Brewery. The Brewery used hardly ever to be mentioned in conversations but at our recent Third of a Millennium party I learned more of how bitter resentments between members of the family must have been. Our cousin Victor Hoare told me that as a young man of about 21 he had gone in to our Park Lane branch to cash a cheque and found himself summoned in to a back room to meet the resident Partner, Col Geoffrey Hoare. Geoffrey then gave Victor a powerful ticking off because, alleged Geoffrey, Victor's grandfather had been responsible for losing Geoffrey's family share of Hoare's Brewery!

I do not think that my father would mind our linen now being washed in public. Time is a great healer. What would certainly absolutely delight him, as it does me, is to see the eleventh generation firmly in place, working away, not personally greedy, and coping successfully with technical complications which my generation, and the nine generations before, could never have contemplated. He would be proud of them, as am I.

Henry Hoare, 2005

# SIR RICHARD AND THE GOLDEN BOTTLE 1672–1719

Hoare's Bank owes its name and much of its character to its founding father Richard Hoare. As a young and recently qualified goldsmith he bought a business from his late master's widow in 1673 and, by a series of astute alliances, rose to become a highly regarded figure in the City of London. His surviving letters indicate a man rooted in his religious beliefs but driven by a desire for success. Throughout his career he displayed energy, determination and integrity, qualities which earned him a fine reputation and a profitable business, and which he took great pains to pass on to all his sons.

Richard's father, Henry, was one of several sons of a yeoman farmer who lived in Walton, Buckinghamshire. Henry and his wife, Sicilia, had come to London where Richard, their only son, was born in 1648. The family lived near Smithfield Market, where Henry made a respectable living as a horse dealer. He is reputed to have earned around £400 a year, which was about the annual income of a middling merchant of the times. In 1659 Henry bought a house in Chiswell Street, in the parish of St Giles Cripplegate, and was elected an Overseer of the Poor, an important post in local government involving the distribution of poor relief in the parish.

Nothing is known of Richard's early childhood or schooling, but from the manner in which he was to raise his own family we can guess that it was a household where religion provided the structure and the habit of hard work was expected. He was brought up at a time when the Bible was unchallenged as the source of all truth, and the hand of God was perceived at every turn. The Civil War in England had left a legacy of unresolved religious issues in the country. The Church of England with its bench of bishops and Book of Common Prayer was restored in 1660, and as Overseer Richard's father would have been compelled to

Sir R Hoare Kn Ol

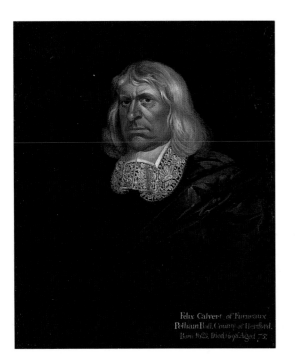

Felix Calvert of Furneaux
Pelham Hall, County of Hertford,
Born 1623, Died 1698 Aged 75.

*Felix Calvert of*
*Furneaux Pelham,*
*Hertfordshire, 1623-*
*1698. His name appears*
*as the opening entry in*
*the Bank's first current*
*account ledger.*

take the sacrament according to the rites of the Church of England; so Richard must have been raised to pledge his loyalty to the same church. However, many non-conforming groups of Protestant worshippers dissented from Anglicanism. There was also widespread fear that Roman Catholicism might be reimposed on the country, as it became increasingly likely that Charles II would be succeeded by his Catholic brother, James Duke of York. To protect the established church, the state imposed a series of penal legislative measures to limit the possibility of Non Conformists and Roman Catholics playing any part in civic society.

The earliest record of Richard's education is his indenture as an apprentice to the goldsmith Richard Moore in 1665, the year of the great plague which claimed the lives of more than one eighth of London's population. Perhaps on account of Moore's death, Richard was turned over to another City goldsmith, Robert Tempest, to complete his seven-year apprenticeship. On 5 July 1672 he was entered as a Freeman of the Worshipful Company of Goldsmiths and so permitted to trade in his own name. The date marked the beginning of Richard's career as a goldsmith. The timing was propitious. In 1672 Charles II's reckless spending compelled him to suspend paying interest on all government loans, half of which were owed to goldsmith-bankers. Referred to as the 'Stop' on the Exchequer, this action forced many of these lenders out of business including Oliver Cromwell's banker, Edward Backwell, and the King's financial confidant, Sir Robert Viner. Others such as Francis Child and Charles Duncombe survived the crisis, but enough of the competition had been removed to encourage Richard to purchase Robert Tempest's business when he died in 1673.

Some of the purchase would have come from his wife's dowry, for by then he had married Susannah Austen in Lincoln's Inn chapel. The couple chose to be married by licence rather than by the public reading of banns, in order to keep the ceremony private and avoid the necessity of being married during Divine Service on a Sunday witnessed by the entire congregation. Whether or not this was a love match, each had made a judicious choice. Susannah's father, John Austen, had been an Alderman and had owned a substantial house near Hornchurch in Essex. He had carried on his own business as a goldsmith at the sign of the Star in Fenchurch Street, and in 1667 had been elected Prime Warden of the Goldsmiths Company. This was not far from where Richard was working for Tempest, at the sign of the Golden Bottle in 'Goldsmiths Row', Cheapside, a stone's

Receipt, dated 11 July 1676, for the sum of £54 10s 10d, on the back of the earliest known cheque drawn on Richard Hoare. It was returned to the Bank 250 years after it was written.

throw away from the Assay Office at Goldsmiths' Hall in Foster Lane.[1]  (All businesses were identified by means of a sign before street numbering was introduced in the late eighteenth century.) Austen must have met the young apprentice and singled him out as a suitable match for his daughter; when he died in 1670, marriage plans between the two young people had already been agreed.

Richard's father had died in 1669 but his widowed mother survived her husband by six years. At her death her son and heir, Richard, inherited a legacy of £400 which, together with rents from property in the vicinity of St Martin's le Grand and West Smithfield, left to Susannah by her father, gave the young couple enough for a comfortable start to their married life at the sign of the Golden Bottle.

Goldsmiths at that time were not only makers and dealers in gold and silver wares, but also bankers for their customers. The term 'banker' was rarely used on its own before 1700. In 1677 a trade directory for the City of London entitled The Little London Directory named fifty-eight goldsmiths who kept what were known as 'running cashes', by means of which the goldsmith-banker took money on deposit and issued a receipt. These receipts, known as goldsmith's notes, were the prototype of the modern banknote, being payable on demand and circulated instead of coins. The goldsmith-banker lent money out at interest (in most cases) and also paid interest to his depositors. Richard suspended paying interest to depositors in order to finance interest-free lending which he used, with discretion, as part of his strategy for building up the business in the early years.[2]

By 1690 Cheapside had declined in popularity; so Richard moved his business to Fleet Street. The western district of the City reaching along Fleet Street where it joined the Strand at Temple Bar (the City boundary) was now, after Lombard Street where the goldsmith-bankers served the merchant population, the most

Receipt, dated 28 December 1677, signed by Fulke Bookey, Richard Hoare's head clerk 1676-81.

important focus for the goldsmiths' trade. It gave access to all types of customers: to local trades people with relatively modest requirements; to the lawyers in the Inns of Court (traditionally also the home of the Scriveners who in earlier times had performed many of the functions now assumed by the goldsmith-bankers); and to the wealthy country gentry and nobility who had their town houses in nearby Lincoln's Inn Fields and the newly developed squares of Bloomsbury and St James's. The Fleet Street goldsmiths' shops, all situated just within the City limits, carried on their trade making and selling plate and jewellery, avoiding competition from the Huguenot craftsmen, who had settled round the Court in Westminster, and the Jewish diamond cutters in Aldgate, who were classified as aliens and forbidden to compete with the Freemen of the City of London on their own territory.

London then was the largest capital city in Europe. At half a million inhabitants it had a greater population than Paris and it was a serious commercial competitor to its rival Amsterdam. Despite the high level of mortality — Richard and Susannah lost ten children, in infancy, of the seventeen born to them — its numbers were increasing, because of high levels of migration into the capital from the provinces and the arrival of Huguenots and other religious refugees from abroad. One in ten English people lived in London and perhaps one in six resided there at some time in their lives. Country gentry and members of the aristocracy came during the Parliamentary Sittings or to attend at Court. Those who were not MPs or courtiers came on matters of business and for the social and cultural experiences that only London could offer.

*Mortality Bill. A record of christenings and burials, and the causes of death, for the year 1684-85. Sir Richard and Lady Hoare lost ten of their children in infancy.*

This country clientele needed cash during their stay in the metropolis both to spend and to invest. In most cases the source of their income was their rural rents, so when they needed to move their cash to town, cattle and sheep drovers, who travelled regularly from around the country to the central markets, were used as couriers to carry up landlords' rents to London. There they would meet an appointed agent, often the landlord's banker, in the market or at a nearby inn, a receipt was handed over and the cash would then be safely deposited in the bank. In the absence of any form of co-ordinated banking system, cash and receipts payable on demand travelled up and down to London in the safekeeping of these trusted individuals in an attempt to meet the demands for ready money in both places.

The Bank's own records illustrate how the system worked. Sending a letter by 'The Northants bagg' to Francis Saunders Esq. at Brixworth, dated 13 June 1702,

Countess Fauconberg, 1637-1713, by Michael Dahl. Often referred to as 'Princess Mary' she was the daughter of Oliver Cromwell. She opened her account with Richard Hoare in 1680.

Richard explains he cannot entrust a bill for £150 to the post but 'There will be one Mr Morton a grocer which will be at Northampton faire which will pay £150 upon delivery of our note seeing your name on ye back of it, he is a very good and substantial man, he is known by most people thereabouts.' The regular payment of rents was never guaranteed and shortage of cash was a constant worry. A short-term solution to this problem was to bring silver plate to London in order to exchange it for guineas. Customers of high standing wishing to do this could expect a visit from Richard Hoare's clerk who would wait on them at their London address, weigh the silver and exchange it for its exact value in coin.

The nature of their stock-in-trade made the goldsmith-bankers very security-conscious and this meant they were able to offer their customers the reassurance that their money and precious goods would be safe while in their hands. This was a vital service at a time when the personal cheque or 'drawn note' was only just beginning to emerge as an alternative to carrying cash. Customers needed a place to store their money and precious possessions safely when they had no immediate use for them.

Richard Hoare not only kept valuables under lock-and-key for his customers but also acted as an intermediary after they had been lost or stolen. The London Gazette of the time carried frequent reports of robberies which were a constant threat to people travelling around the City's streets. Money and valuables were obvious targets: 'Lost on Saturday night a Gold Snuff box, engraven with Juno drawn in a chariot by peacocks' (5 January 1692 ); 'Lost on the 24th instant on

A tankard, c.1675-80,
a rare item of silver plate
known to have been
made by Richard Hoare.
A ledger containing the
Bank's trading records in
South Sea stock during
the 'Bubble' years. A
17th century leather
bottle adapted for use as
the Bank's 'shop' sign.

or near The Royal Exchange a letter case with 13 Exchequer Bills, 4 Bank Bills, current money and other valuables' (30 September 1697). The return of the lost items to 'Richard Hoare at The Golden Bottle over against St Dunstan's Church in Fleet Street' carried a reward; in the first case ten guineas was offered and in the second the reward was £20 or a proportion thereof if only part of the haul was handed in. Bank customers who were robbed in their homes also called on their banker to try to recover their losses. The Earl of Anglesey, Lady Morris, Sir Henry Goodrick, The Earl of Burlington, Earl Fauconberg and Lady Stringer all had engraved plate stolen and offered rewards payable by Richard Hoare for the arrest of the culprit as well as the return of the goods.

Robbery with murder was dealt with in the same way. After the murder of The Duke of Hamilton and Brandon in 1711 Queen Anne offered a reward of £500 for the arrest of the suspect George Macartney to which the Duchess, through Richard Hoare, added a further £300. An unusual case concerned the kidnap of an heiress, the eleven-year-old Mary Burrows who 'was taken by force out of a calesh', on 21 May 1692, in the 'forest of Sherwood, by three persons upon bay horses, armed, one of middle stature, bow legged, with his own hair, dark brown, with a blue coat laced or embroidered on the sleeves'. News of the child brought to Richard Hoare would carry a reward of £10 with expenses. Thieves were usually caught as a result of information supplied by a fellow-goldsmith when stolen goods were brought into his shop to be valued, sold or pawned.

The Golden Bottle kept its own stock of plate and jewellery. The ledgers record items made for 'ye shop', mostly fashionable pieces for visiting customers. The bulk of the goldsmithing business came from orders to make new plate or refashion old plate and for this Richard would use his extensive network of journeymen-goldsmiths and engravers. The Bank's 'Goldsmiths work Books' of the period are a catalogue of this trade in luxury goods. There were personal items such as boxes for combs, powder and patches, silver buttons, rosewater bottles, chamber pots, toothpicks, embroidered gloves and dog collars and the usual complement of household plate: porringers, teapots, tankards, trencher plates, sconces, candlesticks, sugar casters, chafing dishes, salts, snuffers, pepper boxes, looking glasses, basins and ewers, andirons, monteith dishes, candle boxes, sand boxes, cups, covers and stands, knives, forks and spoons − and so the list goes on. A frequent entry is for silver plate sent in to be melted down or 'boyled for the shop'.

'The shop' employed the leading craftsmen of their day. Benjamin Rhodes was one of the engravers of heraldry who worked for Richard, and his notebook of armorial designs covering the period 1693-98 is preserved in the Bank's archives, a rare survival. Two items engraved by Rhodes for Richard Hoare are still in the possession of their original owners. The goldsmith John Bodington made up precisely 17,753 oz 14dw (penny weight) of silver into articles ordered by Richard between 1697 and 1701. For this he was paid £733 10s 10d. One of the commissions was for a 'Knurl'd Cup and Cover' for Trinity College, Cambridge, engraved with the College arms and those of the donor Henry Boyle, MP for the University and later Chancellor of the Exchequer. Under a similar arrangement through Richard Hoare, Godfrey Clarke gave a smaller cup and cover engraved with the arms of the donor and college to Magdalen College, Oxford. Charles II's consort Catherine of Braganza sent several pieces of 'old plaite'. Judge Jeffreys, when Lord Chancellor, sent in a gold snuff box to be coloured while Samuel Pepys, who had brought his bank account to Richard Hoare in 1680, also used the alteration services that were on offer: 'March 29th 1686, Recd. A Cup and Cover of Esq. Pepys to take out the arms 36s 17d.'

The move to Fleet Street brought an increase in business. The Earl of Nottingham, the Duke of St Albans and the Duke of Rutland were among the aristocratic patrons to submit orders for plate and to borrow against plate deposited in the Bank's vaults. On the receipt of two boxes of silver ingots and pieces of plate from the Earl of Nottingham, on 7 July 1705, the contents were carefully weighed

*Caudle Cup and Cover 1685-86. Commissioned from Richard Hoare for Magdalen College, Oxford, in whose possession it still remains. Benjamin Rhodes' design for the engraving is in the Bank's archives.*

15

at Fleet Street and a courteous note sent to his lordship assuring him that his steward, Mr Armstrong, 'may draw bills on me for ye value so soon as he pleases (wch to be sure will be upwards of £300) and they shall be paid on sight by your lordship's most humble servant'. The entries debited to the Earl of Derby's account for 1694-95 provide details of his diverse instructions to his banker and neatly illustrate the duality of the role of the goldsmith-banker: for colouring and mending a coronet, £1 0s 0d; for new lining the cap with 'Fur Irmin'd round', 17s 0d; for making a new coffee pot weighing 21oz 2dw, at 7s 6d per ounce, £7 18s 4d; for putting an advertisement for a horse race into 'Ye Gazette', 10s 0d; and 10 per cent interest charged for 6 months on a loan of £80. In 1702 Richard was asked to lend silver plates to Queen Anne for her Coronation.

As overseas trade expanded in the decades before the wars with France began in 1689, scope for private investment, which had been largely confined to mortgages, extended to the purchase of stock in the great trading monopolies: the Royal Africa, the East India, the South Sea and the Levant Companies. Further opportunities lay in loans to the Exchequer and, after its foundation in 1694, to the Bank of England, the first joint-stock bank in the country. But in offering a means whereby their wealth could be stored and by careful management increased, and by extending banking facilities, which included the discounting of bills, the goldsmith-banker developed a range of services to keep his customers

facing page
*Samuel Pepys, 1633-*
*1703, by John Hayls,*
*1666. A customer and*
*friend of Richard Hoare,*
*Pepys left him a*
*mourning ring in his*
*will. No fewer than*
*twelve different spellings*
*of his name are recorded*
*in the Bank's ledgers.*

satisfied. Moreover, the long years of war which followed the accession of William and Mary to the throne in 1689, and which occasioned fiscal crises at home and interrupted trade abroad, did not threaten the operations of the private banker and his clients. So long as the Government needed money and raised enough in taxes to pay interest on its borrowings, the individual investor and his agent or 'private' banker could make money without the risk which the trading population and their 'merchant' bankers in Lombard Street were inevitably exposed to.

Richard Hoare conducted business with men and women he knew, or at least with those introduced to him on a reliable recommendation. In the City of London he was on sure ground with strong connections. One relationship, in particular, illustrates the nature of such partnerships that served him so well. The 1st Baron Ashburnham, who had represented Hastings in the Tory interest during the 1680s, had retired from active politics when he brought his account to the Bank in 1690. His peerage, bestowed in 1689, probably derived from his usefulness to the crown as a wealthy and influential landowner. He had large but dispersed holdings in Sussex and Bedfordshire and half-a-dozen other counties as well as property in London. Ashburnham kept copies of every letter he wrote and happily these have been preserved (as doubtless he would have expected). Copies of the replies to his letters from Richard and his son, Henry, survive in an early 'Letter Book' in Hoare's Bank and thus for a few years, between 1701 and 1706, we have a complete correspondence between banker and customer.

*Letter wrapper, addressed to Richard Hoare at The Golden Bottle, Fleet Street, from his customer Lord Ashburnham, dated 12 May 1698.*

Ashburnham wanted his money to 'pay'. He would have his money 'allwayes going', he was 'not sensible of the advantages of estates in land but by the produce of them' and his letters reveal a compulsive urge to shift his money about, from 'Bank [Bank of England Stock] to tally [loans to the Exchequer represented by receipts in the form of tally sticks] to the New East India Company and so on'. During William III's war with France during the 1690s, while the tax burden went up, profits could be made by the monied class, such as Ashburnham, from advancing loans to the Exchequer on the promise of repayment with interest at 6,7 or 8 per cent from future taxes raised, whether land taxes, poll taxes or levies raised on malt and coal. On 10 January 1698 Lord Ashburnham wrote to Richard in typically peremptory style: 'Sir, I must desire you will look back into your book of accounts from the beginnings of our dealings to find out ten pounds payed for my use by Mr Morgan the merchant and in case you find anything of it certfye the same to me in your next. I desire that all convenient despatch may be given to finishing the silver plate I bespoke, and that the glass sconces may be allsoe gotten ready at the same time. Yesterday became due to me 6 months' interest for my money lent on the Poll Act which I desire may be received for my use.'

We know that Ashburnham's trust in Richard was absolute, and his habit of pre-empting his banker reflected only his passionate concern for his own interest. His demands were tempered by the occasional expressions of genuine appreciation: 'May 12th 1698, Upon all occasions [you] have soe eminently shewed your affection, care and diligence in promoting the welfare and interest of mee and myne, in admiration whereof I shall never be wanting nor those that belong to me.' Asking Richard's son Henry, recently made a Partner, in August 1702 how much the interest of my 'Tenn thousand pounds came on the Malt' and if 'the orders in the Exchequer are gotten out for my foure Thousand on the present land tax', Ashburnham concluded with a complaint: 'your father's last letter was folded upp soe singly that every word might be plainely and easily read without opening or breaking the seale and by being soe much rumpled I am confident had passed the scrutiny of more than one curious examination.'

Any interval in the exchange of correspondence was hard for Ashburnham to bear. A few weeks' silence from London prompted him to approach Henry again: 'Decr. 27th 1702, Having not lately heard from your father, possibly he may not be in Towne, or indisposed; I therefore desire you will acquaint him with my concern for him and hearty kind wishes, hoping to receive a letter from him next post. I desire to be informed observing the Queene has passed a money Bill, what is the borrowing clause of it, for you are sensible that it will not be long before my £4000 on the present land tax will come in and I have thoughts of disposing that money on this new act, soe as it may stand out at interest for one yeare and I am desirous that noe time may be lost in the management of this business.' A swift reply from Richard, dated 29 December, offered a perfectly reasonable explanation: 'Not any business relating to your lordship's affairs … has been the onely occasion of my not writing to your lordship … your lordship's £4000 on this present yeare's land tax is payable after £1,060,000 [has been] raised. If your lordship is desirous to put that £4000 on the land tax, if you shall be pleased to send us the order … I will lend the money againe after sutch a manner.'

Ashburnham kept meticulous records of all his transactions and, when two of his tallies worth £1000 each went missing, he was quite sure that the fault lay with his banker and not with himself. He wrote to Richard from his house in Westminster on 7 December 1703: 'I came home before eight this evening on purpose to search my memorandums, my books of accompt, my scrutoires, and boxes for the two tallies on the malt tax … I am very confident that I have no such tallies in my keeping nor never had, and that if at any time any tallies were brought me by Mr Arnold [Richard's clerk] I gave them him back, and only retained the orders in my owne custody. If you please any morning to call upon me you shall see my memorandums and books of accompt that concern this affaire wherein I desire that you should receive all due satisfaction.'

Banking and investment management was only part of the service that Ashburnham expected from his banker. Writing to Richard from Sussex in September 1698, Ashburnham kept him informed of his requirements: 'Your son Harry ... did promise me in your absence that he would take order for tenn welsh runts of about £5 a pair to be gotten and sent down hither to be maintained this winter in my grounds and made fitt for table earlye the next year.' Tea at forty shillings a pound was procured by the Bank and pronounced very good. Ashburnham wrote to Henry on 5 August 1699: 'My wife desires to have two pounds of it in a right Indian pott and that you will keep it for her until we come to town in our passage into Sussex.' His lordship's repeating watch was broken, losing 'one third part in twelve hours going and often stands still. I believe it is very fowle having beene three years in my pocket and nothing done to it.' The solution was to send the watch to Richard via his chaplain with a request, dated 2 February 1696: 'I must desire you soe to give it to Tompsion [Thomas Tompion] your neighbour. I would have [him] sett it in perfect good order against my coming upp which will be speedilye, and if by that time he gets me ready an excellent newmade sylver watch that will endure to worn in fox hunting and all rough exercises by sea or land, and yet keepe its going right and true, I shall willingly gratifie him for it.'

When weightier matters had to be dealt with Ashburnham turned again to his banker. Writing on 12 June 1703, he asked for help in finding a tenant: 'if amoung your great number of acquaintance and friends in the world you could recommend my iron works and woods to some honest and able dealer, I conceive such a person would have reason both to acknowledge and be thankfull to you for the favour, even in as high a degree as myself, you would oblige us both. Here are all the things necessary and inviting for making warlike stores commodiously and the sea att hand to embarque goods when made ... old Mr Western gott above forty thousand pounds by this single iron work of mine in times when iron was not soe necessary, nor soe deare.'

Diamond dealing and pawnbroking were practised by some goldsmiths, including Richard. He never called himself a pawnbroker, but when he lent money against collateral in the form of jewellery, gold and silver plate, Westphalian ham, Tuscan wine or a fine sword hilt he was in effect pawnbroking. He abandoned the practice when he realised that the greatest number of defaults in the payment of interest resulted from these loans and that the delay involved in selling the collateral led to an overall poor rate of return. Under the usury laws interest rates were restricted to 6per cent until 1714 and to 5 per cent thereafter. Hoare's Bank were generally in compliance with these laws and Richard may well have thought that given the restrictions he was operating under with his lending he needed to look elsewhere for a chance to increase his profitability.[1] So, while he continued to devote time and effort to the development of his nascent banking practice, he simultaneously made strenuous efforts to break into the diamond trade. The scale of his investments in diamonds put him on an equal footing with the great London jewellers of the period such as Sir Steven Evance and Sir Francis Child, who was for a time 'jeweller in ordinary' to William III. London had become the world centre for the distribution of diamonds because the East India Company ships brought home consignments of stones from the Indian mines.

Richard ranked among the highest bidders for rough diamonds at the East India Company auctions in 1682-84, buying stones to the value of £3364. By 1707 he had taken a Mr Marcus Moses of Amsterdam into co-partnership and had largely delegated to him the task of buying rough stones, then cutting and setting them, while reserving for himself the role of retailer. However, it is clear that Moses drove a hard bargain and demanded for himself a share of the retail prof-its in addition to what he was paid as a supplier. The principal markets were abroad, in Amsterdam, Antwerp and Hamburg, and were dominated by the Jewish dealers who had established themselves in the Low Countries where they had fled from the Inquisition in Spain and Portugal. In the year from April 1707 Moses provided Richard and his son, Henry, with a stock of thirty-seven jewels with a value of over £16,000 and these, by consent of all the partners, were then despatched by 'four severall yachts … to Amsterdam and from thence to Mr Walter Beckhoff at Hamborough, these to be sold at the best price'.

Richard never travelled abroad himself but used his youthful and inexperi-enced sons as agents, in an effort to break into the closed circle of merchants, in particular the diamond dealers, in Germany and the Low Countries. Richard sent his eldest son, referred to in the Bank ledgers as 'Richard Junior', to Holland to learn basic business skills when he was a young man. In January 1700 a younger son, John (born 1682), was packed off on a similar mission to Messrs Scudamore and Henshaw in Genoa. His father revealed his anxiety to them on John's arrival: 'I hope my son John will behave himself with the industry and application in your business that will be to your content and satisfaction.' He was further troubled by the likelihood of a new war on the Continent – there had been a brief period of peace since 1697: 'I heartily wish that all these apprehensions may blow over and that peace may long continue in Europe … At present the generall apprehension of warr has made many of our best merchants desist sending goods abroad.'

His worst fears were realized when England joined the Grand Alliance against France in the War of the Spanish Succession in 1702. Nevertheless Richard stuck fast to his desire to see his sons educated abroad. He wanted them to be business-men not scholars and, while John was in Genoa, Jimmy, another son, was at school in Amsterdam, 'to qualify himself for the merchant service'. He encouraged them to learn French and Dutch, to be diligent in improving their skills in account keeping, to write well and spell correctly and above all to learn how to live within their means: 'Let me receive an account of your expenses every six months and a letter every month.' He repeatedly warned against the pitfalls of excessive drinking and the company of women – 'you have the least reason to suspect to be given to any vice or a lewdness' – and was admant that they remain steadfast to the Protestant faith and avoid all disputes concerning the 'Romish religion'. He was keen that John should keep an eye on his older brother Richard's affairs at Leghorn which, by 1703, had run into difficulties. 'The warr which makes trading very bad and dangerous has tied up your brother Richard's hands.' John was lazy about writing home but he corresponded with his brothers and Richard had to be satisfied with that.

When John's time with his Genoese masters expired in 1705 Richard could not refrain from confiding his disquiet about his son's plan to move on. 'In your last I find your inclinations of going to Rome about March next,' he wrote, 'I think it will not be convenient for you to goe thither unless you can find some sober good humoured gent. to Beare you companye and I do not question but you will take care to preserve yourself from the infection of the religion of that Country … If any persons shall begin arguments about religion tell them your business is only to travel and see the country and not to enter any disputes and therefore desire to be excused.'

Once established in Fleet Street, Richard and Susannah had looked for a country house. They found one in Hendon, a village ten miles to the north, where their enthusiasm for creating a garden was somewhat tempered by the fact that, to begin with, they were able only to rent the house. Nevertheless, in his excitement for his new project, Richard sent to John for some exotic species, a request he had quickly to revise once he experienced the limitations of gardening in northern climes: 'I shall not trouble you to send me any orange or lemon trees nor tube roses but if you can send me some roots or seeds of fine flowers or anything that keep green all the year about they will be acceptable to me … there is not any green house … and I shall not build one myself unless I can have it to be my owne therefore I doe not intend to have anything growing in the garden that will not endure our certaine climate.' In the event Richard sent to Holland, being a little nearer, for his 'roots of fine flowers' but later he wrote that the ship 'that they were sent by was taken by the French so that my garden will not be soe good as I intended it'. John was also given permission to draw on his masters for the sum of £200, because Richard wanted 'some small pieces of painting about 18 inches to 24 inches but let them be good of the sort for I doe not care for bad painting'. 'For your mother and sisters,' he added, '… I would have you buy them any sorts of silks that are very britte.'

Richard kept the boys informed of all family events, and in among the bulletins he sent reporting births, marriages and deaths there are occasional glimpses of himself. Writing to John in June 1703 he mentioned that he was about to go to Bath for a month, taking with him Susannah and their daughter Mary. He later revealed that the visit had been undertaken 'to remove the remains of severall colds and sharp paines I had in my head', and that to his great relief the waters had had a most beneficial effect.

Thomas, born a year after John in 1683, started his working life in the Bank, but even under the stern eye of his father he fell into dissolute ways. Two clerks at the Golden Bottle, Tom and William Cooke, appeared to have defrauded the Bank. Richard never accused his son directly of any complicity in the fraud, and Thomas on 30 October 1707 offered the only likely explanation of how the money could have gone missing. 'If [Tom Cooke] has wronged you of anything I believe it must be in your cash accounts for you know it may be possible for a bookkeeper to doe it but I hope he has not and if he has I doe assure you it is not toe my knowledge and I am altogether a strainger to anything of that nature concerning him.'

There were further confusions at Fleet Street over missing plate, lost credits, overpaid bills, irregularities in a mortgage and a misplaced gold necklace. The Cooke brothers denied any involvement and no prosecutions were brought. Understandably Richard could not bring himself to believe that he could have been robbed by his own son, but Thomas's outburst of bitter self-reproach in a letter to his brother Henry in January 1708 reveals a young man tormented by more than guilt over the usual excesses of loose living. 'You may see by these actions which I have transacted how base and vile I have been in my trust and how many ways the devil putts thoughts and actions into one's mind to deceive and defraude ... I would not for ten thousand worlds live as I have lived for some years past which are abominably wicked and vile in my own eyes and my sins are more than ye hairs of my head and I have gained nothing thereby but shame and confusion of face.'

It was resolved that Thomas should go to Amsterdam. Richard hoped that he could be useful in furthering the sale of his diamonds but the price put on them was too high, by as much as 30 or 40 per cent, and Thomas was not proficient enough in Plat Dutch, the language of commerce there, to negotiate on behalf of his father. Thomas became thoroughly discouraged. He couldn't break into the closed circle of dealers who 'are as cunning and close in their affairs as any people in the world ... they would sooner lose a limb as to informe any boddy in there affairs', and he complained to Richard that unless he set lower prices on his gems they will 'remaine here till Domesday'. Marlborough's victories over the French gave hope for peace in the winter of 1709, but a new war brewing between Denmark and Sweden kept trade flat. In Thomas's view Richard would find 'little or noe incouragement in your affairs in these parts till such time as there is peace among our neighbouring kings'. Thomas removed himself to

Lisbon in 1712 where he died from consumption after a few months. He hadn't seen his family in over four years and, both before and during his absence, he had been a perpetual cause of worry and frustration to his father. He was not up to the job he had been sent to do and Richard knew this. He kept only a selection of the letters written to him from abroad by John and Jimmy, but he preserved every letter which Thomas wrote home.

Jimmy too had died while in Amsterdam and his body was brought back to be buried in St Dunstan's in the West in Fleet Street, directly opposite his father's bank. He was the first member of the family to be buried in what became the Hoares' family church. Then John returned to England. His future as a trader with Constantinople had been disrupted by war and Richard felt obliged to help him but did not consider him eligible for partnership in the Bank. John married and had four children but died suddenly in 1721, at the age of 41, from a fall from his horse while out riding near his home in Edmonton.[3]

Richard's eldest son, his namesake Richard Junior, did no better than his brothers as a Continental trader, and also had the onerous responsibility imposed upon him by his father of supervising his younger brothers' expenditure abroad. In the family annals he has been dismissed as the eldest son who failed to live up to expectations as heir and is referred to, perhaps a little unfairly, as 'Naughty

Richard'. Apart from the fact that he is due a certain amount of recognition by generations of Bank partners who trace their direct ancestry back to him, he should be seen as more unlucky than venal. At the start of Richard Junior's working life Richard senior was very happy to put up the capital to establish his firstborn son as a merchant trading in the Mediterranean and to act as his agent. War, however, which had cut a swathe through the diamond business, also brought trade in other commodities to a standstill and young Richard's money quickly became tied up in 'severall sorts of merchandize and remittances and bills of exchange to forreyne parts', and any money he did receive quickly vanished in interest repayments and warehouse rents for the goods he couldn't shift. Between 1701 and 1709 nearly £30,000 was paid in interest. Entries in this ill-starred account reveal the fantastic variety of commodities which Richard traded in: anchovies, brimstone, nutmegs and mace, coral, crabb's eyes, cochineal, bays [baize], shalloons [Flemish lining material], aniseed, capers, diamonds, gold ingots, seed pearls, wine, sugar, spices, wool and tobacco, cocoa, coffee, paper, rice, leather and lead.

Richard senior began withdrawing from any active engagement in this trade in 1703 and Richard Junior managed to keep his debts and credits balancing until a crisis occurred in 1712 when a bill for over £15,000 was drawn on him, which he couldn't pay, and his father was obliged to take over his overdraft of £36,822. His original debt had been nearly twice that sum and he had managed to reduce it only by the sale of all his assets. Even if this was partly due to bad luck, Richard's bad management had clearly compromised his position as the eldest son. In return for Richard Junior formally relinquishing any claim on his father's estate, Richard senior left instructions in his will that all his son's debts, which by that stage had been substantially reduced, should be paid off in full.

Even after peace came with the Treaty of Utrecht in 1713, the depression in the diamond trade on the Continent continued. Those who had money chose to keep it rather than lay it out in goods and, although there were rumours of great

*Cheque, dated 18 December 1695, addressed to Brother Hoare and signed by Richard's brother-in-law John Austen, with an instruction to pay Brother Benson £300. All parties were related by marriage. Benson's daughter Jane married Richard's son Henry.*

consignments of rough stones arriving in the East India ships, those that appeared on the market were of indifferent quality and the price of all stones remained fixed at a discount of up to half of their top value. Paris proved to be no better as a market for Richard, and his agent there, Monsieur Masson, spent five dispiriting years from 1712 to 1717 trying to sell diamonds for him. On the single occasion when he succeeded in finding a buyer for a brilliant ring priced at £950 or 1350 livres he nearly

*Christ's Hospital, by Samuel Wale, 1748. Richard Hoare's governorship began a long association with the Bank. Until well after the Second World War many of the clerks were former 'Bluecoat' boys.*

exhausted himself in pursuit of the debt.

Richard always showed a great reluctance to relent on price, and he was convinced that the low offers he received were not a true reflection of the market but a conspiracy to force the hand of a foreigner. He did not benefit from a high turnover in this business and thus became increasingly committed to holding out for a good price. He was inflexible in other matters as well. When assured by David and James de Neufville of Frankfurt that his 'great earrings', which he had entrusted to them to sell, might have a buyer in the King of Poland if only he could see them, the chance of a sale was lost by Richard's refusal to revise his previous instructions that his gems were not to be loaned out on approval. By 1716 the de Neufvilles were politely requesting that Richard should cease to supply them with any more diamonds; the 'great earrings' valued at £9000 were still in their hands and although well known to all the jewellers in the area no purchasers were forthcoming.

In addition to Richard's own mistakes Marcus Moses let everyone down. He accepted money in advance for his buying trips to India but became notorious for his failure to deliver in either quantity or quality. In the period 1705-9 Moses was the largest single debtor to the Bank, borrowing £34,296, about 20 per cent of money lent overall.[4] He probably defrauded Richard and was a significant contributor to the challenge the Bank faced to return a profit in 1710, when it had to rely for survival on personal funding from Richard and Henry. In any case the writing was on the wall for Richard's experiment with the Continental gem markets. Increasingly he concentrated his efforts on developing banking skills while reducing the work at Fleet Street associated with goldsmithing. In the 1702 Balance Sheet 38 per cent of the Bank's assets still related to aspects of the traditional business, whether it was in the form of loans to customers for buying or refashioning plate or in the stock-in-trade of gold, silver, diamonds and pearls. This proportion gradually declined throughout Richard's lifetime representing his deliberate abandonment of the craft origins of his new profession.

By contrast with his and his sons' efforts abroad Richard's career at home prospered.[5] In 1702 he received a knighthood from the new sovereign, Queen Anne. Although he described the honour as unexpected it seems to have galvanized him into seeking election as an Alderman of the City of London. His public career was only just beginning, but he was now fifty-four and aware of the infirmities of advancing age. He wrote to a customer, William Jessop, on 29 September 1702 asking him to find him a horse: '... a guelding that trots and gallops easily…you know I grow old therefore must not have a rough trot for I have a days hunting but not to have my boanes very sore after it.' On 16 September 1703 Sir Richard was elected Alderman for Bread Street Ward, on the nomination of three prominent Tory Aldermen, Sir William Pritchard, Sir John Fleet and Sir Francis Dashwood. City politics and charitable affairs now began to dominate his life.

From 1661 until 1832 the City of London returned four members to Parliament and often all four were Aldermen. After two unsuccessful attempts in 1705 and 1708 Sir Richard was elected as an MP for the City in 1710 and again in 1713.[6] Appointments were showered on the new Member: Colonel-in-Chief of the Green Regiment, one of the Trained Bands of the City of London 1710; a Director of the South Sea Company 1711; Commissioner, with his son Henry, for the Building of Fifty New Churches in London in 1711; and in 1713, after twenty years serving as a Governor of Christ's Hospital School, he was elected President. The school was principally a charity giving free education to poor children. Samuel Pepys, a Governor in the previous century, had been instrumental in the foundation of its famous Mathematical School, which was established to teach much needed navigational skills to boys intended for the Royal Navy and merchant marine.

Sir Richard's loyalty to the Tory party and the Church of England is indisputable but he never made the mistake of allowing political considerations to obscure his commercial interests or destroy his friendships. He declared his opposition to the Bank of England on its establishment in 1694, not just because the bank was creation of the Whig Ministry, which came into power at the Glorious Revolution of 1688, but because it might harm Hoare's Bank. It was established to manage the astronomical public debt created by William

*Broadsheet listing objections to the foundation of the Bank of England in 1694, co-authored by Richard Hoare who was one of its leading opponents.*

III's war programme. Funds were raised from the public and lent to the Government at a high rate of interest, and the subscribers of the initial £1,200,000 were constituted into a joint-stock company. In addition to the management of the public debt it was awarded a number of privileges as a bank including the discounting of bills, the circulation of its own notes and protection against competition by legislation, passed in 1697, which forbade the establishment of any further joint stock banks in England. The establishment of the Bank of England alarmed the goldsmith-bankers, and Richard was one of the authors of a list of objections they made public in a broadsheet issued in 1694. Their principal argument was that the Bank would have a monopoly over borrowing and lending; it would 'engross all the ready money in or near the city of

London which is the heart of trade' and drive out competition, bringing depression in its wake. The calamitous effects of a monopoly were spelt out in twenty-one clauses and, when the original Bank Charter came up for renewal several years later, the private bankers repeated their objections.

In 1696 the Exchequer was put to further expense by a re-coinage, which was introduced to replace a debased over-clipped silver currency which had lost its value. The re-coinage stimulated a demand for new coins and there was a rush to exchange Bank of England notes for silver. The consequent run on the bank could have had very serious implications as it had issued notes far in excess of its deposits. It was saved by a fortnight's moratorium but Richard, who was well known as a critic of the bank, was accused, with others of his profession, of orchestrating this run. He later refuted the charge in March 1707 claiming that if he had intended to 'promote a run for money on the Bank he could have done it … having by him, all the time that the great demand for money was on the Bank, several thousand pounds in notes payable by the Bank; and also there was brought to Sir Richard by several gentlemen in the time of the run on the Bank, notes payable by the said Bank, amounting to a great many thousands of pounds, which he was desired to take, and receive the money presently from the bank, which he refused to do until the great Demand on the bank for money was over.'

Thomas Wharton, later elevated to the peerage as the Marquess of Wharton and Malmesbury and acknowledged as one of the most powerful Whig leaders in England, kept an account at the Golden Bottle from 1695 until his death in 1715. Another 'Opposition' customer, John Dolben, called Richard 'a damned Tory' but admitted he did have 'the fairest character and is the most secure of any of his calling'. (Dolben's political opinions were shared by the goldsmith Sir Steven Evance who could not, however, share Dolben's admiration of his rival. Evance was dangerously ill in 1708 and concern arose over what to do with the famous Pitt Diamond which was in his custody. Dolben put forward the suggestion that Sir Richard Hoare should take charge of it, whereupon Sir Steven, 'flew into a passion and disorder that was very near carrying him off [and] I was forced to leave him to recover himself'.)

The year before he first entered Parliament Richard was appointed Sherriff of the City of London. He kept a diary of his Shrievalty, entering every appointment associated with the office and, with the exception of an occasional reprieve when the Lord Mayor was absent from town for a few days, he was in constant attendance, often on a daily basis. Details of Church services, dinners, Sessions at

Playing cards depicting the impeachment of Henry Sacheverell in 1710. His intolerance of religious Dissenters won the approval of Richard Hoare and many of his high church customers.

the Old Bailey, the Guildhall and the Sessions House in Southwark, meetings of the Court of Aldermen and Wardmotes fill the pages, interspersed with exceptional activities such as the election of a new Lord Mayor and the remarkable public incineration of the sermons of the Divine, Dr Sacheverell.

Henry Sacheverell, a high churchman, conducted a relentless campaign against the Whig Party's toleration of Dissenters and controversially preached on this subject at St Paul's in November 1709, which led to him being put on trial. On the evening of 23 March 1710, during the trial, Henry Hoare, under orders from his father, instructed two of the Bank servants to extinguish a bonfire that had just been lit 'on the other side of the way neare the kennel opposite to our dwelling house', which they did in his presence and 'which I gave my father immediately an account of which he very well approved'. The instigator of the fire was unknown but there can be little doubt that he was suspected of intending to burn the writings of Sacheverell. This odd occurrence, noted by Henry as being 'the only bonfire that has been made during the tryall of Dr Sacheverell or since between Fetter lane and the west end of St Dunstan's Church', took place three days after the Doctor was found guilty by the House of Lords, suspended from preaching for three years and had his offending sermons burned by the common hangman. His sentence was considered light and a triumph for him and his supporters who included the proprietors of the Golden Bottle. It increased his public support, and the Whig Ministry was swept away by the revelation of their unpopularity. Robert Harley

came in as Queen Anne's Chief Minister at the head of a Tory Ministry. On 29 July Richard noted in his Diary that Harley wished 'to speak with me to know my thoughts whether the Queen might be supplied with £200,000 by the City'.

Richard's eventual election to the office of Lord Mayor came in September 1712. Nine months later he rode at the head of the official procession from the heart of the City of London to a spot at the bottom of Chancery Lane, very close to his banking house, where he heard a public reading of the peace treaty with France. Although always a supporter of a peace, when the commercial treaty with France was debated in Parliament he voted against it, alongside the Tory merchants, convinced that British interests would not benefit enough by its terms. His role as a financier to the Harley Administration stopped soon after and although he was returned as an MP again in the election of 1713 he never regained the

*Thomas Wharton, 1st Marquess of Wharton and Malmesbury, by Sir Godfrey Kneller, c.1710-15. Sitter and artist were members of the famous Kit Kat Club. The club was a focus for the Whigs, but more than half of the members banked at Hoare's.*

29

influence he had enjoyed three years earlier. He did not even contest the City election of 1715 when the Tory candidates were trounced by the Whigs.

His Mayoral year was thus his final year of strenuous public duty. Traditional gifts of venison were sent to him by his grander customers, among them Lord Ashburnham, Lord Guernsey and Lady Hastings. The Duke of Rutland regretted he could not attend the Lord Mayor's entertainment at Goldsmiths' Hall: 'tho I never wished myself in town on 29th Oct. yet now my worthy friend Good Sir Richard Hoar is Choose Lord May. I own I should have bine very well pleased with the sight and to have bine one to have payd my respects to him and his Lady and wished him health, prosperity and hapynes in his great office. I know you will have so much venison for the toast yt I would not send a doe against that time, but whenever else you will like best to have owne and will give me notice one of the best I can procure shall be sent to you.'

Richard died at Hendon in January 1719 at the age of seventy. He had been 'seized with an indisposition' a year before his death which, in spite of a good recovery, caused him to retreat from the world in order, said the *Weekly Journal*, 'that he might without interruption apply all his thoughts and hours to reading, meditation and prayer … an actual preparation for death added to a good life … exemplary and exact.' After lying in state his coffin was carried from the banking house across the street to St Dunstan's, the pall 'above the chair was born by six Aldermen' and the cortege was led by Bluecoat boys from Christ's Hospital walking two by two and singing hymns. He was then interred in the new family vault and in due course Henry commissioned Thomas Stayner to carve his memorial tablet. There were many mourners in attendance and the occasion was further marked by a generous distribution of alms. Richard was survived by his wife and six children, all of whom were beneficiaries of his will, but only on the condition that they signed a release to Henry of all their claims to Richard's real and personal estate.

At Richard's death the diamonds and pearls in his possession were valued at £24,800 10s, nearly one third of the Bank's assets, but these were merely what remained of his unsuccessful flirtation with the diamond trade abroad, and did not represent any ongoing interest in the jewellery business. Loans against interest and lending for the purchase of securities rather than plate represented the largest single category of assets.

Few of the forty-two private banks in London in 1700 survived the first two decades of the eighteenth century, and Richard Hoare was exceptional in that he not only survived – he succeeded. He and Henry were pioneers in those early years of private banking and they had to learn as they went along. In 1710 they had been obliged to make a substantial personal investment in the Bank and take very little income for some years subsequently. If they were in business simply to make money they weren't doing very well at that stage and they would have got as good a return on their equity by investing in government bonds as they were getting from the Bank. Yet Richard was determined to carry on regardless of the dip in profits and despite the restrictions on what bankers could charge for their money. In 1714 the legal maximum rate of interest was fixed at 5 per cent. As the government's requirements increased so it needed to keep down the cost of its own borrowing. As a consequence the Hoares had to develop a strategy. They restricted the amount of credit they gave, eliminating numerous small loans to their more modestly placed clients, which were costly to administer and scarcely profitable. Instead they focused their attention on building up a prominent, well-heeled clientele with large and regular borrowing requirements: people with the best security who posed very little risk. They lent most of their money to around twenty of their top borrowers. Between 1700 and 1710 a hundred new names were added each year to Richard's customer list.[1] Thereafter the rate slowed considerably and the social profile of the list became increasingly blue-blooded as Richard and Henry identified those who were most likely to be the source of their future profits. It was a strategy that would stand the Hoares in good stead in the years to come.

*Marble memorial to Sir Richard and Lady Hoare. Designed by Thomas Stayner in 1723, for which he was paid £40.*

SACRED TO THE MEMORY OF
Sʳ RICHARD HOARE KNᵀ WHO DIED IANᵛ
VI MDCCXVIII. AGED LXX. AND OF HIS RELICT
DAME SUSANNA HOARE WHO DIED SEP: XXIV.
MDCCXX. AGED LXVII.
BOTH EXEMPLARY IN THEIR PIETY AND STRICT
ADHERENCE TO THE CHURCH OF ENGLAND, IN
THEIR CONJUGAL AFFECTION & IN THEIR SINGULER
CARE OF THE RELIGIOUS EDUCATION OF A
NUMEROUS ISSUE, THEY HAD ELEVEN
SONS & SIX DAUGHTERS: THREE ONLY
OF WHICH ARE NOW SURVIVING.
HE WAS EMINENT FOR HIS FIDELITY
HUMANITY. DILIGENCE CIRCUMSPECTION
STRICT IUSTICE & CHARITY IN Ẏ SEVERAL
TRUST'S & OFFICES OF LORD MAYOR
ALDERMAN, & SHERIFF OF LONDON, OF
MEMBER OF PARLIAMENT FOR THIS CITY
& OF PRESIDENT OF CHRIST'S HOSPITAL
AND THE                         LONDON
WORK                            HOUSE

THIS MONUMENT
WAS GRATEFULLY
ERECTED BY HENRY
HOARE ESQ.ʳ THEIR
SON & SOLE EXECU-
TOUR. AN: DOM:
MDCCXXIII.

# GOOD HENRY
# AND THE CHARITIES
# 1718–1725

On becoming a Partner in 1702 Henry married his first cousin Jane Benson, the daughter of Sir William and Lady Benson. Benson was a wealthy iron merchant and a political crony of Sir Richard's in the City, and his wife was Henry's aunt. Henry and Jane were obliged to live in the banking house at Fleet Street as a condition of his partnership. They and their four surviving children (seven died in infancy) born between 1703 and 1708, shared the accommodation with Sir Richard and Lady Hoare, four or five clerks and a similar complement of household servants. With two generations in residence there was no room for the apprentices whom Richard had previously taken on for the goldsmithing business. Henry and Jane's two boys, Henry and Richard, spent their formative years under the close watch of their grandparents. The future of the family and the Bank rested with them for, when Henry erected the monument in memory of his father in St Dunstan's Church in 1723, he, his youngest brother Benjamin, then just thirty, and his sisters Mary and Jane were the only survivors of Sir Richard and Lady Hoare's numerous offspring. Thirteen of their siblings were dead, including six infants as a result of 'Convultions', 'Feaver' or 'Gripes' who were buried in the Hoares' old parish church, St Vedast, Foster Lane.

The original Banking House in Fleet Street had a narrow frontage of less than twenty feet, with a decorative iron balcony at first-floor level. The basement housed the kitchen and a cellar; at ground level there was 'a faire shoppe' (the Banking Hall is still referred to as 'the Shop') and a 'parlour'. The dining room on the first floor faced St

Dunstan's Church with 'a fair chamber behind', and on the second and third floors there were four decent bedrooms and then two garret bedrooms at the top of the house. On each floor extra accommodation was made by squeezing 'little lodging rooms' out of the space between the front and back rooms. The house, known prior to 1690 as 'The Golden Hinde', was leased from a goldsmith, John Pargiter. In 1711 Sir Richard renewed his lease and bought the next-door house on the east side[1], which he had held on lease since 1705. The Golden Bottle thus doubled its size, occupying the sites later numbered as 35 and 36 Fleet Street.

The kinship ties, strengthened and formalized by the business, which bound the Hoares and the Bensons so closely together, were mirrored, to an extent, on the clerical side of the business. Here a similar pattern of succession of father by son was considered the most reliable means of acquiring dependable clerks. Despite their suspicions that at least two members of the Cooke family might have acted fraudulently in their conduct of business, Richard and Henry employed three of them – John, Thomas and William – over the period 1698-1717. An even more impressive record was provided by John Arnold and his son Christopher. John came to the Bank in 1685, in its Cheapside days, and in 1698 took up the post of head clerk, which he retained until 1722, making him the longest-serving head clerk in the entire history of the Bank.

Henry succeeded his father at the Bank only a few months in advance of a period of excitement and potential danger that could have brought financial ruin to the Golden Bottle. The investment frenzy, known as the 'South Sea Bubble' was a six-month orgy of trading in South Sea Company stock between March and October 1720 which made a few men and women rich but, more significantly, crippled the vast majority of shareholders, victims of corruption at the highest levels. In its infancy the South Sea Company was conceived of as a trading company targeting the precious resources of gold and silver from South America. These, it was believed, would be used to buy English cloth while the Company would profit at the same time from a stake in the lucrative slave trade between Africa and the New World. Robert Harley, and his impecunious war-weary Tory government had a more audacious plan for it, in addition to its trading monopoly. Harley proposed that the South Sea Company should also operate as a financial institution, taking over part of the National Debt by offering government creditors shares in the new Company in lieu of the money they were owed, and granting the government such favourable rates of interest on the debt that the

South Sea Stock Ledger showing the astronomical rise in stock prices during the 'Bubble' speculation, 1718-20.

Bank of England would find itself outmanoeuvred and struggling to compete. This was a Tory-inspired project from the start and Sir Richard Hoare was one of the many bankers who packed the Court of Directors of the Company at its inception in 1711. Not one of them had any experience of trading with South America. A disadvantageous peace in 1713, which failed to deliver the trading privileges desired by the Company, conspired with the Company's own mismanagement to give the Spanish the upper hand, and the Company failed to profit from either sales of cloth or the trade in human cargo. With a new declaration of war with Spain in 1718 the great trading Company ceased all overseas trade.

Sir Richard had survived in office within the Company to this date but, with the replacement of the Prince of Wales as its Governor by the King himself and a new Whig administration under Sir Robert Walpole, the entire Tory interest in the South Sea Company was voted out and their place taken by Whig businessmen, MPs, and office holders led by John Blunt. Henry Hoare, so much his father's son in many respects, did not attempt to become a director of this reconstituted South Sea Company but like thousands of others who had money, or access to it, he became an active player in the game of buying and selling stock. Under Blunt's direction the South Sea Company made a convincing bid to purchase the entire National Debt and, bolstered by Government backing, this led to a rapid escalation in share price. The South Sea Bill passed through Parliament in April 1720, and in authorizing a new share issue for the South Sea Company it opened the way for hundreds of imitation 'Bubble' companies to lure investors into their schemes.

Only a handful of these imitators survived in competition with the South Sea Company, but new deals were cut with its investors: in a series of four subscription issues new stock could be bought by instalments with no restriction on selling. With each issue Blunt made the terms increasingly generous, to the point of absurdity. Sales were pitched at members of both Houses of Parliament, and leading Government ministers became owners of stock they never paid for.

Totally unaware of the conspiracy between Parliament and the Directors to inflate the share price people competed fiercely to buy stock, which could be bought on credit. In addition the Company recklessly offered loans to investors secured on old stock, to buy new stock. As a result in one week in June 1720 the price for 100 shares, which had been £508 leapt to £830 in the space of four days. The highest price quoted was £1110 which valued the Company at £300 million, ten times the National Debt. At the same time it was owed £60 million by its investors. The end came when, in the fourth and final money subscription opened on 22 August, with the stock priced at £1000 per 100 shares, the Company offered a 50 per cent dividend for ten years and the investors finally suspended belief. Confidence in this magical corporation faltered. Some of those made rich on this speculation were already investing in land, and prices and rents had risen accordingly; some prudent investors from 1711 had sold out by June but there were those, tempted into the market by the subscription offers, who were left in debt to the company and with declining assets.

It had been noted that although the Company's books were full in June 1720, 'the sober cloths of merchants and bankers were scarce in the throng' to buy, and Hoare's were certainly to be counted among the cautious. Throughout 1718 and 1719, once South Sea stock had risen well above par, they bought and sold steadily on their own and their customers' behalf. Henry's private account and the Bank's loan ledgers for the purchase of stock, record active buying of stock for twelve months to April 1720, with the sale of stock reaching into October of that year. The prices held reasonably well but the amount of stock which could be offloaded had clearly shrunk. Share prices crept up during March and April and Hoares traded intensively, paying £182 for 100 shares at the beginning of March and selling at over £100 more in April. The highest price paid in their books was £473 when on 27 May £9460 was paid for 2000 stock, but this marked the end of their systematic purchasing and by June, although they were selling 1000 stock at £760, they were realistically valuing their remaining holdings of 14,575 stock at £250. Although they managed to secure an even higher premium at £773, the amount of stock being sold between June and September had fallen dramatically and by December no price for South Sea stock could be quoted. Henry managed to sell his shares and the only setback suffered by the Bank was a loss over an unwise decision to buy more stock in the fourth money subscription.

JONATHAN'S COFFEE HOUSE *or* an Analysis of CHANGE ALLEY
With a Group of Characters from the Life - *Inscrib'd to Jacob Henriques.*

Overall the Bank had earned profits of £19,355 from trading in South Sea stock during the period February to mid-September. Its success has been attributed to the fact that it timed the market with considerable skill, and this was demonstrable also in the excellent returns it achieved on other securities, principally Bank of England and two smaller firms, Ram's Assurance and the Royal African Company. In 1720, however, their main exposure was to South Sea Company stock and the investment activity related to this far outstripped any trading in other shares, both in the number and value of the transactions.[2]

The Bank's balance sheet for the year ending 24 June 1720 looked very healthy in the calm before the storm, with Henry and Benjamin dividing the profits three-quarters to one-quarter, according to Partnership Articles drawn up after Sir Richard's death, giving them respectively £29,119 5s 8d and £9,706 8s 7d. The following year the Bank's assets and liabilities had shrunk by over a half reflecting the ravages made on customers' wealth by the Bubble debacle. However the Partners' profits remained undiminished. It seems likely that during these years Henry and Benjamin kept most of their profit in the business: it was not until November 1721 that they were paid £21,000 and £7000 out of the Stock ledger. In the following years, as they worked to rebuild customer deposits against a falling market, their profits were reduced to half the level they had been in 1720-21, years when their earnings had probably amounted to more than the total profits of the preceding twenty years. The aftermath of the bubble led to the imprisonment of some Directors of the South Sea Company and the resignation of Government Ministers, but Walpole arranged a substantial cover-up to protect those he could, in order to ensure the survival of his party and himself at its head. The Government wrote off a hefty proportion of the amount owed by subscribers and shareholders, who had taken out loans to buy stock, and permitted investors to trade in their shares at a loss. The stock market quietened down and its activities no longer occupied centre stage.

One of the best-known of those who profited from the South Sea affair was the bookseller, Thomas Guy, who directed in his will that his fortune of £240,000, made out of prudently timed speculation, should be spent on founding a London hospital

*Jonathan's Coffee House, Exchange Alley, where stockbrokers met, c. 1763. It was the centre for trading during the South Sea Bubble and later became the City's first stock exchange.*

*Westminster Hospital (left), Broad Sanctuary, 1842. Founded in 1719 at the instigation of Henry Hoare, it was rebuilt, with the help of Charles Hoare, in 1832.*

bearing his name. At the same time Henry Hoare was playing a similar role in the foundation of Westminster Hospital. Although the hospital does not bear his name, it is an acknowledged fact that he was the inspiration behind its foundation. He supplied a combination of money and a radical idea. On 14 January 1716 he met with three others – William Wogan, a writer, Robert Witham, a vintner, and the Reverend Patrick Coburn – at St Dunstan's Coffee house (the site of which lies beneath the western part of the Bank premises) to 'consult upon the most effectual methods for relieving the Sick and Needy'.

At that time only two hospitals, St. Bartholomew's in Smithfield and St Thomas's in Southwark, offered any help to the poor in London and they were overwhelmed by demand. The meeting produced a 'Charitable Proposal': 'if the Necessitys of those who are in health be still so incompetently provided for, how deplorable must the condition be of such persons whose poverty is accompanied with sickness who not only want the necessarys of life but are rendered incapable either by their labour or otherwise to procure them, and are destitute of all remedys and helps that may be proper for their recovery. What but a languishing and inevitable death can be the consequence of such complicated Miserys, what except a timely relief from charitable persons can prevent it?'

The St Dunstan's Meeting had grand designs to provide a free medical service all over London, for those who could not pay, and to raise funds by means of charitable societies which would attract voluntary contributions. Henry Hoare flourished ten pounds, which he had about him, and urged the company to start at once on their good works. The first practical measures taken were organized visits to the sick inmates of London's prisons. It soon became clear that their efforts, to be effective, must be restricted geographically, and thenceforth their work was confined to the parish of St Margaret's Westminster. The charitable society there had a faltering start but, due to Henry's determination, by 1721 it had established the first Westminster Infirmary in a house near St James's Park, with eighteen beds, offering free medical care to in-patients and out-patients. Henry lived to see a second, larger infirmary built, but within a decade of his death there was a rift between the trustees, which led to the creation of yet another hospital, St George's. By 1734 there were five hospitals in London: St Bartholomew's, St Thomas's, Westminster, Guys' and St George's – a radical improvement on the situation in 1716.

Westminster Hospital maintained its association with Hoare's Bank for over two hundred years. In Hoare family folklore Henry's reputation as a devout man with a social conscience and a practical nature has earned him the title of 'Good Henry'. He has also been referred to as 'the ubiquitous Henry Hoare' in recognition of his energetic pursuit of good causes. The codicil to his will contained a list of established charities who were his beneficiaries: Christ's Hospital, St Bartholomew's Hospital, Bridewell, Bethlem Hospital, the Society For The Promotion of Christian Knowledge, The Society for the Propagation of the Gospel in Foreign Parts, the Society for the Reformation of Manners and the Corporation of Clergymen's Sons. There were also legacies for other charitable purposes. Principal among them were sums of £2000 for the erecting and maintaining of two Charity Schools or Workhouses in the parish of St Dunstan's, and £2000 for the establishment of the Henry Hoare Bible Fund. Smaller amounts were given for: poor housekeepers, 'deemed fit by my wife' in the parish of St Dunstan's; and for eight 'poor and decayed' goldsmiths or their widows; for poor persons 'on the road to Stourton' as recommended by the Minister and Churchwardens at Stourton. The vicar of St Dunstan's was to receive £5 annually on condition he celebrated Communion on all the Saints Days and Festivals, in the Anglican liturgy, in addition to Sundays.

The donation to Stourton reflected another of Henry's interests. He was planning his own country estate, encouraged by Jane's brother, William Benson, an extraordinarily ambitious young man who was to succeed Sir Christopher Wren as Surveyor-General (chief government architect) in 1718. Benson scarcely merited the post on grounds of ability but he had put himself in the vanguard of fashionable taste in architecture. He settled in Wiltshire soon after his sister's marriage, taking a lease on Amesbury Abbey near Stonehenge. In 1709 he bought an estate nearby at Newton Toney and embarked on building a fine neo-Palladian villa he named Wilbury. In the same year Sir Richard wrote to his son Tom that Henry had gone 'to Coz Benson's in Wiltshire and from thence to some other places' and it seems likely that he was looking around for some suitable purchase in the neighbourhood for himself. With the Bank absorbing much of his personal fortune at that time, the decision to buy was delayed until 1717 when he bought the Manor of Stourton, including old Stourton House, from John Meres whose father, Sir Thomas Meres, had taken over the heavily mortgaged estate from the thirteenth Lord Stourton in 1714. In search of the pleasures of country life, Henry was also making an investment which would bring him good financial returns and introduce him and his family to the ranks of landed gentry.

Henry was only one of a band of distinguished men who gave large amounts of their own money for public purposes in the early decades of the eighteenth century, continuing a tradition of private philanthropy which stretched back to Elizabethan times. Philanthropy gave Henry the opportunity to work unofficially as a public servant. With the Whigs firmly in power, politics was no longer an option for Tory partisans such as the Hoares. Henry was not prepared to join the Jacobite cause, although he had friends and customers who were Jacobites. Robert Nelson, an intimate friend (Henry was his executor) and a pre-eminent Anglican writer of his day, whose works were as much referred to as the Bible and the Book of Common Prayer, remained a Jacobite all his life. He remained faithful to the Stuarts and until 1709 belonged to the ranks of non-jurors who could not swear allegiance to Queen Anne. Henry knew many of this non-juring circle, and he no doubt sympathized with those clergy who had been deprived of their livings on account of their beliefs, but he remained detached from it and certainly took no part in the Jacobite risings of 1715 and 1719.

The established Church at that time was concerned by both religious opposition and by the widespread irreligion and immorality in the growing capital. The Tory and Anglican administration that came to power in 1710 set out to serve the spiritual needs of expanding London and its growing population and to educate the young in the doctrines of the Church of England. In 1710 the Act to appoint a 'Commission to build Fifty New Churches in London and its Suburbs' had received the approval of Queen Anne and thereafter bore her name. The Act was seen, in part, as a counter-measure to the Dissenters who were free to establish meeting houses and chapels wherever they liked, unhindered by the restrictions of the parish system. Sir Richard and Henry were both appointed to the First and Second Commission, in 1711 and 1712. Their responsibility was to determine where the new churches were to be sited. Both also served on the smaller Committee, with Sir Christopher Wren and Sir John Vanbrugh, which instructed the Surveyors and considered and reported on proposals received from the parishes. We find Henry recorded in the minutes as taking on the proprietor of the Three Cups Inn in Holborn over the purchase price for land to build a new church there and beating him down in price from £2200 to £1900. He then went with a party, including Nicholas Hawksmoor, one of the Commission's Surveyors, to visit a site for a church in the parish of St Giles in the Fields.

There were numerous friends, acquaintances and Bank customers on the Commission: the clergy were represented by the Rev. William Stanley, and the Rev. George Stanhope, Robert Nelson and no less than six bishops. These included Francis Atterbury, intimate friend of Henry and Jane Hoare who, until his banishment after the failed Jacobite Rising of 1719, was the Old Pretender's chief representative in England. There were several lawyers including Vigerius Edwards who acted as solicitor to the Third Commission and also acted for Henry in his purchase of Stourton, and John Skeat who was solicitor to Queen Anne and was subsequently appointed Agent to the King George Commissions. Thomas Archer,

Thomas Bateman and Sir John Vanbrugh gave architectural assistance. Then there were Henry Smith the Commission's Treasurer and, from Parliament, Secretary of State William Bromley among others. [3] In the first fifty years of the Bank's history it was with professional men such as these, rather than with their landed clientele, that the Hoares shared an identity of interest and common purpose. Subsequently the funding for the new churches, which was meant to derive from the tax on coal, became problematical and when the Commission was wound up in 1734 only nineteen new churches had been built or procured.

Beyond the immediate circle of active Commissioners there was a wider group of dedicated men who, like Henry, approached the issue of spreading the influence of the Church of England through schools and societies with almost obsessive concern. Henry's name appears as a trustee or member or banker to many of the societies. Given the Hoare family's commitment to the Established Church as the driving force for moral reform and political stability, it comes as no great surprise to find the two great Protestant Missionary Societies, the Society for the Propagation of Christian Knowledge and its close relation, the Society for the Propagation of the Gospel, among the customer lists of the Bank. Both were founded in the heat of the Anglican revival. Dr Thomas Bray, the theologian and founder of the SPCK in 1699, was also a personal customer. [4]

Dr Bray concentrated most of his efforts on establishing parochial libraries in England and the new colony of Maryland where they were to become the first public libraries in America. Between 1706 and 1713, 6730 books had been received into the repository for the libraries, the majority written by the principal theological writers of the day including Henry's close friends Robert Nelson and Thomas Bray. Those willing to be benefactors to the SPCK were desired to 'pay the sums they shall contribute to Mr Henry Hoare, in Fleet Street, London'. After a flourishing start the 'Account For Parocheall Librarys' rather petered out in the late 1720s but the loss of impetus there, was, to some degree, compensated for by Henry's personal enthusiasm for the cause of publishing and distributing Bibles, Books of Common Prayer and other suitable works. Interest on the £2000 bequest in his will to the Henry Hoare Bible Fund was spent in this way, and the trustees of the Fund held their first meeting at the Bank on 1 July 1725. For two hundred years thereafter the minutes of the annual meetings were recorded in a single slim volume. Now it is in the care of Messrs Hoare Trustees although the family connection is still maintained, with three of the Partners acting as Trustees. The Fund's objectives remain the same, and the stipulation that each volume supplied should carry a bookplate acknowledging 'The gift of Henry Hoare Esq', which is a precise reproduction of those originally engraved for the Fund, continues unaltered.

Henry's other major charitable bequest was to Charity Schools and Workhouses. During Queen Anne's reign well over a hundred Charity Schools had been erected in the City and Westminster. The master in charge of one at

Clerkenwell was criticized at a meeting of the SPCK in 1711 for allowing his pupils and himself to appear in a public performance of *Timon of Athens*. This was considered by the Society to be 'a great reproach to the design of Charity Schools'. Sir Richard and Henry were asked to intervene to prevent any further performance taking place, and the master, Mr Honeycott, subsequently had his licence to teach withdrawn by the Bishop of London.

The Hoares also played a central part in organizing a very different kind of public exhibition involving Charity School children. In 1713 after the signing of a peace with France which ended the War of the Spanish Succession, a thanksgiving service was held at St Paul's Cathedral celebrating the provision that the thrones of Spain and France should never be united, the recognition of the Hanoverian Succession, and the gaining of Minorca, Gibralta and tracts of new territory in North America. Nearly 4000 charity children 'new clothed with their masters and mistresses were placed on a machine or gallery in the Strand, which was in length above 600 feet, and had in breadth eight ranges of seats one above another, whereby they were put in full view of both Houses of Parliament in their procession to St. Paul's on that occasion'. This exhibition was repeated the following year on the new King George I's triumphal entry into the City of London.

For a brief period between 1719 and 1725 the two brothers, Henry and Benjamin, ran the business together. There were sixteen years between them, but Benjamin was evidently well regarded. He did not live at Fleet Street, but in a house in St Martin's Lane and, with his father's legacy of £4000, augmented by a

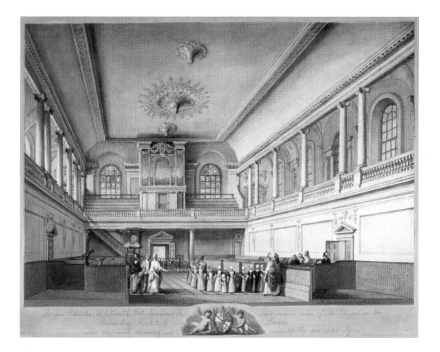

*Chapel of the Foundling Hospital, founded in 1739 by Thomas Coram for the care of abandoned infants. Hoare's were bankers to the charity; Benjamin was a governor.*

Benjamin Hoare on horseback with his groom, by John Wootton, c.1732. Painted at Boreham, Essex, with the spire of Danbury church in the background.

further £2000 from his brother's estate in 1725, he began buying land in Essex, near Colchester.

In 1730 he borrowed £28,500, at the rate of 4.5 per cent interest, from the Bank to purchase the New Hall estate which had been owned by the Duke and Duchess of Montagu. They had a sizeable mortgage on it from Hoare's. The estate included a beautiful but ruinous old house, which Benjamin used as a source for the internal fittings for the new house he had already begun to build himself at Boreham, on the Colchester Road, using Edward Shepherd as his surveyor. At exactly the same time Shepherd, who had opened his account at Hoare's in 1724, was engaged as architect and builder by the actor-manager John Rich to build the first Theatre Royal on the Covent Garden site (now the Royal Opera House but in those days a playhouse) which opened on 7 December 1732. In 1730 John Rich, flushed with success from his production of John Gay's *Beggar's Opera* in his theatre in Lincoln Inn Fields, issued a Prospectus for a capital issue of £15,000, but it is clear that Shepherd had to finance the Covent Garden project personally at the beginning and relied on the Bank for loans. Shepherd kept his account at the Bank for as long as he was in debt to the Partners and his final repayment of £250 was made in 1747. Had Good Henry been alive it is most unlikely that the Bank would have become involved in a scheme for a new theatre in London.

The tradesmen and craftsmen employed to work on the theatre were in many cases the same men Shepherd had used to build and decorate Boreham, which cost Benjamin £19,000. His new house was criticized by Lord Oxford who would doubtless have been even more censorious had he known the true cost of it: 'Such is the fine taste of a banker on Fleet Street. He has laid out about £12,000 and had

*East front of Stourhead 1725. Engraving of Colen Campbell's design, showing a projecting portico, abandoned by Good Henry and added by Charles Parker in 1839.*

eight been laid out upon the old house when he first bought it he would have had one of the best houses in England.' Benjamin sold off the New Hall portion of the estate in 1738 for £11,367, but Boreham remained in the family for three generations until it was sold in 1783. The John Wootton equestrian portraits of Benjamin, his adolescent son Richard and their huntsmen, which were commissioned shortly after Boreham was finished, to display the splendour of the setting of the new country house, now hang at the Bank in Fleet Street. Surrounded by the more conventional portraits of their relations, they are a reminder of the lure of the country estate for the newly enriched city men, who after the sobering example of the South Sea affair, assiduously banked their assets in land and indulged their taste for refinement by building and adorning increasingly grand houses.

In this, among the Hoare family, Sir Richard himself had led the way. By the terms of his marriage settlement in 1672, Sir Richard Hoare had agreed to buy a freehold property worth £150 per annum in or near London or land worth £50 less if it was situated in the country within thirty miles of London. During his lifetime his rented house at Hendon fulfilled the role of a country house for him and Lady Hoare. However it only comprised a house and garden and thus, in accordance with the marriage agreement, in 1700 he bought 242 acres at Staplehurst in Kent from Lady Gerrard for £1700. Her husband Sir Samuel Gerrard had had several judgements against him, in the King's Bench Division, for non-payment of debt including a sum of £600 plus costs which was owing to Richard Hoare from 1688. It is probable that the purchase of the estate in Kent was in part settlement of the debt. Staplehurst was held in trust during the lifetime of Sir Richard and

Lady Hoare and thereafter was settled on their otherwise disinherited eldest son 'Naughty Richard', and from him it passed down the senior line of the family.

Good Henry purchased his own estate at Stourton in 1717 for £23,000, but he did not begin the building work until 1721, employing the Scottish architect, Colen Campbell. Henry's brother-in-law, Benson, had employed Campbell to design Wilbury, which was planned on a modest scale as a house for occasional rather than continuous occupation. Plans and elevations of the house, described as 'invented and built by himself in the style of Inigo Jones', appeared in the first volume, of Campbell's great illustrated work *Vitruvius Britannicus* or 'The British Architect' published in 1715. This covered the work of Wren and Vanbrugh. It also introduced the work of Andrea Palladio and Inigo Jones, the English exponent of Italian classicism, to a wider audience in Britain. Campbell paid tribute to Benson for having rediscovered Inigo Jones and showing at Wilbury 'a particular Regard to the noblest Manner of Architecture in this beautiful and regular Design'.

*18th century pewter sand shaker used for drying ink. Blotting paper was a mid Victorian invention.*

Campbell's reputation as the leading Palladian architect of the day was further enhanced by the patronage offered him by one of the Bank's customers, Richard Boyle, 3rd Earl of Burlington, who employed him as architect for the remodelling of Burlington House in Piccadilly and for his new house at Chiswick. In 1718 Benson appointed him his deputy during his brief tenure as Surveyor-General. Henry would have known Campbell from his time on the Commission for Fifty New Churches and had witnessed his rise to stardom. Given his familiarity with the man and his work and the endorsement Campbell had received for his ideas from Benson and Lord Burlington, we can assume that Henry needed little persuasion to choose him as the architect for his own house. When he posed for his portrait for Michael Dahl he chose to be represented, not as a banker, but in his newly acquired position as a wealthy landowner, dressed in a coat of rich brown velvet and displaying in his hand Campbell's drawing of his house, the designs for which were published in 1725 in the third volume of *Vitruvius Britannicus*. He called the house Stourhead.[5]

Although Henry gives every appearance of being well established as a country gentleman in Dahl's picture, the truth was he never had more than a short taste of life as a landowner. Nevertheless he quickly developed a fondness for Stourhead and in his will, drawn up in 1722, he stipulated that he should be buried, not with a fanfare in St Dunstan's in the West, but 'in a private manner in a leaden coffin in the vault I have built in the parish church of Stourton'. The building work on the house was not finished at his death; the last entry in his building account is dated 27 January 1725 and is for £50 0s 9d for communion plate for St Peter's Church at Stourton, the total spent up to that date being £10,150 10s 5d. All the while the house was being built he bought household goods and furniture to fit it out.

After his death his widow Jane, by his specific instruction, was to be allowed to continue to live at Fleet Street with her children until his heir, Henry, reached the age of twenty-one. If Henry then wanted the Banking House for his personal use, he must furnish his mother with the means to rent a house elsewhere. In fact Henry went to live in a house in Lincoln's Inn Fields. Jane and Henry were also charged with finishing the work at Stourton, work which included providing a water supply to the house and making a garden. Henry left £3000 to complete the works in addition to all the rents which were in the hands of his 'stewards, bailiffs or receivers' at the time of his death. His personal legacy to Jane was £4000, while the whole of the estate at Stourton was settled on her in jointure and all expenses relating to the repair and maintenance were to be met by Henry. If she required further sums over and above the £3000 to be spent at Stourton, she should be obliged so long as she made her request in writing.

It seems that Hendon was abandoned at this stage. It had hardly been occupied since Lady Hoare's death in 1720 and Jane took to living at Stourton. Henry's legacies to his own family and relations were generous. He left £2000 to his 'loving brother' Benjamin, although he had to work for it: 'When my said brother Benjamin shall have made up a fair and just account of such part of my personal estate as belongs to the said co-partnership and shall have paid or delivered over to such person or persons to whom the residue of my personall estate is hereinafter bequeathed ... then only the said legacy ... shall be paid to my said brother Benjamin.' Furthermore he was 'recommended' to take Richard, his younger nephew, as 'an apprentice in his trade ... and if he continues to behave himself well until he attains his age of one and twenty years then to give him the rest of his time and take him in a partner with him in his trade.' This Richard, later to become the second Lord Mayor in the family, was left £4000 by his father, as well as his place in the Bank, but no property.

Through their successful 'riding' of the South Sea Bubble, which resulted in a profit for the Bank of £28,000, Henry and Benjamin had made a crucial contribution to the prosperity of the Golden Bottle, though there is evidence that the experience predisposed them to increase their already conservative cash–liability ratios.[6] The ascendancy of the Whigs under George I put a stop to any political ambition Good Henry may have had. Paradoxically though, his close relationship with William Benson and his natural desire to improve his social position in line with his increase in wealth, led him to become one of the earliest supporters of the 'Whiggish' taste in architecture. His purchase of the Stourton estate propelled the Hoare family from their membership of the merchant classes into the ranks of the landed gentry and his building of a neo-Palladian villa put them in the vanguard of good taste. It was a position his son and heir, Henry, was to exploit fully in his remarkable creation of the 'Paradise' of Stourhead.

# Chapter Three

# Henry the Magnificent and the Paradise of Stourhead 1725–1783

I n 1725, over fifty years after Richard Hoare entered the first customer's name in his own ledgers, the third generation of his family took on the task of running the Bank. This third generation was dominated by Henry the Magnificent (1705-85) whose wealth and personal charisma spectacularly overshadowed his Partners in the Bank. They were all committed bankers, unhesitatingly loyal to their predecessors' creation, but they were led and largely controlled by Henry.

Henry was an unusually fortunate young man. In addition to a large country estate, he had inherited freehold property in London, including the Bank premises, and a large share of the business. His half share of the profits was endorsed in the partnership deed of 1732 which, in terms of the distribution of shares between himself and the other Partners, remained unchanged until after his death.[1] Added to these advantages he had a good brain and generally robust health, remaining active well into his seventies, which enabled him to direct the Bank's affairs for sixty years. His unequivocal devotion to the business was remarkable, given that he was a man of outstanding cultural refinement whose pleasure grounds at Stourhead, and collection of works of art in the house there, have traditionally been regarded as his pre-occupation and his greatest achievement.

Not much is known of Henry's childhood. He was educated at Westminster School, and we must assume he moved between Fleet Street and Hendon while under the charge of his parents. As a young man he spent time at Quarley in Hampshire, not far from Amesbury, conveniently situated half way on the road

facing page

*Henry Hoare II, painted as 'the Magnificent' by Michael Dahl and John Wootton for Stourhead in 1726, the year of his marriage to Anne Masham.*

from Stourhead to London. Good Henry had bought Quarley as a first step towards his move to the country. It was here, as he later told his grandson, Richard Colt Hoare, that Henry the Magnificent enjoyed himself with his friends: hunting, shooting and drinking until he found the 'gay and dissolute style of life' was affecting his health. He also had considerable responsibilities. He was only nineteen when he came into the business and twenty-one when he married Anne Masham, the daughter of Lord and Lady Masham (who, as Lady-in-Waiting to Queen Anne, had brought the Privy Purse account to Sir Richard Hoare in 1710). Anne died in childbirth in 1727, within a year of their marriage, leaving Henry a widower with an infant daughter. In 1728 he married Susan Colt of Clapham, and in 1734 he was elected MP for Salisbury and bought Wilbury from his uncle William Benson. Although Henry did not take up residence at Stourhead until his mother died in 1741, he was keenly interested in finishing the house and in the period 1726-34 spent £10,000 on building works and £3000 on furniture.

It was also a time that he spent reading. In correspondence with his nephew, Richard Hoare, in 1755, he advised him to spend his leisure hours at Fleet Street 'looking into Books and the pursuit of that knowledge which distinguishes only the Gentleman from the Vulgar and teaches him to adorn his fortune he acquires or possesses and which, without the lessons in History (which is Philosophy teaching by example) the most envied height of Fortune will not be enjoyed'. We know from his letters that he was familiar with the works of Pope and Milton, Virgil and Ovid, authors whom William Benson admired. Through him Henry was also introduced to the painter John Wootton, the sculptor Michael Rysbrack and the architect Henry Flitcroft, all of whom he went on to employ at Stourhead. In 1737 Henry travelled to Italy on a belated Grand Tour and over the following three years spent considerable sums on 17th and 18th century Italian masters[2] which he shipped back to Stourhead.

His ambitious plans for the garden did not begin to take shape until after

1743, the year Susan died leaving him with three young children. Richard Colt Hoare wrote that his grandfather 'did not think of seriously improving his place by plantation till he gained the age of forty years. When he began he proceeded *con spirito* upon a widely extended scale.' In the absence of any surviving documents for his grand scheme, historians have seen Henry's manifest interest in the authors of the classical world and the great artists who visualized it, as the key to his intended purpose at Stourhead. His garden was a re-creation of a classical

'*A Conversation of Virtuosis …*'*at the King's Arms, by Gawen Hamilton, 1735. This club of artists included John Wootton, Michael Dahl, Michael Rysbrack and George Vertue, all of whom were patronized by the Hoare family.*

landscape designed with a lake as its central feature and temple-like buildings, set against wooded slopes, marking stages in the prescribed route around its shore. His composition did not include the house, which was invisible from the low ground he had chosen for the garden.

Henry took twenty years to realize his plans, directing the works himself with the assistance of Henry Flitcroft, a protégé of Lord Burlington. Flitcroft worked with Henry from the beginning and became adept at interpreting his ideas. The lake, planned from the outset but not completed until 1754-55 (when a sizeable dam was built to raise the level of the existing ponds, which were merged to form a single stretch of water), was the key element in his design, and the circuit around its undulating shores was created to take the enlightened visitor on a journey of discovery. Perhaps, as has been suggested,[3] he wished this journey to be recognized as an allegory of Aeneas's wanderings from Troy to Italy where he founded the colony from which the Roman people traced their origin. The heroic Aeneas was thus celebrated as the founder of a dynasty strongly associated with a place, and it is not too fanciful to conjecture that Henry was making a similar claim for the Hoare family at Stourhead.

He expected his allusions to the classical past to be understood as was made clear from the inscription from the sixth book of Virgil's *Aeneid* on Flitcroft's first building for him, the Temple of Ceres (now called Flora), which greeted the visitor on entering; 'Procul o procul este profani' ('Hence,oh hence, ye that are uninitiated'). Four years later Henry began work on his subterranean Grotto further round the lake. It was lined with tufa-like rock and a jagged window opening at water level revealed a sublime view across the lake to the village church of Stourton. The pedimented entrance, now gone, carried another inscription from the *Aeneid*. The gloomy interior was lit dramatically from above, and, in a dark

recess in the main chamber, lay the statue of a sleeping nymph, sculpted in the classic style by John Cheere, above a pool representing the source of the Stour and lines from Alexander Pope's translation of a Renaissance Latin inscription: 'Nymph of the grot these sacred springs I keep...' From the entrance the eye was drawn to an imposing statue of the River God, 'old Tiber himself', also by Cheere, which in Henry's time was accompanied by an inscription from Ovid's *Metamorphoses*.

Henry saw the planting of his garden with the eyes of an artist. He observed in 1752 that 'the greens should be ranged together in large masses as the shades are in paintings: to contrast the dark masses with light ones, and to relieve each dark mass itself with little sprinklings of lighter greens here and there'.[4] With the building of Flitcroft's Pantheon in 1753-54, designed to house Rysbrack's statue of Hercules, the pictorial imagery directly influencing Henry became more apparent. A ledger entry in his 'Wilberry' account book for 5 December 1746 refers to his purchase of a painting by John Wootton as a companion to his Claude Lorrain. This is the first indication we have of Henry's interest in Claude. The Pantheon appears in a number of Claude's paintings, but the most important for Stourhead was his 'Coast view of Delos with Aeneas' (now in the National Gallery), which was on sale in Paris in 1737 and which Henry may well have seen on his travels. Claude's buildings and the relationship between them bear a striking resemblance to Henry's Pantheon and Temple of Flora in his created landscape at Stourhead. He completed his landscape 'after Claude' by adding a stone bridge over the end of the lake in 1762 which enhanced the view from the Pantheon over the lake to the village and reminded him of the work of Gaspard Dughet, a follower of Claude. He wrote to his daughter, Sukey, on 23 October 1762: 'The bridge is now about. It is simple and plain. I took it from Palladio's bridge at Vicenza, 5 arches, and when you stand at the Pantheon the water will be seen thro the arches and it will look as if the river came down thro the village and that this was the village bridge for publick use; the view of the Bridge, village and church altogether will be a Charming Gaspd. Picture at that end of the water.'[5]

The last monument of Henry's classical scheme was the Temple of Apollo built on high ground overlooking the gardens. Again designed by Flitcroft, it was based on an engraving in Robert Wood's *Ruins of Balbec*, which Henry bought on its publication in 1757. The Temple was finished in 1765, and its completion marked the end of Henry's 'Virgilian period' and his move, inspired by Horace Walpole's transformation of his house called Strawberry Hill on the Thames at Twickenham (which Henry visited in 1763), towards a taste for Gothic. In 1765 he added the fourteenth century Bristol High Cross to his 'Charming Gaspd. Picture'. The Cross had been presented to him in pieces by the Dean of Bristol Cathedral; he restored it and placed it by the entrance to the gardens. The following year he acquired another discarded antiquity – a fifteenth-century pump from St Peter's Church in Bristol – which he set up on a Grotto base over the springs at the far end of Six Wells Bottom.

Stourhead was admired as a showplace by contemporary observers. Garden visiting was fashionable, and the new 'garden circuits' such as it boasted provided gracious out-door entertainment for the leisured classes. Stourhead had its rivals, notably at Stowe where over thirty garden buildings had been completed by 1760; nonetheless it excited great interest and admiration. Some visitors, like Horace Walpole, who visited it in June 1762, had seen dozens of other country seats with which they could compare it, but he declared it 'one of the most picturesque scenes in the world' and the Pantheon as having few rivals 'in magnificence, taste and beauty'. John Wesley's impression was less favourable 'because I cannot admire the images of devils and we know the gods of the heathens are devils [and] because I defy all mankind to reconcile statues with nudity, either to common-sense or common decency.' He noticed however that 'others were delighted with the temples'.

Parson Woodforde, whose nephew, the artist Samuel Woodforde, was to enjoy the patronage of both Henry and Richard Colt Hoare, came to Stourhead in 1763, the year Samuel was born. He spent the whole day there with a large party of friends and relations, noting, typically, how 'we dined at the sign of the old Merlin at Stourton upon a boiled Round of beef and 2 fowls ... The Temple of

*Stourhead Garden. The Bristol Cross, by Francis Nicholson, who was employed by Colt Hoare to make watercolour drawings of Stourhead in 1813.*

Hercules must have cost Mr Hoare £10,000, it is excessively grand – the Grotto where the sleeping nymph laid struck me much more than anything else there.' Five years later he returned and dined at the house: 'I was introduced to Mr Hoare by Justice Creed and received very graciously – Mr Hoare's House is as well furnished a house as any in the Kingdom, not excepting any, and his pictures are the best without exception – Mr Hoare is a tall thin gentleman, and very familiar, and as rich a man as any in the Kingdom.'

Henry did not work in isolation at Stourhead. He was a pivotal figure in the development of landscape design but he was also one of a group of 'gentlemen gardeners' who borrowed ideas from one another. Charles Hamilton, Henry's contemporary, started his garden project at Painshill in Surrey four or five years before Henry set to work at Stourhead. Both men designed and directed the construction of their gardens themselves. They also appear to have kept a close watch on one another. There was a certain amount of rivalry and some imitation, though

*Mr and Mrs Samuel Hoare at Heath House, Hampstead, c.1820, previously the home of Christopher Arnold. Though a City banker, Samuel was only distantly related to the Hoares of 'The Golden Bottle'.*

Hamilton's garden had 'no declared theme, no political or artistic "signposts" for the visitors to read and follow'.[6] The essential difference was in their respective financial circumstances. Henry could afford all that he did at Stourhead, whereas Hamilton overreached himself. In 1747 Hamilton opened an account at Hoare's and borrowed £6000 on mortgage to finance his improvements, but eventually the money ran out and in 1773 Painshill was sold.

Stourhead may be the clue to Henry's meticulous management of the Bank. To pay for his creation of a paradise on earth he was in turn obliged to pay very great attention to affairs at Fleet Street. It was income from the Bank which brought his dreams to reality, a fact which he never allowed himself to forget for one moment and which he spelt out to his nephew Richard in a letter dated 28 January 1755: 'What is there in creation … Those are the fruits of industry and application to Business and shows what great things may be done by it, the envy of the indolent who have no claims to Temples, Grottos, Bridges, Rocks, Exotick Pines [pineapples] and Ice in Summer. When those are won by the industrious, they have the best claim to them provided their foundations are laid by the hand of prudence and supported by perseverance in well-doing and constant watchfulness over the main chance.' Henry and his uncle Benjamin were effectively joint senior Partners, although Henry's capital share was twice that of Benjamin's and four times that of his younger brother Richard, aged twenty-two, and the former clerk Christopher Arnold.[7]

Christopher Arnold had entered the business under his father's wing in 1707 and as a young man, like his father before him, served his apprenticeship and was duly made a freeman of the Goldsmith's Company. On Henry's premature death in middle age, in 1725, Benjamin and Henry naturally turned to their loyal servant and fellow-goldsmith, Christopher Arnold, to join the partnership in the same year. In Hoare's Bank, Christopher's partnership was unique, but generally speaking such a promotion would have been considered an unexceptional event at the time when apprenticeship was the automatic route to enter and rise in certain professions. These would have included among others: apothecaries and surgeons, architects and survey-ors, solicitors and attorneys as well as merchants of all kinds includ-ing goldsmiths. In Christopher Arnold's case this move at once took him from a clerk's salary (with bonus) of £50 a year to a profit share which fluctuated but never fell below £800 and in peak years during the 1740s and 1750s yielded over £2200, although he remained a minority shareholder

Sale document relating to Henry Thrale's Anchor Brewery which was sold to Messrs Barclay and Perkins after his death in 1781. Thrale was a Bank customer; his youngest daughter, Sophia, married Henry Merrick Hoare in 1807.

in the profits of the business until his death in 1758. By 1744 he had made enough money to buy Heath House, a substantial brick-built house with one and a half acres and magnificent views still to be found on the crest of Hampstead Hill, in addition to renting a country retreat, Rectory House in Datchet, Buckinghamshire. The Arnolds' name became associated with Datchet over succeeding generations in the same way, if not quite on the same scale, as the Hoare name became identified with their estate at Stourton. Christopher Arnold's memorial is in Datchet Church and he and his wife are remembered to this day in the village for their generous bequests to the parish.

England went to war with Spain in 1739 over the Spanish monopoly of trade with South America, and, for much of the rest of Henry's life, was engaged in full-scale wars or military skirmishes in Europe, India or America. England's 'War of Jenkins' Ear' with Spain evolved into war with France and Prussia over the issue of the Austrian Succession, lasting until 1748, while at home the Young Pretender, Bonnie Prince Charlie, attempted to reinstate the Stuart dynasty with the support of France in 1745. In 1756 hostilities with France erupted again in all three con-tinents and were not concluded until the Treaty of Paris in 1763. There followed a respite for over a decade until Britain's humiliating loss of her North American colonies, a prelude to revolution in France.

At the beginning of this prolonged period of hostilities, in the 1740s, government borrowing was reasonably light and the Dutch, at that stage a friendly nation, continued to invest on a scale which kept interest rates buoyant. The Bank nevertheless began to build up its cash reserves and restrict loans, raising deposits from £460,000 in 1740 to £610,000 five years later, the year of the Jacobite Rising. It managed to keep the ratio of cash to liabilities high but deposits were halved in the year 1745-46. Victory over the Jacobite rebels at Culloden heralded a period of slow retrenchment throughout the private banking sector. The Bank began to rebuild its deposits and lend again cautiously, but demanding first that old loans be repaid.

Although they were switching their own resources into interest-bearing government securities, such as Navy and Victualling bills and Ordnance debentures, where good profits were to be made trading in the sharply rising discounts, the Partners were not prepared to offer loans to their customers who wished to do the same thing. Money was tight and the Partners made it clear that they would not sell their own government securities to finance loans to customers who wished to purchase further government paper for themselves. Nevertheless the crisis in credit caused by the demands of war from 1758 onwards did force them to realize their securities; roughly one fifth of their assets were then invested in these 'Funds'. Although deposits remained low throughout the period 1758-64 these sales of government stock, which cost the Bank dearly at the time, enabled them to maintain a healthy cash-to-liabilities ratio during a period when, as Henry described it, 'there was a crisis of stagnation of money and a consuming war without prospect of end'.

In such circumstances growth was not possible in the private banking sector. Profits shrank to £5974 in 1756, the year when the Seven Years War began. Government borrowing increased

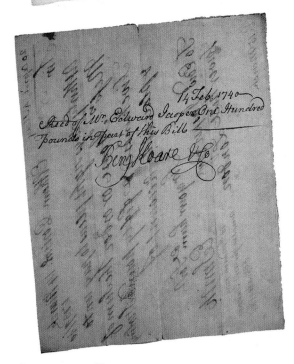

dramatically two years into the war and Henry, recognizing a crisis, was firm in dealing with his customers although, as he later revealed in a letter to a customer, Thomas Parker, written from Stourhead on 15 September 1759, it was never a position he relished: 'it is a mortification to live in times when it is not in our power to oblige and obey the commandments of our Best friends.' In the same year, Richard promised William Mildmay, who was pressing again for a loan he had already been refused six months earlier, that he would show his letter to Henry, but 'I have … to add that at this time we do not advance money to any person whatever'. Henry's letters of refusal to the many requests he had for loans, on any security, tell the same story. He had a stock explanation which he used to refuse his customers: 'The uncommon supply of millions upon millions granted now to be raised again obliges all of our Profession to be prepared for these payments coming on so that instead of lending money out we have called it in.'

*Lord North, by George Romney, 1780. Prime Minister 1770-1782 and bank customer. He lived and died in debt.*

  Where necessary, Henry added a little extra pressure. On 15 October 1759 he wrote to George Cooke calling for the repayment of £1000 lent on bond: '… we have been calling in tens of thousands from our best friends who have been so good as to consider us at this critical time and without scruple have paid us off with chearfullness … everyone must take his share with us in suffering inconveniences for the publick troubles.' On 18 January 1759, he had sent a peremptory demand for the immediate repayment of an eight-year-old loan of £13,000 to the Duke of Newcastle, a loan which, as Henry pointed out, was given on slender security and at only 3 per cent (money at that time could not be had for less than 5 per cent, often with the addition of a premium). He added reprovingly that as First Lord of the Treasury nobody was in a better position than His Grace to judge the uncommon scarcity of money and the critical state of credit. After threatening legal action for the recovery of the debt the loan was paid off in October of that year.

  Debt chasing, which particularly pre-occupied the Partners during the war years, was a way of life in their dealings with some of their customers. Thomas Thynne succeeded his father as third Viscount Weymouth in 1751 and, to satisfy his trustees, Hoare's were prepared to lend him several large sums as a mortgage to enable him to pay off his debts. Weymouth borrowed the astronomical sum of £94,000 overall and on 19 September 1758 Henry was constrained to write to him directly expressing great indignation at the fact that rather than paying back thousands of pounds annually to reduce the debt, as had been agreed, Lord Weymouth had boldly increased it by making further substantial drawings, and it now stood

Thomas Thynne, 1st
Marquess of Bath,
c. 1795. His borrowings
from Hoare's were double
the amount ever loaned
to any other person.

at a sum 'larger by more than double than we ever advanced to one person'. This
debt became known as 'The Affair of the Mortgages' and was the subject of anxious correspondence between Henry and Weymouth's man of business, Euan
Thomas. The mortgages may have been the 'best of securities' but, as Henry
explained in a letter to Thomas a month later, there was likely to be a call for funds
of £13 or £14 million for the war effort, sums larger than had ever been known
before and far greater than anyone could have foreseen, and the Bank, wishing to
perform its patriotic duty in bearing its 'share in the Publick Troubles' by buying
into 'the Funds', requested that at least one of the large mortgages should be repaid.

Among their landed clientele Hoare's had developed something of a speciality
in lending money out on mortgage and, where that was not possible, in finding
other lenders for customers who had good mortgages to offer and who were in
need of cash. For these arrangements they often had to look further afield than
their own customers. One such 'outside' lender was Colonel (later Lord) Clive of
the East India Company, Pitt's 'heaven born general', whose campaigns in the sub-
continent had won him fame and a nabob's fortune. Clive had already paid off the
£13,000 debt owed to the Bank by the Duke of Newcastle and, much encouraged
by this, Henry did not hesitate to urge Mr Thomas to gain Lord Weymouth's consent to allow Clive to take over one or other of his outstanding mortgages.

The Bank's loan ledgers record several unusually large borrowings by noble
customers throughout this period, notably the Duke of Northumberland, the
Duke of Kingston and Lord Milton, as well as the Jamaican sugar baron, Alderman
William Beckford MP. None of them, as Henry pointed out, amounted to even half
the amount borrowed by Weymouth, who made his bankers work hard for their

money. By 13 June 1761, the year government borrowing reached its peak, Henry's frustration with Lord Weymouth had reached such a pitch that indignation broke through the deferential manner he customarily employed in dealing with his noble clients: 'Indeed my Lord there is no such thing as carrying on business at this rate, punctuality is the soul of it and must be insisted on. I will affirm that no House in the City would have been so regardful of your Lordship's interests as we have been from the beginning of our transactions with yourself and farther in prejudice to our own.'

Weymouth appeared deaf to his entreaties until threatened with legal action, whereupon he wrote himself to Henry, lamenting that it was much more disagreeable for him not to be able to discharge his debt than it was for the Bank to continue to bear it, adding that it was the impossibility of finding the money rather than callousness which prevented repayment. He reasoned that if Hoares so desired the money perhaps they could find somebody willing to take over one of the remaining mortgages and he, Weymouth, would pay any rate of interest that was asked for. Although there is no evidence to suggest that he was particularly influenced by the fact that Weymouth was a near neighbour of his in Wiltshire, Henry backed down in the face of this insouciant response. Predictably Weymouth's vague reassurances about clearing his balance amounted to nothing and his debt continued to grow. Some of the money was spent wisely on the improvement of his estate at Longleat, but as a young man he had spent recklessly, and his taste for gaming and drinking at Brooks' and Whites didn't diminish with age. Although interest on his loans was paid in full and on time, which Weymouth believed entitled him to make further drawings without limitation, a principal of £64,000 still remained outstanding and was not repaid until May 1789, the year Weymouth, always a favourite of the king's, was created Marquess of Bath, and four years after Henry's death.

Bankers were at some disadvantage in their dealings with their aristocratic customers. The richest and most powerful social and political group in the country, they were immensely attractive as clients and the long-term advantages of keeping them and their families on the books outweighed many of the short-term difficulties of keeping their borrowings under control and their creditworthiness under surveillance. They borrowed to consume, to cover debts incurred at gaming and from high living, to build, to make improvements in agriculture and transport and to make the necessary arrangements for marriage settlements. To exercise any financial control over individuals with such unbridled influence required fine judgement and strict rules.

The private banks in Fleet Street, the Strand and Charing Cross – Hoare's, Child's, Gosling's, Coutts and Drummond's – all had landowning customers, and were keen for their business, but they could also be distinguished from one another by their particular affiliation to other groups.[8] Drummond's, for example, founded in 1717, built its reputation on its virtual monopoly of business from the

*Richard 'Beau' Nash, by William Hoare, c.1749. A Bank customer, he transformed Bath from a provincial spa into the leading fashionable resort of the century.*

regimental army agents, while Gosling's, at the sign of the Three Squirrels in Fleet Street, had a special relationship with the book trade, based on Sir Francis Gosling's connection with publishing. When Sam Bennett, a retired East India trader, joined the firm in 1743 he brought his East India Company connections with him. Child's, too, had strong associations with the East India Company but in other respects closely resembled Hoare's in terms of its size and profile. Although Coutts had its origins in Scottish banking, Thomas Coutts made it known that he wished to attract aristocratic custom and was averse to any connection with industry. Among the smaller firms, Wright's in Covent Garden specialized in holding the accounts of the Catholic gentry, and Herries Bank in St. James's Street specialized in the issue of travellers cheques for gentlemen going on the Grand Tour.

The Golden Bottle was perhaps the first in the field to make a distinct reputation for itself as a money lender on mortgage security and as a broker in mortgage loans, keeping control of its credit by careful scrutiny of all securities and insistence on retaining all the legal writings to the loans until the interest and the principal was paid in.[9] Henry was outraged when, in 1764, the Honourable Thomas Harley attempted to withdraw his security of a mortgage deed, which he had deposited with Hoare's against a loan of £3000, on the pretence of repayment, while in fact he wished to use it as a security to raise a further £3000 elsewhere.

The financial affairs of two customers, Sir James Lowther, the 'bad' Earl of Lonsdale, and Thomas Pelham Holles, the first Duke of Newcastle, illustrate how Henry's careful attention to the management of debt was crucial for the Bank in protecting itself from the profligate among its noble customers. Lowther spent prodigiously on electioneering in his native counties of Cumberland and Westmorland, but it was his addiction to the gaming tables at Arthur's that really worried Henry. Henry was chasing repayment of a £31,000 loan, and he realized that repaying one's banker was not the priority where gaming debts were concerned.

Banking was a very personal affair between the banker and his customer and the proprietor and his clerk. Henry wrote to Sir James on 20 November 1758: 'I am concerned that I was not in Fleet Street yesterday when you honoured us with your commands and would have paid my respects to you myself this morning had either of my partners been in the way to permit my absence. I have therefore as you are pleased to direct sent one of our clerks Mr Dawes the Bearer to receive your commands.' It was an accommodation worth making so as to get his debt settled and, after Mr Dawes' visit, Henry was moved to write as much in direct terms to the baronet: 'I will wait on you any morning and hour that you are pleased to name to enforce more, if possible what I have now wrote.' Leaving no stone unturned, he suggested the same to Lowther's London agent, Fletcher Norton, proposing he would call on Norton in his chambers in the Temple before he left for the Law Courts in Westminster in the morning or on his return, when Henry could call in after his departure from the Bank at his habitual time of 3 pm. That was when he went home to dinner.

Henry followed Lowther's gambling fortunes closely, noting in a letter to Fletcher Norton, on 18 December 1758, that it was publicly known Sir James's name had been drawn in the ballot to appear at the next 'dangerous party of play at Arthur's' and raising the understandable concern that, if he should have a bad run, 'is there not a danger of his laying hold of this £31,000 to pay what he thinks a debt of honour, preferable to ours, as he certainly did in his loss at Newmarket?' The stream of letters from Fleet Street to Mr Norton had the desired effect on Lowther, who requested Henry to stop writing. In this case Lowther was true to his word and his debts were settled by 1760, with interest, which in this case appears to have been charged at an exceptionally high rate of 10 per cent.

*Henry Fielding, engraving after William Hogarth, c.1750. The novelist banked exclusively at Hoare's; apart from his bank account few of his own papers have survived.*

Newcastle's dealings with the Bank have already been touched on. The scale of his overspending was well known in his lifetime and the patience required of his bankers is worth describing in detail, although it pales to nothing when compared with the trials he inflicted on his trustees. His brother, Thomas Pelham, was Prime Minister from 1744 until his death ten years later, when Newcastle succeeded to the highest political office in the land. He was the owner of vast estates in eleven counties with large houses, which needed upkeep and improvement, in Nottinghamshire, Surrey, Sussex and London. He did not have any children, so his attention was not focused on passing on an estate unencumbered by debt to a son or on providing a suitable marriage portion for a daughter. His attitude to money was patrician in the extreme and he seemed unable to grasp the connection between what he needed to spend and what he had at his disposal. When his financial affairs became hopeless they were taken under the control of trustees. The one area of autonomy left to him was the leasing of lands, but even here he

showed no regard for his desperate need for cash, remaining firmly opposed to raising rents. He was fearful such a move would alienate his tenants which would be to the detriment of his political interests in those constituencies where he relied on support from his own people.

Newcastle's father, Lord Pelham of Laughton, had begun banking with Richard and Henry Hoare in 1696, and his two sons used the bank exhaustively during their lives. Ray Kelch, Newcastle's financial biographer observed, 'It would be difficult to overemphasize the role of Hoare's bank in the Duke's financial history.'[10] The Duke opened his account in 1714 at the age of twenty-one, the year he finally took possession of his inheritance from his uncle, one of the richest men in England with an annual income of £25,000 and no debts. He began spending on a grand scale almost at once and by his thirtieth birthday he had borrowed, from various creditors, a total of about £100,000, by which stage he was obliged to live on less than half his original income. The borrowing increased with time. To service the growing debts, his trustees were forever devising schemes whereby the Duke should live on less and less. Constant overspending characterized his relationship with Hoare's. When his credit failed elsewhere the Bank would usually come to his rescue.

A judicious combination of loyalty to the Pelham family and an awareness of the honour bestowed on the business at Fleet Street probably accounts for the Bank's continued support. Certainly the interest they were paid by his trustees was never generous. In 1751 the Partners agreed to accept a low rate of interest on a loan (3.5 per cent) knowing it would stand a better chance of getting paid at that rate, rather than at the usual 4 or 5 per cent. But they were always meticulous regarding the security, and if dissatisfied on that score they would not hesitate to call for the loan to be paid in. In 1751 they had agreed to the £13,000 loan, with the Duke's 'beloved' Claremont House in Surrey as security. Five years later, as they tightened their belts, they felt Claremont alone was inadequate and proposed that they would reduce the interest by a half a per cent if Newcastle House in London was added. This was eventually agreed to, but only after a tart exchange with Newcastle's solicitor. Henry's caustic observation that, if Claremont on its own was as good as was claimed, then the first Lord of the Treasury would have no difficulty getting the cash 'from some other friend', appears to have done the trick. The Partners clearly believed that Newcastle was a risk worth taking, or more probably, they didn't consider him a serious risk at all. With his immense landed wealth and other treasures, income from his political appointments and the management of all his money in the hands of trustees (who also banked at Hoare's) there was no danger that the Duke would be declared bankrupt.

The rents which Newcastle's stewards remitted to the Bank were sent from the country in cash, but never came anywhere near meeting the drawings from the Duke's account, which only balanced nine times in his life. On these occasions

*facing page*
*Thomas Pelham-Holles, 1st Duke of Newcastle, by William Hoare, c.1752. Hoare's most distinguished debtor of the 18th century.*

the ledgers would be taken to him at Newcastle House in Lincoln's Inn Fields where he would gather his accountants to examine them and then, in the customary manner, 'allow' them by adding his signature. There doesn't seem to have been any personal connection between the Duke and Henry, although they both had houses in Lincoln's Inn Fields, and, as we have seen, the same stern treatment was meted out to Newcastle as it was to others who were deeply in debt. After the final £13,000 was paid off in 1759 neither the Duke personally – nor his trustees – made any further borrowings from the Bank. When he resigned from office in 1762 he spent his few remaining years living comfortably off his income without the enormous costs associated with occupying high office. But if he managed to rescue himself and satisfy his bankers in the end, he paid a very high price along the way. A lifetime of spectacular indebtedness broke up the magnificent estates which his Pelham, Holles and Cavendish ancestors had increased and invested in over generations.

The Duke's unassailable position, as holder of the highest political office in the land and of the highest hereditary rank in the British peerage, and as landlord of extensive estates all over the country, provided Hoare's with the best security they could ask for. However much it cost the Bank in constant vigilance over his affairs and anxiety in times of stringency, it made good business sense for Hoare's to consolidate their increasing status as one of the principal bankers to the landowning classes by accommodating this notorious spender. It is a tribute to Henry's judgement that he recognized this and was prepared to act as one of Newcastle's major creditors, confident that the Bank could not lose, even during those unpropitious years when private credit was at a standstill and a contemporary witness reported that many of the great houses in the City 'were tumbling down one after another'.

If banking was testing during the middle decades of the eighteenth century, Henry was further stretched by the distresses and demands of his personal life. Left a widower for a second time in 1743, he became responsible for his two daughters, Susanna, known as 'Sukey', and Anne whom he called 'Nanny'. His only surviving son, Henry, died of smallpox in Naples in 1752 while on the Grand Tour. Henry never married again and had to manage, alone, the delicate business of guiding his daughters' entry into the marriage market, where their fortunes would be well known. In Sukey's case she married well, twice in the space of eight years, but these happy events were expensive for her father and, in the case of her first marriage in 1753 to Charles Boyle, Viscount Dungarvan, heir to the 5th Earl of Cork and Orrery, caused Henry untold trouble on account of her in-laws.

Henry gave the married pair a fully furnished house in Lincoln's Inn Fields, which he estimated cost him £10,000, along with jewellery worth £3000 and new clothes worth £1000 for his daughter. To the Earl came the welcome gift of over £25,000 as his daughter-in-law's portion, which should have been laid out on his son's inheritance, Marston House near Frome in Somerset, but was instead used to pay off Lord Cork's Irish mortgage with only £6000 being reserved for Dungarvan. (Lord Cork had inherited his Irish titles and estates from his kinsman Richard Boyle, 3rd Earl of Burlington, who died a few months before Charles and Sukey were married.) The Earl and Countess, both Bank customers, looked favourably on this union to begin with, as they had little money and their inherited estates were heavily encumbered with debt. Susanna's fortune was irresistible to them, as Lady Cork's remark on the proposed marriage inadvertently revealed: 'My Lord made no hesitation of giving consent although she was of birth far inferior to those ladies of noble houses from whom both my lord and his son were descended.'

Relations with the Bank, and Henry in particular, quickly soured. He realized that the Corks were in a distressed condition and persuaded them that their affairs

*State Lottery Tickets. The 1753 Lottery raised money to found the British Museum. The antiquities collections of Sir Hans Sloane, a physician and Bank customer, were purchased for the nation for £20,000. By 1815 lotteries had become discredited through private contractors parading absurd chances and were outlawed in 1823.*

must be put into the hands of a trust while they lived abroad. The Earl and Countess left for Italy with their youngest children, while Henry and Dungarvan, as the nominated trustees, attempted to manage their affairs at home. The trouble began when the Corks' agent in Ireland, under their instruction, creamed off all the revenues from the estates in Caledon in order to pay debts which had been concealed from the trustees. Henry, meanwhile, had felt obliged to pay off the Corks' small creditors himself without receiving a penny from the trust. Once he became aware of the deceit, 'his style to his noble customers was thenceforth cool and altered', as Lady Cork observed.

The Corks continued to make applications to the trustees for funds beyond the income they were allowed and made all manner of secret arrangements regarding money which they did not disclose to the trust. In one instance they were in dispute over who should pay for young Hamilton Boyle's school fees of £200 p.a. Christopher Arnold was brought in to give added weight to Henry's

Henry the Magnificent,
c.1758-60, pastel by
William Hoare, probably
made as a study for a
more formal oil portrait.

resolve not to pay: 'Mr Arnold observing the trust is debtor for £8,566 5s 6d has protested against paying any more till the remittances from Ireland enable us to do it, on which an order of refusal was given at Fleet Street.'

In 1755 the Corks returned to England. The dispute with Henry developed into open hostility; Lady Cork took great offence at Susanna's coldness towards her and her husband, which she viewed as a serious case of lese majesty and, in the

face of all evidence to the contrary, she made a defiant stab at placing all wrong-doing at the doors of Hoare's Bank: 'We have gone as far as any persons can or ought to go with an intention to preserve harmony between us and the family into which Lord Dungarvan married and the failure has been entirely on the side of Mr Hoare and his daughter.' In answering this charge Henry pointed out that he had never been told the truth. He had been informed that the Corks' debts were in the region of £5000 or £6000, at the time of the marriage, when in fact they were at least three times as much, and then he discovered the deceit over Ireland: 'Is it to be wondered at that I altered my conduct to them and that I had spirit to show I was not quite as tame an animal as not to resent such treatment which has been a dagger in dear Lord Dungarvan's heart?' Lady Cork retaliated by writing an abusive 'open' letter to Henry at Stourhead from Marston, a distance of less than ten miles away, which she circulated widely in the neighbourhood.

Dungarvan died in 1759 but Sukey's interests had to be looked after and Henry had a grandchild, Harriot, who was a descendant of the 'noble house'; so he continued to pay off clamouring creditors out of his own pocket. Though he endured 'abuse, calumny and opposition' from the Corks he had no wish to see what had become his own family's interests prejudiced by the claims of creditors.

Sukey's second husband was Lord Bruce of Tottenham Park, Wiltshire, who was created the 1st Earl of Ailesbury in 1776. They were married in 1761 and her portion, this time, was £23,000. Bruce was a Gentleman of the Bedchamber to George III and as Hereditary Warden of Savernake Forest was interested in matters relating to the English landscape. He and Henry corresponded over estate matters, and relations between Stourhead and Savernake were close. (Henry left Bruce £10,000 in his will.) In 1764 he urged him to consult Lancelot 'Capability' Brown, a Bank customer, on how to put his ideas for improvements into effect: 'I am glad your lordship has got Mr Browne … He has undoubtedly the best taste of anybody for improving Nature by what I have seen of his works. He paints as He plants; I doubt not that he will remove the damps and the too great regularity of your garden, far better to be turned into a park.'[11]

Sukey was now Henry's sole surviving child, as 'Nanny' had died shortly after giving birth to Richard Colt Hoare, known as Colt, in 1759. She had married her first cousin, Richard Hoare of Barn Elms, the eldest son of Henry's brother Richard, who had gained distinction by serving as Lord Mayor in the year of the Jacobite Rising and was knighted in 1746. The manor of Barn Elms in Barnes had been bought by this Sir Richard Hoare in 1750 and it passed to his son, Richard, after his death in 1754. The Barn Elms connection was an important one in the history of the Bank. Young Richard, always referred to as 'of Barn Elms' became very close to Henry when he lost his father. Henry, now having lost his brother too and without male heirs himself, pinned all his hopes on his nephew, who had also become his son-in-law. It has been suggested that, with one daughter expecting to become a countess and, the family's position in the upper echelons of society secure, Henry decided that his other principal concern, the Bank succession, could best be settled by a match between his younger daughter and nephew. Furthermore nephew Richard was a grandson of Good Henry who had purchased Stourhead. This gave him a moral claim to the estate and so could allow Henry to feel easy in his mind in bequeathing it in its entir-

*Barn Elms, Surrey, by John Buckler, 1818. Owned by members of the Hoare family from 1750 until 1820, the estate is now part of the London Wetlands Centre.*

ety to him, thereby avoiding the necessity of dividing it between the girls. Such an arrangement guaranteed that the ownership of Stourhead and the Bank continued in the hands of those bearing the name of Hoare.

Fortunately for Henry, who had confided to his brother in a letter of 8 September 1754, his wish 'that kind Providence would direct that our dear children might unite our name and family, with the firmest affection and most sincere love for each other', both Nanny and Richard had been most willing participants in this scheme. Henry, anxious that he should be properly understood, laid out his conditions for Richard entering the Bank to his brother a week later: 'It is very obvious how absolutely necessary it is that the strict residence and attendance we and our fathers have given at Fleet Street should be continued in the person of my dear Nephew who would forfeit all claim of relief from his descendants unless by following in the steps of his predecessors he continues that care and example which has been the credit, support and security of us all and without which the profession so much envy'd us must unhappily be transferr'd into other hands. God forbid it. If I know my own heart I will dye in my calling to prevent it.'

The pair had not married until 1756 by which time Henry had taken his young Partner under his wing. Henry wrote constantly to Richard from Stourhead on the theme of 'attention to business', warning him 'not to devolve that great care and concern on another who may be willing enough to take it on him that his expectations may rise higher and be gratified accordingly, but it is in our interest to keep down such expectations by our own attention to what ought to be the first and last of all our thoughts and chief happy business and employment of our whole lives.'

Henry instructed Richard to spend his leisure hours, at the Bank, in the parlour, reading, in the 'pursuit of knowledge', the lack of which would present him with an insurmountable obstacle to the enjoyment of his fortune whether made or acquired. During working hours Richard was to be 'in the shop as much as you can and appear willing and ready to receive and despatch all that enter especially persons of condition from the highest to the lowest. All have a right to it from us and the more we are seen in the business the better surely.' Typical of the communications between uncle and nephew is the letter sent as Henry went off with Nanny to take the waters at Bath for a couple of days. Henry entrusted Richard with some investment business for the Bank, buying India Bonds, but he told him to keep an eye on the rising cost of the stock and on the political situation, that no advantage might be lost to the House.

*Charles Wray, head clerk 1766-91, by Nathaniel Hone, a Bank customer.*

At the Bank long service was customary. Fair pay and full board in return for dedication and loyalty was the bargain struck between the Partners and their clerks throughout the eighteenth century. The basic annual pay of £30 for a clerk was raised in 1755 to £80-£100, but the system of paying additional gratuities was then discontinued. In 1796 it was raised again, according to length of service, with a ceiling of £140. (On this occasion it was noted in the Partners' Memorandum Book that: 'Noble, Morgan, Willoughby and Claridge thanked for increase in salary. Lainchbury and Babbage said nothing.') Charles Wray held the distinction of being the longest-serving clerk. He came to the Bank in 1737 and was promoted to head clerk in 1766, a post he occupied until 1791. The developing custom of commissioning a portrait of each of the Partners was extended to include Mr Wray on account of his long service to the Bank, and he was painted, quill pen in hand, against a backdrop of a shelf of ledgers, by the Royal academician, Nathaniel Hone, who was a Bank customer and probably well known to the head clerk. Charles Wray had close competitors in terms of service: John Noble worked for 52 years between 1758 and 1810, William Atkinson for 35 years from 1731 to 1766 and Joseph Graham for the same length of time from 1759 to 1794. Writing a Christmas letter to Richard from Stourhead in December 1755 Henry reminded him that the clerks would need a holiday, which they might be hesitant in suggesting for themselves: 'You will take care the gentlemen of our shop are not baulked of theirs as we Messrs can take our holydays at any time.'

*18th century tally sticks used as receipts for loans to the Exchequer.*

The private quarters at Fleet Street

top

*An early 'Messrs Hoare and Co' printed cheque, dated 4 March 1763. Made out to David Roberts for £5000 and signed by John Calcraft 'the most important regimental agent of the 18th century'.*

above

*Promissory note, 12 May 1769, signed on behalf of the partners by their head clerk, Charles Wray.*

could only accommodate one Partner and his family, with their servants, at any one time, along with the bank clerks who 'lived in'. The total establishment remained much the same size throughout Henry's time: a modest complement of domestics (cook, manservant and maid) and five or six clerks. Two more were taken on in 1779, followed a decade later by a further two. Richard's father, Sir Richard, was the resident Partner in Fleet Street from the time he entered the Bank in 1732. As was the case with his father, Good Henry, this was not simply a matter of choice but was stipulated in the partnership deed of that year. He was to pay Henry, as owner of the freehold an annual rent of £120 from the joint stock of the Bank, for the house and the shop, and was in turn given an allowance of £230 for all household expenses.

Detailed weekly accounts survive from 1753 with every item of expenditure entered. Meat, poultry, fish and butter were the heaviest burden on the budget, partly because they were consumed regularly. Fish and meat prices changed frequently. Other expensive items cost less in total, such as chocolate at 4s 6d per pound since they were bought less often. Asparagus was bought throughout the year and a weekly delivery of ass's milk was among the regular staples ordered by the cook. Many of the household tasks were regularly contracted out such as cleaning the pewter (monthly), all the laundry (weekly), the carriage of fresh water to the Bank (daily), most of the baking (in charge of Mr Parish the pastry cook), and special but infrequent jobs such as beating the carpets and scouring the wainscot. From the allowance all wages were paid, including those of a 'chear' woman who came in once a week and charged a shilling and all sundries paid for including replacement chamber pots and basins, china plates and wine glasses. 'Gardin stuff' and peas for fattening the hogs kept at Barn Elms, rare treats of 'purstachou nuts' and strawberries, and a single weekly newspaper, were also covered by the allowance. Although it was raised to £300 in 1742, and to twice that in 1785, the resident Partner was naturally expected to make a substantial personal contribution to the household expenses which, for the year 1755-56, totalled £464 3s 6d.

Soon after Sir Richard's untimely death in 1754 his elder son, Richard of Barn

Elms, took up residence at Fleet Street where he was joined by Nanny after their marriage. This arrangement gave Henry, his father-in-law and uncle, much satisfaction, but everyone's happiness was destroyed by the death of Nanny on 9 December 1758, after the birth of her only son. Richard remained in residence at Fleet Street and in 1761 got married again to Frances Anne Acland, who was the first of three members of her family to marry into this branch of the Hoare family. By 1765 Richard and Frances had two small children, and they moved out of Fleet Street. His younger half-brother, a *bon viveur* known affectionately as 'Fat Harry', came to live at the Bank with his new wife, Mary, whose maiden name also happened to be Hoare although she was not related to her husband. Mary was the daughter of a well-known portrait painter, William Hoare RA, who lived and worked in Bath.

William Hoare was a learned man as well as a skilled artist, and he and Henry took pleasure in critical discussions of the techniques of the Old Masters. Henry became his patron and their friendship was cemented by the marriage of Harry and Mary. During the 1760s William was a frequent visitor to Stourhead, where he would sketch in the park, and copy pictures in the house. (Henry greatly admired 'three of the finest heads he ever did from my Judgement of Hercules' by Poussin.)[12] In 1765 Henry engaged William on the interior decoration of the Temple of Apollo and of the Pantheon, where his grisaille panels on the seats still remain. Several of his fine pastel portraits of the family hang in the Little Dining Room at Stourhead. Mary was an accomplished artist herself and William discussed

*left*

*Richard Hoare of Barn Elms, by Francis Cotes 1757. He was created 1st Baronet 1786, died 1787.*

*right*

*Frances Anne Acland, by Francis Cotes. She married Richard of Barn Elms in 1761 and was the mother of three Partners of the Bank.*

'Fat Harry' Hoare, a gregarious man and keen breeder of bulldogs, drawn by his father-in-law, William Hoare, who was not a blood relation, c.1765.

his ideas on her training with Henry.

Fat Harry's tenancy lasted until 1777, the year he became a Partner, and another Henry, the grandson of the founder's eldest son, 'Naughty Richard', entered the Bank. He took on the responsibilities of resident Partner, sharing the duty with his cousins to suit each individual circumstances, and continued to stay at the Bank periodically even after he had bought his pleasant suburban estate, Mitcham Grove, in Surrey. Henry of Mitcham had known the Bank all his life, having been brought up in Henry the Magnificent's household in Clapham from the age of three. His father William, had died in 1753 and his widowed mother Martha went to live with Henry, as his housekeeper and companion taking the infant Harry with her. Martha was also Henry's niece and this close family relationship, combined with their individual personal circumstances, made this arrangement very satisfactory for all parties.

The requirement that the Partners should be in constant attendance at the Bank meant that those who did not 'live in' must live nearby. Benjamin lived in a house in St Martin's Lane and, from 1728, after his marriage to Susan Colt, Henry lived at No. 41 Lincoln's Inn Fields, a house he had rebuilt himself after fire had destroyed its predecessor in 1724 (No. 41 is now part of the site occupied by The Royal College of Surgeons).[13] After his children were grown up, he went in search of cleaner air and more salubrious surroundings for himself, which he found in Clapham. Having chosen an elevated site, on the north side of Clapham Common, overlooking the Thames (now Victoria Rise), he commissioned Henry Flitcroft to build him a villa. The house, which he called 'The Wilderness', was pulled down in 1851, but a drawing survives, which shows it to be more of a mansion than a villa. It was put up for sale after Henry's death and the auctioneer described it 'as an enviable retreat for a banker

*Mary Hoare, 'the sweetest of canaries', by her father William Hoare, 1765, the year she married Harry. Mary was a gifted artist and a friend of David Garrick.*

left
*Self portrait by Thomas Gainsborough, 1787.*

right
*David Garrick, c.1770, by Thomas Gainsborough. Artist and sitter were customers of the Bank.*

below and
facing page
*Tradesmen's bills from
Fleet Street addressed to
Richard Hoare, Lord
Mayor of London
1745-46.*

or a merchant, environed by pleasure grounds and gardens laid out with great taste and judgement'. A large bow window on the first floor looked over the gardens to the river and Chelsea beyond. The drawing room had 'walls exquisitely painted in subjects from the Mythology, by an Italian artist', and there was a large library on the ground floor.[14]

It seems that Henry had inherited Nos. 52, 53 and 54 Lincoln's Inn Fields from his father. They were originally part of his grandfather's London estates and eventually passed to Richard of Barn Elms. Lincoln's Inn Fields was much improved by an Act of Parliament of 1734, which provided for the election of trustees, from among the inhabitants, to raise a rate on themselves to fund the enclosure and laying out of the central square and to pay a scavenger to keep it clean. Henry was a trustee and this system of administration remained in force for nearly two centuries.

No. 52 was occupied by Richard of

Barn Elms and Frances on their departure from Fleet Street in 1765, and Henry leased Nos. 53 and 54 to the King of Sardinia as a residence for his ambassador with an adjacent Roman Catholic chapel. The Sardinian chapel was a focus for sporadic outbursts of anti-Catholic rioting throughout the eighteenth century and the chapel was burnt to the ground in the early Summer of 1759 and some damage done to the ambassador's house. The ambassador, Count Viri, made all kinds of spurious claims against his landlord, and Henry found himself involved in a dispute which dragged on and eventually was drawn to the attention of the Prime Minister, Lord Bute. Sukey's new husband, Lord Bruce, was a means of gaining access to Lord Bute, but the Prime Minister had his reasons not to help. He did not want the British government to do anything to alienate the King of Sardinia, in any way, during the Seven Years War, since Sardinia was a helpful ally to Britain against France. Henry reflected sadly in a letter to Lord Bruce that: 'we live in such times when the chiefs of the land desire to be

*Alfred's Tower, Stourhead. Watercolour by John Buckler, 1823.*

excused where justice is called aloud for, for fear of laying themselves under great difficulty and disobliging the party or oppressor because he has always lived on good terms with him. I must now refer this "upright person" [Count Viri] to Norfolk House to the Heads of our Roman Catholics who I believe will apply to the King of Sardinia Himself whose ears as I am told are open at all times to the meanest of peasants.' This strategy worked: pressure was bought to bear by the English Catholic leadership, and the King of Sardinia agreed to meet the full cost of the re-building and repairs.

Henry's dislike of the war was additionally fuelled by the thought of those who had greatly profiteered by it. In writing to Lord Bruce he singled out Sir Lawrence Dundas for particular criticism. Once upon a time Dundas 'had not shoes to his feet', but had made a colossal fortune of £500,000 as contractor for the Army in Germany. 'His immense gains are a glaring proof and shame of what little attention was given to the economy during the consuming war by Mr Pitt.' For all that, Henry welcomed the sizeable territorial gains won by Britain for the inevitable increase in commerce they would bring and there was no doubt too that the Bank's position, after years of anxious management by Henry, was improving after the coming of peace in 1763. Total profits from this time until the end of the American War of Independence in 1782 rose well above the figures for the preceding forty years. The annual figures from 1765 never fell below £18,000 and in several years ranged from £24,000 to £28,000.

At Stourhead, Henry was now considering his latest building project, Alfred's Tower, which he had planned as a memorial to the Saxon king, 'the Founder of the English Monarchy and Liberty' who had reputedly raised his standard against the Danes in 879 on the summit of a wooded hillside above the gardens. The Treaty of Paris of 1763 gave impetus to the project, and Henry's celebration of the British monarchy took on a new meaning. The design of Alfred's Tower owed much to Hamilton's Gothic Belvedere at Painshill. After a visit there in 1762, Henry abandoned his original idea, for copying St Mark's Campanile in Venice, and determined to build his tower in the same manner as Hamilton's, only three times the height. Flitcroft then produced a Gothic-inspired triangular shaped tower of immense height, which created a landmark for the Stourhead estate visible for miles around.

Henry had made a great deal of money in his lifetime but, in a reckoning he made for his nephew Richard, he showed he was also well aware of just how much he had spent. A total of £190,000 was mostly accounted for by his outlay in four major areas of expenditure: the house and gardens and works of art at Stourhead cost more than £20,000; he spent £103,000 on further land purchases; his two daughters' three marriages relieved him of £61,000; and his new house at Clapham was built and furnished for £5000. However this was all within his means, so it was not a feeling of personal financial insecurity which induced the

*Stourhead. The Little Dining Room, with the hunting picture of Henry the Magnificent and his uncle Benjamin, by John Wootton, 1729.*

surprising decisions he took in 1783.

These decisions shook the family at the time and caused deep resentment in some quarters, feelings which were communicated down the generations for many years to come. Until 1783 there had been no doubt about the future of the Bank. Richard of Barn Elms was the heir-apparent. Richard had been working at the Bank for over thirty years, since the death of Henry's son in 1752, in the apparently certain knowledge that he was destined to inherit the twin mantle of owner-ship of the London business and property and some highly desirable country estates, including Stourhead, and land in Wiltshire, Somerset and Dorset. This arrangement was the natural consequence of the entail in Good Henry's will and was referred to as the 'Old Settlement'.

Stourhead itself was an essential part of the business. It not merely helped the reputation of the Bank but it was its reserve capital. The Bank itself had no cap-ital. The partners individually owned capital shares in the business which, after the death of Christopher Arnold in 1759, were increased in total by 2000 to 12,000. In 1783 the shares were divided as follows: Henry, aged seventy-eight, had 6000, Richard (of Barn Elms), aged forty-eight had 3000, Henry (Fat Harry), aged thirty-nine, had 2000 and Henry (of Mitcham), aged twenty-nine, had 1000.[15]

In the summer of 1783 Richard and his brother Harry felt impelled to visit their uncle at Stourhead where he had retired for his customary break from the heat and dust of London. The purpose of this deputation was to request that Henry should consider Richard Colt Hoare's position in the Bank. Colt had been work-ing there as an Agent (a sort of probationary position reserved for family members) since he came of age in 1779 and he was regarded as most satisfactory. He had now declared his intention of marrying Hester Lyttelton whose father, the 1st Baron Lyttelton, had inherited Hagley Hall in Worcestershire from his brother, Sir George Lyttelton, who had been well known to Henry and had shared with him a passion for landscaping and 'improvement'. Nevertheless Henry reacted sourly to this piece of news. Much of the happiness in his private life had been destroyed by the recent death of his last surviving child, Sukey, in February 1783, and the only hope of personal solace he could think of was that Colt should marry his granddaughter, Sukey's daughter, Lady Frances Brudenell Bruce. This idea, which had the ring of the similar plan he had engineered for Richard and Nanny decades before, was a non-starter. Hester Lyttelton, judging by her letters, was a high spirited and entertaining young woman, and clearly Colt had made a very positive choice in selecting her for his future bride.

Henry, rather stiffly, acknowledged defeat, claiming not entirely truthfully

*facing page*
*Mrs Susanna Hoare, wife of Benjamin's son, Richard of Boreham, with her eldest daughter who died aged five. By Joshua Reynolds, 1763-64.*

that 'he had made it a rule never to promote or interfere in a thing of that sort as he thought it better for young people to choose for themselves'. The blow to Richard came when Henry then announced he had resolved to by-pass him as his heir in favour of his son Colt on the condition that Colt should leave the Bank, at once, retire to the country and improve Henry's estates which, at that time, yielded around £6000 a year, roughly what a Partner with 3000 shares in the Bank could reasonably expect to draw. The new arrangement did not stop there because Henry was determined that Colt should inherit the freehold of the Bank as well as Stourhead. This would mean the Partners would become his tenants, a state of affairs which Harry indignantly observed subverted the 'order of nature, right and justice to have the father depending on the will of the son and the uncle on the nephew'.

What impelled Henry was an increasing sense of foreboding about a country shackled by an enormous national debt, coupled with despair brought on by personal loss and an extreme attachment to his glorious creation at Stourhead, which seemed to him to be the only precious part of his life worth saving. The Bank would always be vulnerable, but he could make Stourhead secure. To achieve this, it was vital it should no longer be harnessed to the business. The Bank would have to stand on its own feet without Stourhead as its reserve. Nobody was sanguine that this would be possible, but for the moment the important thing was to keep the new scheme secret, as to broadcast it could seriously prejudice the Bank, as Harry noted in his famous memorandum about the affair: 'The separating of so great an estate from the business would of course alarm many whose chief reason for banking with us [was] thinking the property so great, that let what would happen there could be no loss to them on account of the great assets.'

The two brothers left Stourhead the following morning and returned to London. Two months later all was rearranged at Fleet Street. Colt left the Bank on 2 August and on 28 August Henry agreed that Richard of Barn Elms should, after all, inherit the freehold of the Bank premises with the proviso that a life interest in them should be extended to his Partners, Fat Harry and Henry of Mitcham. Henry handed over to Colt at Stourhead and retired to 'The Wilderness' at Clapham for the last two years of his life. The matter of succession may have been settled, but relationships within the family were now subject to strain, in particular that between Colt and Hester, and, what she referred to as 'the parentage at the Elms'. Richard felt humiliated by Henry and slighted by Colt, all of which Henry would have dismissed as absurd. Henry pointed out to his nephew, Richard, that Colt was Richard's eldest son, 'his good son, his favourite son and the issue of his own loyns'. Colt, for his part, lived with a lingering resentment that he had not been offered a choice and, as he witnessed the Bank's growth and prosperity under the guidance of Henry of Mitcham, he felt he had been materially deprived as well. In a memorandum he wrote on the subject in 1828 he put the blame on Fat Harry: 'By the persuasion of my uncle (Fat and Jovial Hal) my grandfather excluded me (his rightful heir) from any concern in the Banking House.' The tensions between uncle and nephew and father and son were not to last for long since Henry and Fat Harry both died in 1785, while Richard enjoyed a brief moment of glory as a baronet and died, shortly after his elevation, in 1787. Colt's happy marriage was very brief. Hester died in August 1785 and Colt in his distress took himself abroad on a journey which was to occupy him for the next six years.

In his lifetime Henry had succeeded in keeping the Bank afloat through half a century of civil rebellion and war which caused uncertainty in the financial markets and a strain on the Bank's profitability. In his latter years it prospered although it was competing with governments greedy for funds to pay for the armed services – government securities offered high interest rates while bank deposits did not. The deposits Hoare's managed fluctuated, but overall they increased under Henry's management. In 1732 they stood at £286,668, by 1755 they had increased to £723,091, 1759 saw the figures dip to £515,163 but by 1777 they had risen to £860,846.

While others invested in high-yield government stock, during the War of American Independence, Henry, personally, made significant acquisitions of land (in a depressed market), spending well over £60,000 and nearly doubling the size of his estate.[16] This 'last bout of landed investment' ensured that his successor would have a more than adequate rental income without having to rely on a profit share from the Bank. Henry's share from the Bank for 1783 was £11,191 but Bank profits fluctuated considerably from year to year while rental income stayed more or less the same. He may have been mistaken in seeing the inevitable ruin of the nation on account of 'ye great National Debt' but the outcome of his actions was to produce two effective and self-supporting dynasties: the banking Hoares at the sign of the Golden Bottle and the landed Hoares of Stourhead.

## CHAPTER FOUR

# HENRY OF MITCHAM AND THE NAPOLEONIC WARS 1778–1828

The Old Bank, c.1770-80. A warren of rooms lay behind its early Georgian façade. 'The Golden Bottle' was fixed to the pediment over the door.

facing page
Henry Hugh Hoare, c.1784, 'a mighty pleasing young man'.

With the matter of the ownership of the Bank premises settled in his favour, Richard of Barn Elms then applied for a baronetcy. In June 1786 his eligibility for the honour as a man 'eminent for family inheritance, estate and integrity of manners' was confirmed, and he agreed to supply the King with enough money to support thirty foot soldiers in Ulster for a term of three years. From their introduction in the early 17th century baronetcies had been used by the Crown as a source of income as well as a means of bestowing honour. To celebrate his new status Richard ordered from Daniel Smith and Robert Sharpe a spectacular silver dinner service for Barn Elms, big enough to serve a banquet on. At the same time he moved, with Lady Hoare, from the increasingly commercial bustle of Lincoln's Inn Fields to an elegant new house in St James's Square.

A few months earlier his health had begun to be a worry. In April he visited Bath with his wife, and their second son Charles. They were all suffering from different complaints: Frances Anne from an excessively nervous disposition, which a break from London considerably improved; Charles from overindulgence, which a regime of riding, no supper and no dancing seems to have cured; and Richard from something a good deal more serious than the renowned spa waters could hope to mend. He longed to get on a horse, 'for the rides about here are delightful and the verdure beautiful beyond anything near London', but in fact all he could manage by way of entertainment was dancing a quadrille in the evenings. He wrote to his son Hugh that he was gaining strength daily, but any recovery was temporary. All too

*Henrietta Anne, Lady Fortescue, sister of the three 'Adelphi' Partners, and a gifted amateur artist and traveller. Painted in the manner of Rubens by Matthew Peters, 1795.*

soon he was hastily drawing up codicils to his will. He died in October 1787, leaving the freehold of the Bank to his two elder sons by Frances Anne, Henry Hugh (known by the family as Hugh), born in 1762, and Charles, born in 1767, as tenants in common rather than joint tenants. This arrangement gave each of them an equal share but, importantly, allowed them to pass on their share as they pleased (whereas under a joint tenancy the survivor would automatically inherit the share of the deceased). Another son, Henry Merrik, joined the firm in 1791, on a salaried basis, as soon as he came of age, and it was these three, who were most regularly at Fleet Street, and who actually conducted most of the daily business. They were nicknamed 'The Adelphi' but were under the command of their cousin, Henry of Mitcham (always called Harry), who was made senior Partner by the ailing Sir Richard. He explained to Hugh that he felt this arrangement to be the right one for the present but that it was unlikely to be long term: 'You are not quite steady enough for Fleet Street, I have made Harry head Partner. He is not likely to live many years and then you will see the necessity of being a man of business.'

Hugh was to wait much longer for his turn at the helm than anyone could have envisaged in 1787. He was then only twenty-five and had every reason to be optimistic. No doubt he perceived his situation in much the same way as did his aunt, Mary Hoare, who wrote to him in January 1785: 'The arrival of the new year naturally calls forth good wishes but there seems no blessing this world affords of which you are not already in possession. You have youth, friends, health, peace and competence and added to all that you have the damsel of your choice.' She was Maria Palmer, a relation on his mother's side, and by all accounts they were well suited. She, like him, had money and they were an attractive pair. In addition to his rather romantic good looks, Hugh had a warm and generous nature and he inspired great affection among his relations. Shortly after her marriage to Colt Hoare, Hester had written playfully to her brother-in-law, Hugh, from the boudoir of her London apartment: 'I am (now) going to adornize my charms for the Opera, which bye the bye is spick and span new and wonderfully pretty as Lady Gormanton says you are. I wd not have you vain but she whispered to me yesterday that she thought you a might pleasing (I could say pretty but that would be tautology) young man.'

In addition to Colt and the three 'Adelphi' there was a fifth son of Sir Richard, Peter Richard, who did not come into the Bank but qualified as a barrister, and a sister, Henrietta Anne. All of them had been brought up at Barn Elms and enjoyed a very free and affectionate relationship with one another; their spouses were readily welcomed into the closeness of the family circle which included all the relations and in-laws on the 'High Hoares' side of the family, a phrase coined by Peter Richard's son, when referring to all descendants of the 1st Baronet. Henrietta's first husband was her second cousin, Sir Thomas Dyke Acland, 9th Baronet, and, in marrying him, she became mistress of Killerton and Holnicote in Devon. She was aware that her transition from an essentially business background into a long-established landed family might disrupt the easy and confidential relationship she had enjoyed with her brothers and in particular with Hugh. Newly married, she wrote reassuringly to him on this delicate subject: 'Believe me my dearest Hugh … however well I love my husband – whatever prosperity and good fortune attends me or whatever stile of life I may be in it will never diminish my affection for those people who for so many years of my life have shewed me such unremitting kindness … I am certain that if I can make him (Sir Thomas) think of you as you deserve, there is no fear of his good opinion – was I to say nothing your letters would speak your mind – but for my own sake I should wish him to number you amongst the first of his friends.'

Within six months of Hester's death, which prompted Colt to order mourning clothes in such 'great abundance and variety' that it delayed the funeral for over a week, he was in Naples and writing to Hugh whom he had left in charge of his 'Affairs in the West'. He concerned himself in all the detailed matters respecting his tenants at Stourhead, bills to be paid and receipts expected, but declared that he was unable to commit himself on the question of when he was returning home. 'From having been one of the most settled men in the world I am become the most fickle. I hardly know where I shall sleep the next night. How then can I give you hope of returning to England sooner than I originally intended?'

Life abroad was beginning to interest him in earnest and when he reached Rome in the Spring of 1786 he settled in happily, spending every morning visiting antiquities – 'there is so much work for my pencil that I know not when I shall be able to get away' – and otherwise being entertained by a cosmopolitan émigré society with 'dining parties' and soirees, concerts and conversaziones every night. Of particular note was his invitation to the 'Gingerbread Court' of Charles Edward Stuart, The Young Pretender, now 'a lamp nearly burned out' and his daughter the Duchess of Albany, 'a very pleasant and rather handsome woman… Do not think I am turned Jacobite but impute this visit of mine partly to curiosity of seeing a man who once made so much noise in this Country and from the benefit I may reap from an acquaintance with the Duchess.'

*overleaf*

*German landscape on the River Elbe, c.1817, after Richard Colt Hoare, from his tours on the continent 1785-91.*

For all these amusements Colt was always greedy for news from home where he had left not only his responsibilities at Stourhead, but a motherless infant son. Perhaps he sensed that his family might feel that he had too comprehensively severed his ties to England in his flight from personal grief, and that he was taking too much pleasure in his new surroundings, or it may have just been homesickness which caused him to write to Hugh from Florence in April: 'I desire you will not take it into your head that a circumstantial detail of the manner in which you spend your time is *ennuyant* to me – on the contrary I am more interested to hear the news, schemes, engagements etc of the domestic and private Circle of my friends than to plunge myself into the debates and battles of the House of Commons or to canvas the merits of a political pamphlet.' He wanted news of his half-sister, Henrietta, who had just given birth to a boy whom he admiringly referred to as the 'Devonshire baronet', unaware that he would succeed to his father's title before the year was out;

expressed approval that Henry Merrik, born in 1770, would enter the Bank in the course of time to 'ease your burden very much' and entered fully into the discussions of where both Hugh and cousin Harry of Mitcham were to live.

facing page

*Harry Hoare of Mitcham, attributed to George Romney, c.1775-80. He grew up with his widowed mother and his great uncle, Henry the Magnificent, in Clapham.*

However, until the French Revolutionary Wars made the Continent too inhospitable for tourists, Colt felt no compulsion to return. He had been positively excluded from the family business and the prospect of establishing a family at Stourhead had been ruined by Hester's death. Although he was to learn much abroad that was to bear fruit in his later career as a distinguished antiquarian and a dedicated and highly cultivated proprietor of his grandfather's great estate, it was early days for him to reconcile himself to a life that had so unexpectedly changed course and appeared to have taken more away from him than it had delivered.

*Mitcham Grove, Surrey by John Buckler, 1818, bought by Harry in 1786 and home to his orphaned grandchildren.*

Both Hugh and cousin Harry were in search of good sporting estates and given the rota system, which the partners devised for attendance at Fleet Street, they could expect to spend a fair proportion of their time away from the Bank. Colt confessed that it had been so long since he had 'crossed the back of a horse that … I do not know if a pack in full cry would tempt me to follow them' but he was unequivocal in his approval of Harry's choice of Mitcham Grove in Surrey which, as he wrote to Hugh, struck him as having 'every necessary qualification to make it agreeable, viz good hunting at a small distance, good shooting and fishing: pray tell him I shall come and frighten some of his trout when I return to England.' He knew that Hugh's inclinations would lead him to hunting country and was concerned that he and Maria would not flourish if compelled to spend too much time in London. After casting around for several years they found an estate in Bedfordshire, near Woburn Sands, called Wavendon which rather fell into their lap. The previous owner Lord Charles Fitzroy had recently borrowed the £12,000 purchase money from the Bank which he then found difficulty in repaying except by a sale. Hugh kept on the house at Barn Elms, where all sixteen of his children were born, but moved the family to Wavendon in 1797, in the reasonable expectation that before long he would become senior Partner and his new estate, being a comfortable distance from London, would suit his requirements perfectly.

Cousin Harry was believed to have little hope of a long life due to his indifferent health. He was a small slight man but showed remarkable toughness in overcoming his physical weakness. He was to remain in full command at the Bank from 1787, when he was aged thirty-seven, until his death, at the age of seventy-eight, in 1828, even though family circumstances and bouts of illness caused him to take enforced leave from Fleet Street for months, even years at a time. The Memorandum Books, through which the resident Partner recorded and communicated daily matters of business, for the benefit of those not in attendance, are evidence of the fact that nothing of any significance could be decided or acted upon without Harry's express approval.

For forty-two years Harry lived at and ruled from Mitcham Grove, which he bought in 1786. It was a charming house, not overly grand, and set in exceptionally fine grounds of 620 acres on the north bank of the River Wandle west of Mitcham Bridge. The 'Grove' boasted all the elements of a much larger estate: plantations of high trees, which gave it its name, rolling parkland, broad lawns and gravelled walks, a canal and a meandering stream in the pleasure grounds, a picturesque thatched dairy and all the necessary hothouses and greenhouses needed to supply the household, which also had its own piped water supply. The house, with its pleasing aspects overlooking the grounds and the river, had been recently substantially refashioned by Robert Adam for its previous owner, the Lord Chancellor, Lord Loughborough.

Harry's energies were devoted to the Bank and his family. He was not interested in his role as estate owner and farmer and consequently his farms were not regarded as models of good husbandry. Given the enormous contribution he made to the welfare of the people of Mitcham and to the amenities of that place it seems a little harsh that he should have been singled out by James Malcolm in his *Compendium of Modern Husbandry*, published in 1806 for criticism in the one area in which he allowed his standards to fall. Having drawn attention to the poor management of two of his farms, situated to the south of the Grove, Malcolm broadened his attack to include all gentleman farmers: 'As a merchant or banker he may have something else to do besides watching the action of his servant, and being ignorant of the profession, he is at a loss to commend, when to disapprove, or when to recommend a different mode of proceeding; and if his bailiff after paying all the charges, brings in some-

thing more than £5 per cent upon his capital he thinks himself well satisfied, forgetting perhaps, if he had rent to pay and a part of that capital to repay at some future time that it would be a losing concern.'

Harry would not have worried unduly over this. His principal concern was to bring benefit to the greatest number of people in his village community of Mitcham. The ancient church was rebuilt with a substantial personal contribution of his time as well as money: it was his practice to put into the collection plate every week a £5 note with five gold sovereigns to stop it blowing away. He was appointed to the offices of Church Warden, Overseer of the Poor and Justice of the Peace for Surrey. He was behind the foundation of a National School in Mitcham, and he built a cottage for the sick inmates of the workhouse at his own expense. To encourage saving among those who wished to improve themselves he started the Mitcham Savings Bank.

Alive to the threat of invasion from France, Harry was part of the committee for the local Armed Association as well as subscriber to the Light Horse Volunteer Corps raised in the vicinity of the bank. Hannah More, who was a leading member of the Evangelical 'Clapham Sect', and a friend of Harry's son William Henry and daughter-in-law, Louisa, went with them to Mitcham Grove on 17 May 1798 and wrote in her diary, 'I did not enjoy much of Mr Hooare's company, so occupied was he in arming and exercising. He rises at half past four at Mitcham, trots off to town to be ready to meet at six the Fleet Street Corps performing their evolutions in the area of Bridewell, the only place they can find sufficient space, then comes back for a late dinner and as soon as that is over he goes to his Committees, after which he has a sergeant to drill himself and his three sons on the lawn until it is dark.'

*Light Horse Volunteers of London and Westminster, reviewed by George III on Wimbledon Common, 1798. Harry subscribed to the Fleet Street corps of the volunteer force as a protection against invasion from France.*

95

England struggled with a war economy for twenty-three years, between 1792 and 1815, and the Partners at Fleet Street conducted their affairs with utmost caution throughout this period, conscious that they must be ready at all times to meet, in full, any demands made upon them by their customers. When they suffered a 'great decline in the balance' they sold stock, but throughout the 1790s the slump made sales difficult. In a memorandum to his partners, dated 29 April 1795, Harry reported the difficulty, 'Mr Noble was directed to sell 5 per cents, not a shilling to be sold, Mem. A bad stock to hold in case of emergency, there being a ready sale for 3 per cents.' An important element in their careful management of resources was the Sinking Fund established by Harry, in 1799, as a means of meeting any extraordinary expenses or losses incurred or sustained by the Partners. It began with a modest sum of £500 being taken out of the Bank profits each year which was raised to £1000 from 1812-28. The Fund was not to be considered as part of the general divisible joint stock of the business, but as a quite separate account solely for the purpose of paying any losses which arose from overdrafts and trade losses and to provide for the costs of building a new 'House and Offices' on the site of the existing Bank whenever the Partners should consider it expedient to do so.

The Sinking Fund represented long-term strategic planning, but in the short term extreme caution had to be exercised when it came to lending money. During Harry of Mitcham's time normal procedure was for the Bank to decline loans on mortgage, or any other permanent security, on account of the 'critical situation of affairs'. In France the Terror escalated in its ferocity during the early years of the 1790s, tightening its grip on the country. The British government was drawn into war against the Revolutionaries in 1793 and began to introduce a series of repressive measures which were designed to strangle at birth any possibility that similar demands for democratic reform at home would become a mass movement. The situation in England was, nevertheless, volatile. The poor harvests of 1795 and 1796 resulted in rioting over the extortionate price of bread at the same time as news reached England that Napoleon was sweeping through Italy in triumph. Fear of invasion was unsettling and government spies were reported to be everywhere.

Gold was in short supply and, periodically, the shortages reached crisis point. In this climate of uncertainty rumours spread quickly. In February 1797 the Bank of England was obliged to restrict the issue of gold to £50,000 to be distributed among bankers according to the discretion of the Bank's Court of Directors. Word got around that Hoare's had an unusually large supply and, on the basis of this hearsay, Richard Stone, a partner in 'The Grasshopper' (later Martin's Bank) in Lombard Street wrote to the Bank as an 'old friend'. He complained that the 'Grasshopper' was brought low by the drain on their supply and asked that Hoare's should consider lending them their share of the Bank of England's distribution. In the most courteous of terms the Partners replied that they were pressed in exactly the same way as their competitors and the Bank of England had been unable to offer them any further assistance. Old and particular friends they might be but, as Harry wrote to Stone, 'how under the present circumstances can Messrs Hoare be justified in diminishing their stock of specie for the accommodation of another House?'

In this climate financial contracts between the Bank and its customers could not be safely left to roll on year after year without at least being renegotiated, where they were reasonably secure, or terminated, if they posed too much risk. The Duke of Beaufort's mortgage remained but the interest was raised to 4.5 per cent, while Lord Ludlow, whose loan was forty years old and due many years of interest, was pressed for immediate repayment. The Bank refused substantial loans on mortgage, offering temporary loans with stock as collateral. Lord Digby, a friend of Hugh's, secured £10,000, which he needed quickly in July 1796 to pay his sister's marriage portion to Mr Wingfield. He planned to repay the sum in a very short time by the sale of an estate, but rather than lend on mortgage the condition which Hoare's exacted was the 'transfer of a certain portion of stock into our names which shall be retransferred to you as soon as the money is repaid'. Lord Digby was delighted that it was all settled in a week and issued an open invitation to Hugh and Maria to visit him anytime at Sherborne Castle.

Frequently the value of the stock required was worth up to five times the amount borrowed. In the depressed markets of the time customers were very reluctant to sell stock to raise money or to pay off their debts. When Sir John Hussey Delaval pressed the Bank for a loan of £10,000, in December 1794, Harry wouldn't even consider it unless he paid off three bonds on which he also owed interest. In a curt note Harry wrote in the Memorandum Book: 'If he gets the £10,000 he pays them off. Didn't get it.'

In November 1795 Sir Henry Gough Calthorpe wanted £30,000 on mortgage. In reply to his request 'the particular situation of the times' was adverted to and he was refused. Harry described how 'He went away civilly enough' but returned wanting some of the loan on temporary terms which would be in stock transferred to our name and thus be at our command. Harry was unsure how to proceed but knew this much: 'He is an unpleasant genius to deal with but the connection is a very desirable one and must be retained if possible.' The loan on the transfer of stock was agreed a few days later. As was customary in their business

*Receipt for Assessed taxes for £500 paid by the Duke of Beaufort as his contribution to the war effort, 1794. The 1st Duke of Beaufort opened his account at the Bank in 1685.*

97

'A Peep into Westminster Hall', by Robert Dighton, with the Lord Chief Justice, the 1st Earl of Mansfield, known as 'silver tongued Murray', in the left foreground. A Bank customer, Mansfield became fabulously wealthy through his well invested earnings at the bar.

there were always exceptions to the rule. When Lord Suffolk requested a loan of £30,000 for a year to buy a house in Harley Street in April 1796, Harry suggested to the Partners that they should agree to it: 'What say you gentlemen? The money will not be wanted much before mid Summer – though not a capital account now may we not expect something better of his son Lord Andover?' Lord Suffolk got his money but only for six months.

Good relations between the Partners and 'old friends' of the House were greatly valued assets of the business. Viscount Stormont had been readily lent money in 1793 without any further security beyond 'his lordship's note or bond'. When his father, the 2nd Earl of Mansfield, died in 1796 his Executors came to the Bank on 11 October where they sat 'in the parlour all morning' inspecting mortgage deeds and were given 'a good fire, chocolate and sandwiches [and] parted in excellent humour'. It was Stormont, who succeeded his father as the 3rd Earl, who was responsible for the conversion of the Mansfield's Scottish seat at Scone into a magnificent gothic palace. To finance the work he made a further application to the Bank in June 1804 to borrow £8000 in addition to an existing loan of £30,000. The whole debt was to be paid for by the sale of an estate valued at £50,000. The Partners were happy to oblige: 'Nearly fifty years' close attachment to the House claimed an immediate acquiescence.'

The Duchess of Somerset came to Fleet Street, one day in April 1795, and Harry, being in attendance, noted that she was 'in good humour with a large balance. Desired £7000 to be invested in Navy [Bills]... Her Grace asked for Checks (printed cheque forms first used during the 1760s) which were given her without any observations. Mem. I think they should be given to anyone of consequence asking for them as I know it is thought odd to refuse them since they are become so general and has lost us some customers.' Navy Bills paid better interest than loans and Harry recommended that if any of the general balance of the Bank could be spared it should be invested in them. Within the year the Duchess needed to borrow £10,000 to pay off debts. The partners agreed she should be accommodated and proposed her £7000 investment in Navy Bills as collateral, which in the event turned out to be exactly the sum she needed. Both Harry and the Duchess were reported to be 'highly pleased'.

Some longstanding friendships, in this business context, could lead to misunderstandings and, not surprisingly, some connections were open to abuse. For many years Sir Charles Talbot's father had acted as agent for Lord Donegal and had had close dealings with the Bank, and Harry in particular, for his whole working life. In October 1812 the young Sir Charles was much disappointed to hear from Harry that he would not advance him £3000 for the purchase of a farm for which he was prepared to offer any security they chose. Reflecting on the much larger sums which had been repeatedly owed and punctually repaid over the years by his family, he 'could not help but lament that neither this circumstance nor that of my Family having been a real friend to your House (which you voluntarily acknowledged but which I do not pretend to urge as any plea in my favour) should not have secured to me in this instance the loan of so trifling a sum that you would not look upon it as a violation of your resolutions.' He went on to say that 'if my friend Mr Charles Hoare is in town I should hope he would be an advocate.' Harry took offence at the suggestion that there should ever be a breach between the Partners with regard to a resolution they had jointly made: 'After having been very actively involved in the business for near five and forty years and never before having been accused of an indisposition to shew every respect to the wishes of our friends I cannot but feel hurt at an appeal being made to another partner. I trust we are all guided by the same impulse that it is our duty as well as our interest to accommodate those who honour us with their confidence, but there are times in which we deem it expedient to limit our advances. It would be a breach of confidence if I were to acquaint you with the names of some noble and honourable Persons who have recently applied to us but there are many and they have kindly accepted of our excuses, convinced that we are guided by the strictest impartiality and we flattered ourselves that we should have experienced the same at your hands.' In this case there were no damaging repercussions. Sir Charles expressed dismay that he should have provoked such outrage and his death soon after these exchanges removed any possibility of a continuing dispute.

*Charles Henry St John, Earl O'Neill, c.1830, great grandson of Henry the Magnificent, and a drain on the Bank's resources.*

In their dealings with Earl O'Neill the partners found themselves embroiled in a hopeless situation from which nothing could be salvaged. Henry the Magnificent's granddaughter, Henrietta (whom he nicknamed Harriot), only daughter of Lord and Lady Dungarvan, had returned to her Irish roots and had married, in 1777, the heroic Viscount O'Neill of Shanes Castle who then died of wounds in Antrim trying to keep the peace during Wolfe Tone's rebellion in 1798. Their son, Charles Henry St John, created Earl O'Neill, made full use of his family connection to bring pressure to bear on the Bank. His 'fickle and strange conduct' caused them a great deal of bother and concern during the period 1810-1815 when the demands of war restricted credit everywhere, and the Partners to had work hard to keep their balances secured against the possibility of large-scale drawings. He ran up debts of £20,000 at the Bank on

*Queen Charlotte, by Sir William Beechey, 1812. She borrowed money from the Bank, to buy the Frogmore estate.*

which the interest was always promised and never paid and the security, on a part of his estate, was subsequently discovered to be good for nothing since he did not own the land in question.

Much of O'Neill's debt was inherited from his father and the partners felt driven to help him on account of 'Family Connexion and other important Considerations and were fearful that his Lordship's character and influence might be affected if we withheld the advances'. O'Neill was Postmaster General for Ireland and Colonel of the Antrim Militia. His solicitor, William Blacker, felt the Partners would find an account of his frugal manner of living 'gratifying both as relations and friends: his amusements are the least expensive you can imagine being entirely confined to shooting and fishing, one travelling carriage, no horses (excepting three saddle horses) and those necessary for the cultivation of his demesne which is I believe above 2000 English acres and supplies him with everything for the consumption of his house. Two footmen and his own man are the amount of his house servants and he spends only £200 a year. He has no rent roll of his property nor neither does his agent however strange it may appear.' Creditors in Ireland were 'pillaging' him on all sides. Hoare's would be entitled to appoint a receiver to collect the rents but Blacker hoped they would spare the Earl further mortification.

For four months from May to August 1810 no other letters except those to O'Neill were copied into the Partners' Letter Books. Harry, suffering from one of his recurrent bouts of rheumatic fever, was rarely seen at Fleet Street at that time but all correspondence concerning O'Neill was sent down to him at Mitcham. For another fifteen years the Partners wrestled with one scheme after another to try and put order into chaos at Shanes Castle even suggesting that Hugh, accompanied by his lawyer brother Peter Richard, should go over to Ireland to set up a trust to manage the Earl's affairs. This plan was not agreeable to their noble customer who still clung to the fast fading hope that the Bank would rescue him from his creditors. His relations remained adamantly opposed to helping him: 'It appeared clear to us that not Ten, Twenty, or Thirty thousand pounds would be sufficient to silence the clamour of many of the creditors…Silencing one would have made others more importunate and therefore we could not proceed.'

By 1826, after a warning had been sent to Ireland, instructions were given for a writ to be issued. O' Neill claimed he had found another 'monied man' to take over the mortgage but nothing came of this suggestion. In the final resort however, the partners were advised by Counsel that, while they had every right to file a Bill of Foreclosure, there would be so many parties to it that the proceedings would be costly and tedious. Although the interest was paid up by 1828, the total debt of £38,731 18s 11d was written off. O'Neill never married. He and his brother, who succeeded him, both died childless bringing to an end this troublesome family connection which had begun so auspiciously with Sukey Hoare's marriage to the heir of the Earl of Cork and Orrery in 1753, but which had quickly soured in her father's lifetime and then had been stretched beyond the limit, until it was finally severed a hundred years later.

At the Michaelmas meeting with his Partners in 1813 Harry presented them with a strategy document he called a 'Paper on the State of Affairs at Fleet Street', in which he addressed the problems faced by the Bank during this period of restricted credit. The Bank needed money for investment and Harry saw the necessity of reducing the Bank's holdings of permanent securities (mostly mortgages), which could not be easily converted into cash, in favour of lending money on bond with stock as collateral security (with liberty to sell), which could be. He was well aware that the Partners must proceed with delicacy and discretion in order not to offend their customers (he noted seven accounts that were likely to be lost in that year) since it was, as he put it, 'The Age of Accommodation' and there were 'many bankers upon the watch who are ready to advance money to induce people to quit their old Connexion when they cannot get accommodated: this may be one reason why we have yielded, perhaps too easily, to the advances of <u>Money upon Bond only</u> to an amount far beyond whatever our Predecessors did.' He realized that it would be highly imprudent as well as inexpedient to 'say that we will never advance another sum permanently', but he wished it to be the Bank's policy to make every effort to convert its holdings of collateral security into a more liquid form: 'I have given my opinion in a pretty decided manner … upon the absolute necessity of our declining to advance money on mortgage or anything like permanent security: it may be a strong expression but I think the stability of our House depends upon our acting on that principle … [and] on the principle of reducing our temporary securities greatly in order to have a much larger investment on such securities as are speedily convertible into money.'

The well-known shortage of the supply of money did not impede the flow of applications for loans but rather intensified the urgency of the demands, and the Partners, despite Harry's firm guidelines, remained much exercised when dealing with the numerous cases of special pleading. One such came from Sukey's second husband, Lord Ailesbury, who as Groom to the Bedchamber, came to the Bank in February 1806 with a request for a loan on behalf of Queen Charlotte. She wanted 6000 guineas to buy an estate at Frogmore near Windsor Castle. Ailesbury offered the estate as a security and bound himself to pay the interest. Harry hesitated; Lord Ailesbury turned up at Fleet Street, in person, and insisted the Queen should have the money and Hoare's must contrive to get it somehow. This prompted Harry to refuse the application outright, saying the scheme was

*Henry Greathead,
inventor of the lifeboat.
The Bank opened a
subscription account in
his name to alleviate his
financial distress.*

impractical, 'upon which Lord A turned upon his heel and walked out seemingly much disappointed'. A few days reflection brought about a change of heart and it was noted in the Memorandum Book that 'her Majesty is to have the 6000 guineas which will be repaid by half yearly instalments of £1000 commencing Michaelmas day next. Lord Ailesbury to be the Bondsman and undertaking to make the promised payments.'

The Partners' acquiescence in the Royal demand paid off. Several years later an account was opened in the name of the Earl of Winchilsea who held the office of Groom of the Stole to the Royal household. The account was to be managed by Mr Stevenson; £25,000 was paid into it, quarterly, by the Exchequer and from it all the expenses of the Royal household at Windsor were met: 'the salaries are to be paid by us upon the production of proper receipts, and tradesmen's bills also upon them bringing their bills examined and signed by Mr Stevenson.'

Fortunately for Hoare's this period of stringency was also, for them, a time marked by a great increase in the number of their customer accounts. The clerks reported to the Partners that these new accounts were 'considerable in Amount, Respectability and Number' and without them Harry admitted, in his notes to the Partners in 1813, 'I shudder to think what would have been our situation'. Although these new accounts did not have a dramatic effect on the general balance it was reassuring that, at a time when there was a widespread want of confidence in banks, Hoare's retained its reputation of creditworthiness.

The problem of shortage of money, and gold in particular, persisted throughout the war period. The extreme scarcity of 'specie' was constantly alluded to and, on occasion, they had to follow the example set by the Bank of England and restrict distribution to no more than £5 at a time. In 1804 Hoare's secured a supply of gold from a Mr Hanley who collected coin from the turnpikes and other sources which he then sold to banks at a premium. Hoare's contracted with him to supply them with £100 of gold weekly, for six months, for which Hanley charged £1 11s 6d per hundred. There was a difficulty also with banknotes. The Bank of England began to reissue their old £1 and £2 notes 'promiscuously'. This resulted in the circulation of a great many dirty notes which the Partners felt were 'impossible to offer to ladies particularly'. Large balances on accounts at the Bank (of which there were several in the region of £100,000) caused unease, engendering a fear that the Bank might not have adequate cash reserves to meet substantial drawings. The Partners continually assessed the probability of this happening in order to judge the necessity of calling in loans from customers and cashing in their own investments. Calling in unexpired loans was always a risk 'on account of the impression it might make on the minds of the public that Messrs H were pressed for money and it would be the most certain plan we could adopt of making those persons to whom we did apply withdraw their confidence and their concerns together.'

The Bank's balances were falling at a rate to cause alarm; and the rapid decline in government stocks, 'the Funds', 'made everyone, desirous of purchasing [them] and there is no knowing to what extent they may reduce our coffers'. Harry's message in 1813 was a solemn one, 'Our House has stood many a rude blast, and is now in the highest credit, but it cannot be concealed that our resources are alarmingly diminishing and steps must be taken to meet a crisis which seems fast approaching but it must be done with that secret and discriminating hand which the subject and the very great importance of it demands.' As great a forbearance as possible must be exercised in advancing money and, when it was lent, it should only be for a short time and on the basis that there was every probability that it would be repaid at the time stipulated. Harry asked for a more thoughtful and considered approach to business and he devoted his later years to various schemes aimed at establishing codes of practice and rules of conduct for the young Partners and the clerks.

Early 19th century customer pass books, including Harry Hoare's account for Mitcham Grove.

The Partners only met formally together once a year to draw up the balance sheet, a practice which Harry felt was long overdue for reform. The 'awful times' he alluded to in his Paper not only necessitated more frequent meetings but also more time during them devoted to the proper consideration of many pressing subjects which, as things stood, were left unattended. Once the balance had been made it had been the habit of those Partners not officially 'in attendance' to depart without any further discussion. With much of importance then left unresolved too great a burden had been imposed on the Partner left in charge. Attendances were worked out in detail in advance and the distribution of duty weeks appears to have been very uneven. In 1809, for example, only three of the Partners were on the rota for the year. Charles worked for six months, putting in twenty-five weeks, followed by Harry who attended for seventeen weeks and Hugh whose duties occupied him for only 11 weeks. From that time Harry's own domestic responsibilities and his own frailty meant that he was rarely at Fleet Street but he kept in touch daily from Mitcham, while Charles and Henry Merrik, both of whom were childless, continued to take the lion's share of the 'Attendances'.

facing page
Lord Byron, by Thomas Phillips. Byron kept accounts at Hoare's, Kinnaird's and Hammersley's, not wishing to put his money 'into any one banker's hands'.

Arrangements had to be made for their successors and, while it was generally understood outside the confines of the Bank that the business was a family affair, this had sometimes to be explained. In January 1805 the Honourable Mrs Strode had hopes that her son might be introduced to the Bank as a Partner, but she was quickly disabused of the possibility in a letter from Harry, who explained that 'the partnership has ever been formed of our own family name except in one instance and that was for a very short period owing to the want of succession at the time and as there are now many younger branches to succeed it isn't our intention to deviate from the plan marked out by our Ancestors'. Another customer, the Earl of Radnor, had entertained similar hopes for his youngest son Philip Pleydell Bouverie whom he wished to set up in some 'mercantile line and thought of Hoare's, but understanding the idea was quite hopeless [I] never brought myself to mention it'. He managed to find him another situation and then wrote to the Partners on 17 January 1804, giving notice that 'if this treaty with another banking house' were concluded, he would be obliged to move his account there from Hoare's. This did not have the softening effect it was designed to produce, and the Earl closed his account two days later.

When Harry and his wife Lydia had moved to Mitcham Grove in 1796, with their own five small children, they little realized that the house, within the space of a generation, would become home also to six orphaned grandchildren with Harry, by then a widower, as their sole guardian. They were the children of his eldest son, William Henry, and his wife Louisa. Although placed in the Bank as a Partner, with a minority shareholding in 1797, William was never fit enough to be really effective. William and Louisa were both strongly committed evangelical Christians, adherents of the Clapham Sect, and lived, appropriately, in the great evangelical William Wilberforce's old house, 'Broomfield', in Battersea. When their eldest son, Henry, was only a boy of eight and nine both parents wrote him letters of the utmost religious intensity – 'Much did my heart rejoice when you were born – much more and forever shall I rejoice when you are born again,' wrote his mother in 1815 – which, when coupled with the strict moral discipline subsequently learned from his grandfather, inflicted on Henry a youth plagued by fear of a fall from grace.

Louisa died in 1816, the same year as her mother-in-law Lydia Hoare, followed by William in 1819. William bequeathed the care of his children and their disagreeable governess, Miss Holloway, to Harry who had been expecting as much and undertook the task with great commitment and seriousness. Henry's religious education continued. He was kept under strict control when at Eton: a schoolboy prank was regarded by Harry as a catastrophic moral lapse and the slightest propensity to self-indulgence, whether it was the ordering of white trousers rather than the usual nankeen, or the suggestion that he might accompany his cousin Peter to Windsor for an outing one Sunday, was castigated in the bitterest of terms. Harry's position as head of this mushrooming family, with numerous other grandchildren to consider as well, was testing for the elderly widower. He wrote to Henry, on the subject of observing the Sabbath: 'You must remember that I have twenty-six young children who are looking up to me for an example, though by infirmities I am mostly kept at home, yet my most ardent desire is that my family may never desecrate the Sabbath.' Mitcham Grove, like Barn Elms, became a focus for family gatherings. One of the 'High Hoare' relations, Mary Anne Prince, wrote a memoir for her younger siblings in 1861, in which she recollected, 'rather awful Sundays spent at Mitcham … old Mr Hoare's place. He was a very distant relation but head of the House. Such a little man but good natured … I used to be in the schoolroom with Mr H's three orphan granddaughters … they were very strictly and puritanically brought up … I used to pity them and feel very nervous. I remember the church and the girls looking very stiff. I rather think they used to have to write down the sermon.'

The matter of succession was uncontroversial within the family. By 1811 Hugh's two elder boys, Hugh Richard and Henry Charles, were working at the Bank. The brothers, born in 1787 and 1790 respectively, worked closely together.[1] In 1820 it was agreed that after these two the priority of admission into the Bank, subject to their proper conduct and capacities, should be: firstly, Peter Richard, born in 1803, son of the lawyer Peter Richard and first cousin of Hugh and Charles Junior, secondly, Harry's grandson, Henry, who was four years younger than Peter, and thirdly, Hugh's youngest son, Arthur born in 1804. All except Arthur were to become sharing Partners.

Although misdemeanours tended to be recorded at the Bank, whereas satisfactory performance of duties, being taken for granted, was not, the impression is that opportunities for dishonest and fraudulent behaviour were not difficult to find, and so the Partners' scrupulous attention to all matters of business extended to keeping a close watch on the performance of their staff. It was vital that the reputation of their House did not suffer from exploitation by those who worked inside it. A memorandum of 1786 addressed to the 'Gentlemen of the Shop' suggests the Partners were not wholly satisfied by the performance of some of the clerks. They felt obliged to remind the staff that each one of them must be 'dressed and ready to attend in his particular department by 9 o'clock in the Morning', for which purpose breakfast would be on the table half an hour before. Although business finished at 5 o'clock, clerks who were designated to be on duty must remain until the balance was right. On no account should the House be 'left without one clerk in it' and that rule applied to Sundays and to Christmas Day 'which in every respect to be considered a Sunday'. The clerks were to work out their own 'rotation' for attendance after business hours which included those who did not live in at the Bank. No concessions were made to non-resident clerks: 'Any difficulty that may arise from the Distance of their Dwelling from the House at Fleet Street, as it is occasioned solely by their own choice, so it is not to be supposed

Satirical print. 'A New
Banking Drommund
Hoare and Child',
1820.

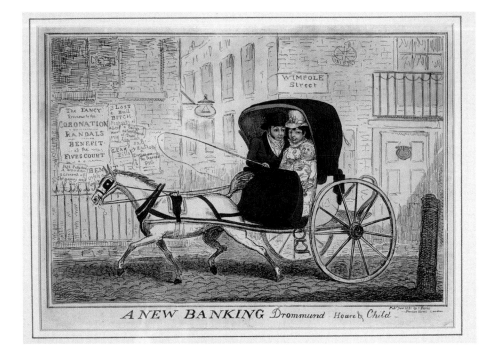

that Messrs Hoare can provide against it.' Those who slept in the House were to
be in by midnight at the latest.

Stern words were delivered on the subject of overpayment on 'those
Gentlemen's accounts whose credit is not thoroughly known and established' and
those responsible for such overpayments would be 'answerable for the sum overdrawn … and if carried to the excess that it has been of late [they] will be called
upon for making good [any] deficiencies.' Food and drink was liberally provided
and Harry greatly disapproved of people bringing in their own sustenance: 'My
directions to my Housekeeper are to provide Plenty, and that of the best kind …
whatever is served on the table must in future be procured by her only. Neither do
I permit Wine or any other liquor more than is provided to be sent for.'

By 1821 the Bank employed fourteen clerks, double the number employed
at the time Harry started in the Bank in 1777. (In the same period deposits had
nearly doubled to over £1.5 million, profits had risen from £25,000 to
£44,000.) Basic salaries had increased from between £80 and £140 to between
£100 and £160 per annum and then remained fixed at these 1807 rates for the
next sixty years. In addition, the two senior clerks could expect to make about
£1000 a year each from a 50 per cent share of the stock broking commission,
the remainder of which was shared out between all the clerical staff in proportion to their seniority either as percentages or as fixed sums. The rules
concerning sharing the brokerage commission were established in 1809. The
Partners, rather than increase the salaries paid to their staff, which would detract
from the general balance, relied on the income generated by the increased activ-

ity in buying and selling stock to meet the need for increased remuneration.

This system led to frequent disputes among the clerks on the fairness of the distribution in relation to the burden of the work. Harry had to deal with one such incident while he was working from home at Mitcham in September 1809. Mr Cottle, who was relatively junior, was paid a fixed sum of £70 per annum out of the brokerage, rather than a percentage, and he complained to the Partners that he felt entitled to more on account of the 'additional trouble he was at in attending on the Brokers'. In the first instance Cottle had taken his grievance to his superior, Mr Barry, who, it appeared, had lost his temper with Cottle and subjected him to 'gross and improper language'. Harry wrote a letter of reprimand to Barry, addressed to all those who had ill-treated Cottle on this occasion, but nevertheless the arrangements remained unaltered.

Vacancies for clerks were rare and highly sought after. The Partners received a regular stream of applications, usually from customers acting as referees for individuals. In addition to taking on only those who came with a personal recommendation, the Bank favoured those candidates with previous experience and those with a family connection. Of the eleven applications for a vacancy, occasioned by the death of Mr Lainchbury in 1802, ten were currently employed by other banking houses and one was Lainchbury's son. On joining, the new clerk had to produce sureties of £1000 and commit himself to 'faithfully and diligently serve according to his utmost skill and knowledge' and promise that he would not 'in any way lose, embezzle, purloin, consume, misspend or keep any money … or any other things whatsoever shall be entrusted to him'. Although strict instructions were given that no speculation should be undertaken which was not directly the concern of the House this was an area where abuses arose, and one particular case, involving a clerk named William Christmas, resulted in very unfavourable publicity for the Bank.

Christmas arrived at the Bank in 1811 with all the right credentials: his father was employed as a clerk in the Bank of England and stood surety for his son. But, as was revealed later, he was evidently one of those 'clever clerks' whom Harry described as 'always rogues'. While working at the Bank William Christmas met Elizabeth Wright, a widow nearly twice his age, whose late husband, Captain Wright, had kept an account at Hoare's. He had died in 1816 leaving £7000 to his widow. In his dealings with Elizabeth, Christmas was 'assiduously attentive and she viewed him with an eye of favour and after a courtship of moderate length they were married'. Having taken possession of her fortune his enthusiasm for his bride waned and the couple separated. From his income of £500 he gave her an allowance of £120 a year. The real trouble between them only started when Christmas, having stopped all payment to her, was seen constantly in the company of a Mrs Chatterley, an actress from Covent Garden. Elizabeth Christmas began a campaign of harassment against the couple which ultimately led to her temporary

Silhouette of Jane
Austen's mother,
Cassandra, who referred
to her bankers as 'those
blundering Hoares ... so
many of us [Austens]
bank with them that it
sometimes puzzles their
heads'.

confinement in St Martin's Watch House. William Christmas and Mrs Chatterley meanwhile had set up house together in Acton in fine style where they lived with her mother under the pretence of being brother and sister. Eventually Elizabeth was driven to exact revenge and in the Spring of 1825 she wrote to the Partners asking them to look into the financial circumstances of her estranged husband since his current lifestyle was clearly not sustainable on a clerk's salary.

Merrik called on the house in East Acton and ascertained that it was let to Christmas, and noted that it was an establishment on a scale 'quite incompatible with that sober regularity and demeanour which Messrs Hoare expect from their clerks'. The implication was that Christmas had other sources of income which the Bank were unaware of. Harry was appalled by the association with Mrs Chatterley 'whether criminal or not' and the manner in which the Bank's name had become connected with her own in the newspapers who had been reporting the continuing fracas between her and Mrs Christmas for the past two years. He could find nothing to say in Christmas's favour: 'He has lived in a style and at an expense far beyond the means of a banker's clerk. He has contrived not to have a friend in the House and has perpetual bickering about his hours for meals; his sentiments are known to be radical and I fear no religious principles are guiding or protecting his slippery path.' In early June 1825 Christmas was dismissed. On 16 July Charles was informed that Christmas had embezzled £1000 of Exchequer Bills. Mr White, the Bank's solicitor, was called in and all the Partners congregated at Fleet Street where they agreed to proceed with a prosecution.

On 20 July Christmas appeared before the magistrate and was committed for trial. The theft had been easily carried out and was as easily discovered. Each year, on the issue of new Exchequer Bills, those holding the old ones had the right to buy new ones or take the money. In September 1824 £475,000 worth of Exchequer bills, paid in September 1823, were called in from Hoare's to be exchanged for new ones with interest. William Christmas signed for the bills having kept back ten of them to the value of £1000 which he subsequently sold to a stockbroker. Each of the bills had a unique number relating to their year of issue and the stolen bills were produced in evidence. Christmas was found guilty and sentenced to transportation to Tasmania. While awaiting departure he wrote abject letters to the Partners from Newgate begging them to intercede with the Home Secretary, Robert Peel, to allow him to conduct himself to his place of exile and 'not suffer to go on a convict ship linked and chained down with a gang of the most depraved and horrible Felons during a long voyage'. A petition (not signed by the Partners) did reach Peel but was dismissed by him as being without precedent and on 25 October Christmas was removed to the hulks at Woolwich to await his passage. The Partners did however write a letter of Recommendation, on Christmas's behalf, to the Colonial Secretary, Earl Bathurst, which resulted in Christmas being employed as a correspondence clerk in the Governor's office in Tasmania.

William Christmas's life thereafter had no further connection with the Bank, but his spirit of enterprise did not desert him and he managed to secure a rare ticket of leave to work in New South Wales for his own benefit, rather than under government control, despite further convictions for forgery and theft. He also managed to return to England. There is no record of his having paid back his debt to the Bank which he so fulsomely promised to do in letters written from Tasmania: 'Yes gentlemen I am determined that you shall not eventually lose one penny by my misconduct.' He married twice more, while his erstwhile mistress returned to the stage and, when no longer in demand there, married the political activist, Francis Place, who, in later life was bitterly to regret the union.

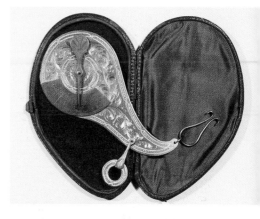

*19th century pocket scales for weighing gold and silver coin.*

The price of war continued to be exacted from the Country through the years of peace following Napoleon's defeat in 1815. Government and local taxes ate into incomes, agriculture and manufacturing no longer benefited from wartime demand and land and property prices stagnated. Henry died in 1828 and Mitcham Grove, which had been bought for £18,000, was sold within six months of his death for £13,500 and the profit from the produce on his estate was reported by his agent to be 'as low now as it was forty years since.' Profits from the business, however, had doubled under Harry's management. In the decade before his death the figures for each year were between £40,000 and £50,000 with the exception of 1825, when the Bank had to ride out a financial panic, which took several other London Houses and many country banks to the wall.

Harry had been taking a half share of the profits, Hugh a quarter and the remaining quarter was divided between Charles and Henry Merrik, two thirds to one third. When Hugh inherited the position of senior Partner he was sixty-six and his brothers were in their late fifties. Although assisted by sons and nephews there was no individual under Harry's scheme of management who had been groomed to take the Bank into its next stage of development. Control was now firmly vested in the hands of the 'High Hoares' with Harry's grandson, just down from Cambridge, being the only representative of the senior line of the family. Hugh chose not to pay him a salary but kept him on an allowance for ten years after he joined the Bank in 1827. Harry left Henry a sizeable income to live off but, having only a life interest in the Bank, there was nothing of the business that was his to bequeath. Once again the senior line of the family were dependent on their cousins from the junior branch for readmission into the ownership of the Bank.

# THE ADELPHI HOARES AND THE RED LION 1828–1866

Stourhead, by John Buckler, 1817, with the pavilions, housing the Library and Picture Gallery, added by Sir Richard Colt Hoare in 1792-94, which tripled the length of the east front.

The 'Adelphi' Hoares, Hugh, Charles and Henry Merrik were now in full control at Fleet Street. An elderly group, they kept a tight grip on the business over the ensuing twenty years. Inevitably the time came for younger relations to be admitted as Partners, but, until 1852, admission into the Partnership was not readily conceded.

Meanwhile, their eldest brother, Colt devoted his resources, both in time and money, to bringing up his son, Henry, embellishing Stourhead and pursuing his topographical and antiquarian interests which he had cultivated during his long stay abroad.[1] During his six years on the continent, Colt added to his grandfather's collection of pictures, including a series of large scale Italian views by the Swiss artist Louis Ducros, and – what he considered to be his most important Italian picture – *The Adoration of the Magi* by Cigoli, which he acquired in 1790, shortly after the demolition of San Pietro Maggiore in Florence. On his return home he promoted the careers of contempor-ary British artists, notably the young J M W Turner, and continued to patronize his grandfather's protégés Francis Nicholson and Samuel Woodforde.

The house he inherited was too small for his purposes. In 1792-94, working from his own designs, he extended it by the addition of two wings projecting to the north and south of Colen Campbell's mansion: one to house a Picture Gallery where his Cigoli took pride of place over the mantelpiece, flanked by two 'mighty canvases' by Maratta and Mengs acquired by Henry the Magnificent (all three are still in place today), and the other to accommodate his extensive library,

facing page.
Sir Richard Colt Hoare, the antiquarian, with his son, Henry, who predeceased him. By Samuel Woodforde, c. 1794, nephew of the diarist Parson Woodforde and protégé of Colt and Charles Hoare.

*The Library at Stourhead, c.1901, Colt Hoare's 'supreme achievement as patron', with all the scholarly comforts of 'an Italian monastery' and none of the disadvantages.*

*Sir Richard Colt Hoare's sketchbook from his tours in England and Wales, 1809-13, when travel on the continent was restricted.*

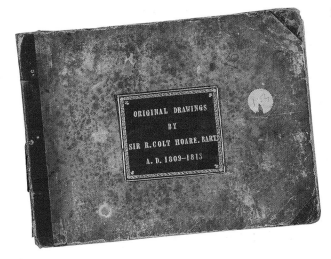

described by Kenneth Woodbridge as Colt Hoare's 'most significant contribution to culture'. In 1825 he gave his collection of Italian topographical and historical works to the British Museum and in its place he collected nearly every book on those subjects relating to the British Isles. All the furniture for the new wings was provided by Thomas Chippendale the younger, who was rescued from bankruptcy in 1804 by the loyalty of clients such as Colt Hoare, who had first employed him before his marriage to Hester and continued to do so until Chippendale's death in 1822.

Colt wished to preserve the lake and the temples from his grandfather's day – though he removed some features, including two of Henry's later follies, the 'Turkish Tent' and the 'Chinese Temple'– but had his own ideas regarding planting. As a fellow of the Linnean Society, he was a considerable botanist (particularly in the cultivation of geraniums) and his knowledge was extended by his association with the nurseryman John Veitch who was employed by his half-sister, Henrietta, at Killerton. Colt began a massive tree-planting scheme in 1791-92, favouring broad-leaf species as against the mixture of beech and fir favoured by his grandfather. He underplanted the trees with laurel, and introduced rhododendrons, which he continued to plant throughout his life, giving the gardens their characteristic appearance much enjoyed today. He commissioned Francis Nicholson to record his maturing landscape in a series of watercolour drawings in 1813.

In London his brothers were also absorbed in building: they were rebuilding. The actual premises had been considerably extended since the seventeenth century by the acquisition of neighbouring buildings, but these were not in any sense purpose-built and, by the early years of the nineteenth century, it was clear that their inadequacies were becoming an impediment to the smooth running of the business. Shortage of space had long been a problem. The setting up of the Sinking Fund in 1799 was a recognition that rebuilding would be needed. The situation was partially eased by the purchase of adjoining premises, to the west of the Bank, next to Falcon Court, in 1801, which became known as the 'Banker's House' and was used by the Partners, and to the east, facing Mitre Court, in 1802.

The family too felt the inconveniences of the lack of suitable space. Henry Charles was put in an uncomfortable position during

The 'Old' Bank shortly before its demolition in 1829, by T H Shepherd, the topographical artist who recorded disappearing London and its improvements. The corner of the old church of St Dunstan's is on the right.

his time as 'Resident Partner' when he was told that it was impossible for his wife to stay with him at Fleet Street. The Partners thought the situation was intolerable, as they indicated in a memorandum to the staff written in 1828: 'this in fact amounts almost to an entire separation of husband and wife for six months of the year. When provision is not made for bed and board in the same house the comforts of the married state are considerably abridged; it is therefore the wish of Messrs Hoare that such accommodation should be provided for Mrs H as may enable Mr H C H to enjoy the society of his wife during the time of his attendance.'

The street façade of the old Bank gave no clue to the cramped and inconvenient arrangement of rooms that lay behind it. Its appearance was virtually indistinguishable from a terrace of town houses, a characteristic it shared with most of the other 'West End' private banks. This derived from the origin of the buildings themselves and from the fact that they functioned as domestic premises, providing accommodation for the proprietors and their staff, as well as business houses with banking halls, offices and strong rooms. The Bank only advertised itself as a business on the ground floor. A discreet sign in the form of a 'Golden Bottle' was fixed under the pediment over the street door which was flanked by two large windows and led straight into the banking Shop.

Hoare's broke new ground when it came to rebuilding their premises. With the exception of Sir John Soane's design for William Praed and Co's banking house at 189 Fleet Street, completed in 1802, any rebuilding or remodelling undertaken by their competitors, clustered round Temple Bar and Charing Cross, had followed

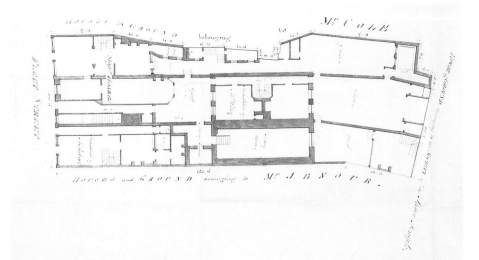

*Ground plan of the 'Old' Bank, c.1780, showing its narrow street façade and Mr Wray's dwelling house in the back yard.*

the traditional pattern of the Georgian town house façade. As a group these private 'West end' banks – which included Hoare's, Child's, Gosling's, Coutts, and Praed's in Fleet Street and the Strand – specialized in serving the aristocracy, gentry and professional classes; so there was no particular requirement for their buildings to have the monumental 'public' character of their erstwhile City counterparts in Lombard Street whose financial activity was now focused on commercial customers.[2] At Hoare's too, from 1826 to 1828, discussions between the Partners concerning the rebuilding revolved round variations on this traditional theme with one or two new ideas for creating more light and space in the Shop. In commissioning the final design for their new building, however, Hoare's decided to give their new House historical 'weight', while at the same time devising a model which would be seen as enlightened and modern and fit for future business. Their solution avoided both imitation and ostentation. They abandoned the town house model and replaced it with a 'sober 19th-century business house, Italian in type but Grecian in austerity' whose façade gave no hint of any domestic function its interior was designed to serve.[3]

Hoare's were prepared to spend a good deal on this project. The estimates and plans for a new stone-fronted banking house, which included rebuilding 33 Fleet Street and constructing two new houses behind it in Falcon Court, a new four-storey set of chambers in Mitre Court for renting out, and alterations for a temporary place of business came to a total of £32,252, of which £19,500 represented the cost of the new Banking House. The architect was Charles Parker, a former pupil of Jeffrey Wyattville, who wrote to Charles on 15 October 1828 after inspecting the plans, that he considered them 'well calculated for the intended purpose'.

Hugh was happy to leave most of the aesthetic decisions to his brothers, Charles and Merrik, and they, in turn, were anxious to have Colt's opinion, knowing him to be a connoisseur in such matters. In writing to Merrik, Colt made no

The three 'Adelphi'
Partners: Henry Hugh,
Charles and Henry
Merrik, c.1830.
Lithograph.

claims for knowing what was right in terms of the 'many separate rooms you want for business and clerks' but urged that the Partners should give themselves a better room than proposed: '25 by 15 is a mere den, little better than the old one – why not throw the bill office into it and make a handsome room of 25 by 26 to receive the noblesse?' He was keen to put the family history on display and expressed his wish to see the new Partners' room 'furnished with portraits aborigine, with the "Lord Mayor a cheval" over the Chimney'. This referred to a painting by John Wootton of Sir Richard Hoare, on horseback, preparing to defend the City of London against the Jacobite army in 1745, a picture that still hangs in the Bank, taking pride of place among the ranks of other, more modest, family portraits.

Colt questioned Parker's proposal to adorn the façade with columns at first-floor level as they might darken the rooms inside. He also objected outright to columns rising from the street level which would produce an inappropriate temple-like effect, but was concerned that dispensing with them altogether might make the front too mean and plain. As an antiquary, he looked for spaces to insert

*Hoare's Bank. The 'Shop'
or Banking Hall as it is
today. Designed by
Charles Parker in 1829,
its central feature, the
bronze stove and lamp
standard, was made by
his brother Samuel.*

shields bearing the arms of the family and the Goldsmith's Company and a tablet commemorating the date of the Bank's foundation. Whatever final decision was taken he was adamant that 'no compromise should be made with their building in order to fit in with the Bank's immediate surroundings: 'I conclude you will not suffer the outside walls to have any conversation with the adjacent buildings.' Charles concurred with him about the columns, being reluctant to have anything which could be seen as too 'magnificent for a House of Business'. He agreed that a pediment over the entrance on the left-hand side of the building 'to receive our signum' would be desirable, but Parker persuaded him to adhere to his original plan of a round-headed arch to the door, and its matching recess on the right-hand side, in keeping with the design of the ground-floor windows.

The estimates accompanied by 'twenty seven detailed drawings containing the construction as well as the manner of furnishing the rooms' were delivered to Hugh on 10 December 1828 with an accompanying letter from Parker who explained that his prices had to take into account the 'very short space of time allowed for the rebuilding and the entire want of conveniences on the spot for workmen'. The only expenses not estimated for were the desks, stoves and bells. Five per cent was allowed against any 'unforseen occurrences', but in the event the final bill exceeded the estimate by over £10,000, which was the sum Praed and Co had paid for their much smaller new building down the road thirty years earlier.

Behind the façade, the dual nature of the new Banking House as a business and a residence became more apparent. The door from the street led into a lobby. This opened into the Shop on the right hand side, but straight ahead a grand staircase swept up to the family's accommodation on the first and second floors in what became known as the 'Private House.' Throughout the building the quality of the materials used in all the fittings and finishes was a testament to the high standards asked of and provided by Parker and his contractors. On the first floor, two rooms – the Saloon, and its ante room at the top of the stairs, furnished with gold framed mirrors by Nicholas Isherwood of Ludgate Hill – overlooked Fleet Street, while Charles's Sitting Room and the Partner's Dining Room overlooked the courtyard. Much of the rosewood furniture, made by Samuel Bamfill of Ludgate Hill for these rooms, has survived and, redecoration apart, little fundamental has changed over the years except minor adjustments in change of use – for example, Charles's Sitting Room is now used as the Drawing Room and the Saloon as a Library and Reception Room. The second floor had three 'sets' of bedrooms and sitting rooms for the Partners which now are offices.

On the ground floor the Bank has remained as Parker planned it. The large round-headed windows facing Fleet Street were designed to back-light the cashiers who were stationed behind an oak counter which curved round two sides of the Shop. It was made by Bamfill, who also supplied round oak tables for the customers' use. The Shop was heated and lit by a neo-classical bronze stove and lamp standard in the

centre of the floor made at the foundry owned by Charles Parker's brother, Samuel. He also supplied a lamp and the columnar iron balusters for the staircase. The Partners were given the spacious room Colt had advocated at the back of the Shop, receiving natural light from the street through a glazed internal partition, and from the south through a large bay facing the courtyard.

*The Partners' staircase, designed by Charles Parker to give direct access from street level to their private apartments without entering the banking offices.*

Charles had no children but he left a lasting legacy to the business and to his family in this remarkable building project, which he undertook almost through force of circumstances but which yielded spectacular and lasting results. He complained about the upheaval involved in rebuilding the Bank, but the decisions he made were impeccable, not least his choice of architect. Charles Parker was known as an academic rather than a practising architect, and Hoare's Bank can claim to be his only complete secular building.[4] (On the strength of his work in Fleet Street, he was commissioned to add a portico to the entrance front at Stourhead in 1838-39, a feature which Colen Campbell had planned but never executed.) Although Parker's plans for the Bank were endorsed by his master, Sir Jeffrey Wyatville, his commission from the Partners was,

*Wooden attaché case constructed as a drawer, used by the Partners. Early 19th century.*

nevertheless, a bold move on their part – one which Charles, in particular, would have made with a good deal of confidence, gained from the very successful completion of his own country house at the beginning of the century.

Charles and his wife, Dorothea, were driven from London on account of her delicate health. During the early 1790s Charles had moved

*Humphry Repton's visualization of the 'modern villa' requested by Charles and Dorothea to be built at Luscombe. From his 'Red Book', 1799.*

*Humphry Repton's trade card, advertising his services as a landscape gardener, designed by himself, c.1788-90.*

from a house in Putney to another in Roehampton and finally to Barnes in search of a place that would suit her. Her health did not improve and in 1791 they abandoned England and spent the whole winter in Lisbon. By 1795 they had settled on the seaside town of Dawlish in South Devon, a small but fashionable watering place, where they rented a house, ordering furniture for it from Thomas Chippendale which suggests they had no immediate plans to move on. However, during a visit there, Colt is said to have drawn his half-brother's attention to a 'beautiful little farm' at Luscombe, a valley which stretched inland from Dawlish church on a gentle incline terminating in a steep ascent into the Halden Hills. The climate of South Devon, untouched by the 'chilling hand of Winter' suited Dorothea and, encouraged by this, and by Colt's advice, Charles bought the freehold of Luscombe farm in 1797-98 followed by further land, known as Luscombe Down, in 1798-99.

Almost immediately Charles engaged Humphry Repton and John Nash, who had been in partnership since 1796, to landscape and to build for him. Following the death of Capability Brown in 1783 Repton had assumed the mantle of his distinguished predecessor as the leading 'improver' of landscapes for the gentry. Both he and his 'ingenious friend Mr Nash' were exponents of the new 'Picturesque' style of country house architecture which threw off the restraints of the classical mould and emphasized the importance of a visual as opposed to an academic approach, with particular attention being paid to the relationship between the architecture of the main house and its setting. Unlike Stourhead, where there was no visual communication between the mansion house and the pleasure grounds, Luscombe was designed as a whole. The valley was landscaped and planted by Repton in harmony with the house and Nash, by means of his intricate planning, ensured the principal rooms in the castle each had a different and splendid view.

By choosing to site the house in a sheltered position halfway up the valley, rather than on top of the hill, Repton elected to sacrifice a panoramic view of the south coast for the sake of the comfort and privacy of his clients. But he argued that nothing of the 'Picturesque' would be lost thereby, for 'the view of the sea … over the beautiful middle distance of town … only requires to be framed by an adequate foreground of highly dressed lawn … gradually feeding into a lawn fed by cattle and sheep and a pleasure garden … on which trees and shrubs may be planted to vary the surface' … to produce 'a beautifully framed picture' which had every advantage over 'an unbroken Stare'. On days when 'Fogs or bad weather may render the sea an unpleasing object' the view could be diverted across the valley where he proposed a 'bank of Lawn beautifully broken by large trees and skirted by a bold sweeping line of plantation across the valley.' The hill at the head of the valley was to be 'cloathed with wood in which a small glade may hereafter be cleared to shew a prospect room or seat from whence is the most extensive view.'[5] Having settled on the site for building, Repton had to persuade Charles and Dorothea that their choice of a neat seaside villa would not fit into his vision of the landscape: 'if the Grecian or modern style were adopted … the roof would be unsightly from every part of the grounds except from the South-East (i.e. below)'.

*Repton's suggested idea for a picturesque castellated house at Luscombe set in a wooded valley. From his 'Red Book', 1799.*

Nash's solution was to build a Gothic castle with a 'bold irregularity of outline and …roof enriched by turrets, battlements, corbels and lofty chimneys' which by its sprawling and asymmetrical nature gave an impression of great size but was in fact no more than a large house. When planning the interior Nash felt at liberty to dispense with the Gothic style (except as dictated by the windows where he freely used stained glass in the upper lights) and to design for comfort and elegance in the neo-classical idiom. The ground-floor rooms – an octagon Drawing Room leading into a conservatory, an Eating Room, a Library and a Staircase Hall fitted with an organ which served as a chapel, and another small book room – were conveniently arranged around a central circular vestibule. Work on the house was nearing completion when Charles ordered his Drawing Room furniture from Thomas Chippendale the younger, in 1803, many of the pieces being very similar in style to the furniture Chippendale had recently supplied to Colt Hoare for his new Picture Gallery at Stourhead. In his choice of modern pictures he commissioned work from the 'Stourhead' artists, Woodforde and Nicholson, and bought work from the Royal Academicians, James Northcote and Henry Thomson.

For the next fifty years Charles spent most of his time at Luscombe, adding to the work begun by Repton in the park and making some adjustments to the house, including an extension to the Drawing Room which would give Dorothea access to the winter sun. When away from the Bank he employed a postboy to collect early morning deliveries from the post office at Dawlish and to take outgoing mail from the Castle. By this system important and urgent messages could pass quickly between Charles and his Partners in Fleet Street. Outside the family Charles's experience in building matters was utilized by the Trustees of Westminster Hospital (his great-grandfather's foundation) when they appointed him, with three others, to undertake the responsibility of contracting for the new hospital building in 1832.

At the same time as the new Banking House was going up, the dilapidated parish church of St Dunstan's in the West was demolished and rebuilt, allowing Fleet Street to be permanently widened at this point and providing extra space for the growing local population. The architect, John Shaw, produced a clever design based on an octagonal nave in the Gothic Revival style with a beautiful lantern tower. The Partners, led by Charles, took a very active interest in the new church, presenting four stained-glass windows (the originals were destroyed by enemy action in September 1940 and replacement copies were made in 1950) behind the high altar which was placed opposite the main door at the north end of the church. Sir Richard

*The new church of St Dunstan's in the West designed by John Shaw. Lithograph by Thomas Shotter Boys, showing the road-widening scheme outside the Bank in Fleet Street, 1842.*

John Nash's octagonal drawing room at Luscombe, furnished by Thomas Chippendale the younger. Watercolour early 19th century.

Hoare, Lord Mayor in 1745, was buried in the church and the rest for his mayoral sword is still fixed to a front pew. His memorial, along with that of his grandfather, was restored and displayed prominently in the new church, with a tablet explaining that: 'This valuable monument … was restored to its original beauty by the inhabitants of this parish in testimony of their grateful sense of obligation to a family whose eminent virtues and munificence it is intended to perpetuate.'

Hoare's acquired new premises at a time when the structure of banking itself was undergoing significant changes. Unlike the Bank of England (the only joint stock bank in existence prior to 1826) private banks were limited by law to partnerships of no more than six individuals. This inevitably resulted in limitations on the size of their resources and this in turn led to closures and failures in times of crisis, such as the financial panic of 1825. This crisis grew out of a spending boom in the early 1820s which included heavy investment in newly independent South American countries. Hoare's was not badly affected and could afford to decline the £10,000 loan offered to them by Colonel Ollney, a concerned customer who was so alarmed by the suffering of 'so many respectable bankers in London as well as the country' that he instructed his bankers to sell stock on his and his sister's account and to appropriate the money to their own use, with the assurance that this offer was made out of a genuine desire to help and not as a consequence of entertaining any suspicions regarding the bank's 'respectability and responsibility'.

Over one hundred private banks, out of a total of seven hundred countrywide, were not in such a happy position and were forced to close their doors and only twenty of them reopened. To help increase the capitalization of the country banks – whose excessive issue of small denomination notes was believed to have exacerbated their problems in 1825 – legislation was introduced in 1826 which lifted the restrictions on the size of partnerships and introduced the principle of joint stock banking. The restriction still operated in London, however, and any-

Certificate for 50 shares in the Bank of the USA, 1832, in the name of the Countess of Pembroke. She used her bankers' vaults and their discretion to hide the family's famous gem collection from her extravagant son and heir.

where within a 65-mile radius of the metropolis. This was to ensure that the Bank of England could not be threatened by joint stock competitors. Its position was further bolstered by the licence it was granted to open branches anywhere in the kingdom. Joint stock banks were finally permitted to operate in London after 1833 but without the capability, which their provincial counterparts enjoyed, to issue their own notes. This privilege was guarded jealously by the Bank of England and in 1833 only their notes were given legal tender status.

The structure of banking in England was complex with private and joint stock banks competing with each other in the country and, to a lesser extent, in London where by 1844 there were only five joint stock banks as opposed to sixty-three private partnerships. This was the year of the Bank Charter Act which was intended to rationalize a confusing picture. The chief aim of the legislation was to restrict any increase in note issue in the country and protect the position of the Bank of England as the sole note issuer in London. One of the clauses of the Act stipulated that if a provincial bank opened a branch in London it would lose its status as a bank of issue. It was anticipated that the private country banks would be quickly absorbed by the more aggressive joint stock operations who, on establishing branches in London, would lose their right to issue banknotes and thus provincial note issue would eventually disappear. This did happen, but only slowly, as the development of joint stock banking did not proceed at the pace expected.

Those private banks that had weathered the difficulties of 1825 continued to prosper by the exercise of sound management. The possible temptation of reduc-

previous page
Luscombe Castle designed by John Nash. John Buckler, 1820. Luscombe was Repton and Nash's most successful collaboration; their partnership disintegrated soon afterwards.

ing their exposure to risk by absorption into a joint stock enterprise was no inducement to successful banks such as Hoare's since, until the 1870s, all banks irrespective of status, were excluded from the protection of limited liability. Besides there was also the matter of trust, as Walter Bagehot wrote in 1873, explaining the connection between the success of the private bank and the personal character of the banker: 'a man of known wealth, known integrity, and known ability is largely entrusted with the money of his neighbours. The confidence is strictly personal. His neighbours know him, and trust him because they know him. They see daily his manner of life, and judge from it that their confidence is deserved.'

Hoare's was certainly one of the largest of the 'West End' private banks in terms of deposits and profits. The figures for the first decades of the nineteenth century show that the scale of operations at Hoare's, for example, was nearly twice that of their near neighbours Messrs Gosling. On the other hand the new joint stock London and Westminster Bank grew rapidly in size after its establishment in 1834 and outstripped many of its private competitors. In some years, as in 1843-45, its deposits edged slightly ahead of those held by Hoare's, but overall Hoare's showed a steady performance at a high level, holding on to deposits well over £2 million without any dramatic fluctuations.

Hugh died at the age of eighty in 1841. As Colt had died in 1838 leaving no direct descendants, under the rules of the male entail, Hugh, his next eldest half-brother, had succeeded to all his estates. So, for nearly four years, once he became third baronet, he had enjoyed the dual position of owner of the Bank and of Stourhead, one which his great uncle, Henry the Magnificent, had seen as such a threat to the survival of his country estates and had taken such pains to prevent Colt from enjoying.

Charles was seventy-four when he assumed the mantle of senior Partner on Hugh's death in 1841, and, although he soon stopped making the arduous journey to London from Luscombe Castle, distance didn't seem to impair his longstanding authority at the Bank. He died in 1851. The last of the 'Adelphi', Henry Merrik, a courteous and generous man, lived until 1856, though by then he was senile, knowing neither the names of his Partners nor his own address, and he had ceased to appear at Fleet Street long before 1852. The control of the Bank now passed on to the next generation.

Hugh had introduced his two older sons into the business at Fleet Street but neither was destined be a senior Partner. The elder, Hugh Richard, on becoming the fourth baronet, gave up his Partnership at the Bank in favour of life as a landowner at Stourhead where he continued Colt's enthusiasm for tree-planting, taking a particular interest in adding ornamental conifers which had recently been introduced into Britain. Hugh Richard was thus the first Partner in the history of the firm to choose to retire, but his uncles were apparently happy to let him go and they agreed that he should be paid an annuity of £5,200 out of Bank profits. Henry Charles who, like his father Hugh, loved hunting and whose attendances at the Bank were arranged around the fixtures of the sporting calendar, died in 1852. The succession therefore went to their cousins Henry and Peter Richard.

Henry, grandson of Harry of Mitcham Grove, had completed his Cambridge education by the age of nineteen, graduating with a double first from St John's, and came straight to the Bank, in a probationary capacity, as an Agent, in 1822. As he was heir to his grandfather's considerable estate, he was given simply an annual allowance of £200 for the work he did and this was not raised and converted into a salary until he was thirty-five. He was made a salaried Partner in 1845 when Sir Hugh Richard retired and it was not until 1852, after the deaths close together of Charles and Henry Charles, that Henry, aged forty-nine, was able to join his cousin Peter Richard as a full Partner. Peter Richard was Henry's near contemporary, being the son of the youngest sibling of the 'Adelphi'. They were not fond of each other, but nevertheless the two men managed to run the Bank together, unaided by any other relations, for a period of twelve years, during which time they learned to accommodate their differences and to master the problem of incipient rivalry by developing absorbing interests outside the business. They organiZed their attendances at Fleet Street so as to coincide as little as possible, but their lives were inextricably connected beyond their affiliation to the family business. In the first place they had married sisters, Lady Mary and Lady Sophia Marsham, daughters of the 2nd Earl of Romney, and both chose to live in Kent. More significantly, they were part of the strong reforming movements within the Church of England although at opposite ends of the religious spectrum, and their shared commitment led to a period of absolute rectitude in the running of the Bank. Daniel Hardcastle in *Banks and Bankers* published in 1843, produced a generalized picture of the 'Private Banker' as a 'man of serious manners, plain apparel, the steadiest of conduct, and a rigid observer of formalities. As you looked in his face you could read that the ruling maxim of his life ... was, that he who would be trusted with the money of other men, should look as if he deserved the trust, and be an ostensible pattern to society of probity, exactness, frugality and decorum.' This description fitted the two devout cousins precisely.

In 1852 the practice of styling the Bank by the name of the current senior Partner was officially abandoned in the new Partnership agreement of that year. 'Messrs Hoare' was designated as the name of the Bank, but the Partners nevertheless continued to sign as 'Charles Hoare and Co' long after Charles's death in 1851. Policy and practice continued to diverge until the style 'Messrs Hoare' was officially replaced by C. Hoare and Co when the Partnership was converted into a Company, under that name, in 1929.

Problems, however, arose over the ownership of the Bank's freehold, which also conferred ownership of all the account books and other papers relating to the business. In 1848 Charles owned the entirety of the freehold: one half came to him directly from his father, the first baronet, and the other half, a life interest, from his elder brother Hugh who had died in 1841. This concentration of influence had never disturbed the smooth working of the Partnership so long as the 'Adelphi' were in control but it became a matter for concern when the younger Partners, Peter Richard and Henry, realized that there was a possibility that their unreliable cousin, Henry Ainslie Hoare, Hugh's grandson, would become heir to the Bank's freehold after Charles's death.

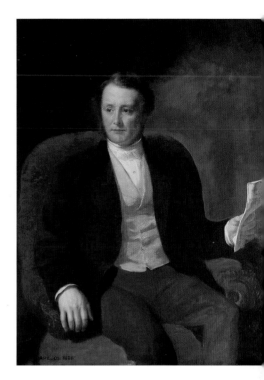

Henry of Staplehurst, c.1852. He ran the Bank with his cousin, Peter Richard. The two men scarcely met, though their wives were sisters.

Henry Ainslie had entered the Bank as a 'confidential clerk' in 1847 and was entrusted with a private key, which gave him access to all the securities and cash belonging to the Firm. No precise details of his misdemeanours were recorded but his conduct was considered so 'irregular' that, within a year, he was dismissed, with the agreement of the whole Partnership, and went to live in Paris. He was a gambling man and the entries in his wife's diaries, kept at Stourhead, indicate that horses were his passion.[6] An anecdote dating from Ainslie's time at the Bank and related much later by Harry of Ellisfield bears this out: 'One day when signing transfers at the Bank of England an old clerk there told me that he recollected how one day Sir Henry Hoare [Ainslie succeeded as the fifth baronet in 1857] had asked to have the transfers ready for his departure as early as possible as he wanted to go to the Derby. This was done and he had a horse waiting for him on London Bridge on which he rode to Epsom – saw the Derby – and rode back getting into 37 Fleet Street in time to lock up at 5 o clock.'

After Ainslie's dismissal his father, Henry Charles, and the two remaining 'Adelphi', Charles and Henry Merrik, changed their minds and were disposed to overlook his past conduct and allow him back into the Bank, clearly with a view to partnership. Peter Richard and Henry were insistent that his reapplication should be refused on the grounds that his conduct abroad had shown no evidence of a reform in his character and therefore the reasons for his dismissal still held good. The matter could not be resolved among themselves and Peter Richard and Henry applied to the Chancery court to obtain a restraining order to stop a majority of the Partnership from cancelling an act done by the whole Partnership.

In an opinion, given by counsel, a number of important issues were now addressed which, if resolved, would have had the effect of creating greater equality of status between the individual Partners. The first step towards achieving this would have been to give the Partnership as a whole full possession of the Bank freehold and thus ownership of the entire business. Moreover on the dissolution of the Partnership, the Bank would have been safeguarded from any act of sabo-

Peter Richard Hoare, c.1845. His devotion to the Bank was not inherited by either of his sons who revealed themselves as unfit for banking.

tage by an individual who under current arrangements would have been the owner or part owner of the property. The advice was not acted upon since the chief concern of the young Partners was to stop Ainslie becoming a proprietor of the business and the remedy to this problem was provided by the deaths of both Charles and Henry Charles, and Charles's decision not to change his will in favour of his great nephew, Ainslie, as Peter Richard and Henry had feared he might.

On Charles's death in November 1851 both halves of his ownership of the Bank premises (freehold and life interest) passed straight to his brother Merrik. Then when Merrik, having been more or less incapable for over a decade, died in 1856, Peter Richard, as Merrik's oldest surviving nephew, inherited a half share while the other half, which was a life interest only, went to Henry Arthur, Hugh's thirteenth child and only surviving son who was in his late forties. Only on his death would the life interest revert to Ainslie.

Henry now saw that the situation as it stood provided him with a great opportunity. Henry Arthur had worked at the Bank for a very brief period before being declared 'unfit for a banker' and dismissed, but he was entitled to a pension. In return for increasing this to a substantial level Henry asked that he should authorize the removal of the entail on his interest in the Bank premises which would allow Ainslie to offer it for sale. The prospect of a pension of over £3000 per annum was enough of an inducement for Henry Arthur, while Ainslie, who was struggling with huge gambling debts, readily agreed to sell his interest to Henry for £25,500. Consequently, although Henry had become a sharing Partner with Peter Richard in 1852, it was only as a result of this acquisition of half of the freehold that he achieved his ultimate goal of bringing back the senior line into the business on an equal footing with the descendants of the first baronet.

He and Lady Mary produced an impressive family of twelve children, not in itself an unusual achievement at the time, except that all lived to adulthood. As he was his father's heir, Henry junior's future was settled, but he had five brothers who were in need of occupation and, remarkably, one way or another the family was eventually able to provide for them in every case. One, Walter Marsham, went into the church becoming Rector of Colkirk in Norfolk, a living owned by his brother Henry. It was joined to the neighbouring village of Stibbard where Walter, true to the Hoare tradition, having seen the lack of provision made by the Post Office for his parishioners, set up a small savings bank, backed entirely by himself, for their benefit. Of the other brothers, Charles and Alfred followed Hugh Junior as Partners in the Bank, while William, known as 'Willie', and Hugh Edward, known as 'Tuppy', joined several of their cousins in Hoare and Co., another Hoare 'family business'.

In 1802 Harry of Mitcham had bought the principal share in the Red Lion Brewery, London's oldest established brewery, in East Smithfield, for his third son George Matthew. The Red Lion Brewery thereafter traded as Hoare and Co and was renowned particularly for the excellence of its porter, a strong dark beer, and for its stout which was popular in London's oyster saloons. With an overall output of 60,000-70,000 barrels a year, it ranked as the sixth largest brewery in the capital. It was situated within the precincts of St Katherine's Hospital next to the Tower of London, a major brewing area in the 16th century. Remarkably it survived the wholesale redevelopment of the area in 1827, when over a thousand homes as well as the Hospital were demolished to make way for the building of St Katherine's Dock.

In 1826 Hoare and Co suffered a severe trading loss due to the rapid rise in the price of malt and Harry was compelled to raise £87,000 to save the brewery. Despite such crises, characteristic of the industry, brewing was very profitable and provided a good return on capital; therefore the purchase of a partnership in one of the thriving businesses was regarded as a rewarding and secure situation for a young man of means. Banking and brewing had become natural partners in several of the prominent London banking families, such as the Quaker clans of

Gurneys, Barclays, Bevans and Hanburys, where younger sons or sons-in-law, with capital, were put into the trade and their family banks benefited in return. Brewers were in constant need of seasonal short-term loans to pay their suppliers of raw materials and extra credit in years when poor harvests or additional taxation forced up grain prices.

The loan to Hoare and Co in 1826 was financed entirely by the family. The Trust set up by Henry's sister-in-law, Elizabeth, Countess Minuzzi, for her four nephews, of whom George Matthew was one, provided about a quarter share, as did Sir Thomas Dyke Acland, who was a distant cousin and also Harry's son-in-law. The Bank and Harry himself provided the other two quarters. Harry assured Charles that he would not solicit aid if had not been assured by Mr White, the solicitor, that 'the concern is perfectly solvent and that no risk can be run by making the advance now required'. While, if help was not forthcoming, 'my son George and this Family must be disgraced forever.'

The brewery effectively absorbed Harry of Mitcham's private fortune; this debt was then bequeathed to Henry who, throughout the time when he was paid only an allowance and then a salary by the Bank, drew the very substantial sum of £8000 in annual interest payments from Hoare and Co. Henry's chief dealings were with Frederick Woodbridge, a non-family partner of the brewery, whom Henry found a good deal more amenable than his uncle and cousins. When George Matthew died in 1853 his son Henry James had already joined the partnership as did, in due course, another son, Charles Hugh and his grandsons Henry Seymour and Charles Twysden who was born in 1851. When Walter Robertson, Willie and Tuppy's nephew and son of the Reverend Walter Hoare of Colkirk, took up the invitation to become a partner in 1889 he was the representative of the fifth and last generation of family partners at Hoare and Co.

*Jane, Countess of Ellenborough, c.1825. Though she married four times – her last husband was a Bedouin sheik – the Bank persisted in keeping her account in the name of her first husband.*

Henry, with such a large capital stake tied up in the concern, was essentially in charge of the brewery and Woodbridge appreciated the fact that any arrangements he made with regard to the profit share and the investment of funds must be adhered to. Woodbridge was conscientious and earned Henry's respect, eventually becoming senior Partner. Woodbridge in turn recognized that 'Henry's superior information regarding the supply and value of money in the City', which had such a direct effect on the price of grain and all other commodities, was of immense value to him in deciding how to pay the best price for his raw materials. Harry of Mitcham had stipulated in a codicil to his will that for fifteen years after his death his Trustees and Executors must allow his loan of £27,000 to George Matthew to continue. Henry made it clear, however, that once this deadline had passed he could sell his interest in the brewery to a third party who would certainly expect to receive half profits. The introduction of a stranger into the business might well therefore impose terms on the present partnership which would be a good deal more obnoxious to them than any proposal put forward by Henry himself. The notion of realizing his capital was intended as no more than a threat to bring his uncle into line.

Henry had little regard for George Matthew as a businessman. Writing to Woodbridge on 10 June 1842 he referred to him as an 'idle man, unfit for business by nature and habits, in short a mere incumbrance'. George Matthew had the good fortune to marry an heiress, Angelina Greene, who inherited part of her father's considerable estates in Lancashire. He clearly resented Henry's influence and was intent on paying him off. Henry was well aware of the strategy and wrote frankly to his aunt Angelina: 'A perseverance in an attempt to pay me off against my will with a view to lessening my power and by degrees getting rid of me is productive only of mischievous consequences which follow. It will not succeed because I am more likely to invest than withdraw money and it tends to raise in my mind the idea of a retaliation and to make me think of paying him off and getting rid of him … not that I seriously think of it but I possess the power to do it.'

*Sir Henry Ainslie Hoare, 5th baronet, by 'Spy' c.1870. He was MP for Chelsea 1869-74, and a JP for Wiltshire, but was unable to keep his position in the Bank.*

No question of paying off could be considered in the catastrophic years of 1846 and 1847 and indeed Peter Richard (the elder) and George Matthew's younger brother, Charles James, Archdeacon of Surrey, were called upon to make advances to the brewery. Potato blight in Ireland sent prices of other crops soaring and Hoare and Co simultaneously plunged themselves further into debt by making huge advances of £39,000 to their publicans to enable them to purchase leases on their public houses in the interests of expanding their trade. On this occasion Henry took a very hard line with Woodbridge over the folly of overstretching resources and of 'acting boldly without consulting me … the whole fault that I loudly complain of is my being kept in the dark'. Woodbridge had to promise that thereafter he would lay before Henry at Fleet Street a quarterly account of all the brewery's loans and transactions. By 1851 the brewery was on its feet again but Henry, having been paid the principal sum owed under his grandfather's will, was content to leave the rest of his accumulated capital in it and continue to have the right to invest more if he so desired. After George Matthew's death Woodbridge, with Henry's agreement, became the senior Partner on half profits with a right to introduce one son as a Partner and another into the firm 'with prospects'. As a result

*Lydia, Lady Acland with her children, by Sir Thomas Lawrence c.1815. The daughter of Harry of Mitcham, she married her distant cousin, Sir Thomas Dyke Acland, in 1808 and became the mistress of Killerton in Devon.*

his name appeared above that of 'Henry James Hoare and Co' on the nameplate attached to the drays which, he explained, 'was the form adopted when Sir Thomas H Buxton became senior Partner in Truman Hanbury's House, it was then Thomas Howell Buxton [and underneath] Robert Hanbury and Co.'

Woodbridge's rise to the top after twenty-five years service to the brewery inevitably caused jealousy, as did Henry's reliance on him in preference to his own cousins. An attempt was made to cause a rift between him and Henry by a suggestion that Woodbridge harboured designs to install his own family as the principal influence in the brewery. Woodbridge, much offended by this, was provoked into writing an impassioned letter of self defence to Henry on 25 June 1853: 'I have resisted to the utmost the opinions of your late uncle and of Harry and Charles that your influence ought to be reduced or that any part of your capital should be attempted to be paid off so long as you desired it should remain at the Brewery.'

Misunderstandings, whether real or imagined, could not be tolerated for long under the pressure of business, and the partners of Hoare and Co quickly proceeded to draw up a new partnership agreement under Henry's direction. They covenanted to pay Henry £8000 to cover the premiums on the life policies he had taken out to protect his investment in the brewery and £6000 interest on the capital in the 'accumulated fund'. By 1855 the Partners were in trouble again and were obliged to default on their payments. This was due to an unexpected rise in the price of malt. An increase in the price of beer did nothing to offset the damage as bread and food prices had also risen and a slump in trade was unavoidable. By now it was becoming clear that the loaned capital was so inextricably tied up in the business that whatever arrangement the creditors desired it was unlikely that withdrawal was going to be an option.

Henry's family was now resident in the low flat country of the Weald of Kent where he had converted an old farmhouse in Little Iden into an extensive Italian-style villa which they named Staplehurst Place. The family had a long-standing connection with Staplehurst. Sir Richard Hoare had bought land there in 1710 to which his great-grandson Harry of Mitcham added Staplehurst Manor purchased from Horace Mann, the British envoy at Florence and a great correspondent with Horace Walpole. Despite this continuing interest in the area nobody in the family appeared to want to live there until Henry introduced himself to the neighbourhood as a young man in 1834. In that year he erected a memorial to his grandfather in the parish church which carried a lengthy description of the pattern of descent of the Staplehurst estate from Sir Richard Hoare to himself.

As Henry was keenly interested in the future of the new Conservative party, and the first of Sir Richard's descendants to have inherited the founder's commitment to politics he set out to canvass the parish of Cranbrook on behalf of the Conservative candidate Sir William Geary. Although a stranger to the locality, he at once assumed a proprietorial role and organized a breakfast at the King's Head in Staplehurst for all supporters prior to the poll. Henry delivered a rousing speech: 'Gentlemen I am as proud as any man of the Weald of Kent. For upwards of a century and a half my family has held property in this parish; and were I to be reduced to my last acre, that acre should be in the Weald of Kent. Warmly do I admire and highly do I prize that noble minded, that unconquerable, that incorruptible spirit which animates no part of the county more than ours – Invicti is our motto; Invicti we are.'

Subsequently, he presided at the first anniversary meeting of the City of London Conservative Association held at the Covent Garden Theatre in April 1836, shortly before his marriage, but he had no ambition to become an MP This was partly because, in the words of his obituarist in *John Bull* (21 April 1866), 'it was not the custom at the time of the banking house of which he was a prominent member to undertake the responsibilities of Parliamentary life', but more probably on account of his growing conviction, as a devout Christian, that the greatest benefit for every individual in the Country lay in the reform of church administration.

Although Henry believed absolutely in maintaining the indivisibility of Church and State, he concluded that this could only be done successfully if the Church followed the secular example set by Constitutional Reform and was given the freedom to develop and govern itself and in its self-government to become more inclusive. No longer should the Bishops rule their church unimpeded, but rather in cooperation with representatives from the clergy and the laity. The introduction of the lay element into church affairs was a radical departure from the past, but for Henry it was the vital element in his campaign for the revival of 'Convocation'. The medieval 'Convocations' or provincial assemblies of York and Canterbury were constituted of representatives from all levels of the clergy. Their powers were drastically reduced by Henry VIII and they were finally prorogued in 1717.

Henry's own religious beliefs were deep seated. His education had begun early at the hands of his mother, the saintly Louisa. She had a strong prejudice against public schools and Henry therefore did not follow his grandfather and father to Eton but was put in the charge of a private tutor, the Reverend Hodson. He shared lessons with Samuel Wilberforce, the third son of William Wilberforce who was his godfather. Samuel – nicknamed Soapy Sam – became Bishop of Oxford and used his considerable influence in furthering the objectives of the Convocation Society which Henry had founded in 1851 with the aim of bringing the issue before a wider public. Ten years later and after a stiff fight, with opposition from both the Archbishops of York and of Canterbury and most of the leading statesmen of the day, they had the satisfaction of seeing their ambition achieved with the restitution of Convocation in both York and Canterbury and the inclusion of a 'House of Laymen'.

Success came at a high price for Henry. He estimated he had spent over a thousand hours in the space of four years sitting in committee on this issue, and seven volumes of this correspondence was published. His obituarist described how it was done: 'he never allowed his business occupation to be an excuse for folding his hands after the work of the day was over. Often he would leave the Bank, take the train and drive miles into the country to attend some church meeting and return by 10 o' clock next morning to Fleet Street.' During the school holidays his sons, who were at Eton, would bring friends back to stay at Staplehurst. One recollected 'old Mr Hoare' suddenly, in the middle of dinner, asking his son Charles to 'state the fifth proposition of Euclid algebraically'. I doubt anyone in Eton had ever conceived such a possibility. It certainly appeared to our minds to be contrary to the laws of nature that anything in Euclid could be solved out of Algebra which was in another book.' Not surprisingly Charles failed the test and was sent to his room where he remained confined for the following day, 'consoled by half facetious sympathy through the keyhole' from his brothers, 'until Mr Hoare dashed off again in pursuit of Convocation when the prisoner was released'.

In London Henry and Lady Mary lived near St Martin's in the Fields where, as church warden, he left his mark in the form of a new school, a mission chapel and a revolutionary 'free' Sunday afternoon service to encourage those without means to pay pew rents to come to church, an experiment which produced very satisfactory results. These concerns, along with 'Convocation', encroached on all aspects of his life throughout the 1850s, and the burden of management at the Bank fell on Peter Richard. In matters of doctrine Peter Richard was firmly within the High Anglo-Catholic tradition of the Church of England, and it was his support for maintaining this tradition within the Anglican church as opposed to Henry's 'Low Church' leanings which gave rise to the family myth that his disagreement with Henry on matters of doctrine was the principal cause of the breakdown in communication between the two Partners. The real issue between them, as far as the business was concerned, was more personal and more intractable.

Peter Richard, who had been an utterly devoted husband, was overwhelmed by grief when his wife, Lady Sophia, died. Never having taken 'that relaxation from business which had been accorded as a matter of course to my predecessors' in his forty-three years as a banker, he now

*Beer bottle from Hoare and Co Brewery. Found in the undergrowth in Luscombe woods, presumably abandoned by a beater.*

longed to be relieved of some of his duties at Fleet Street. He was infuriated by Henry's jockeying for position on behalf of his son, Henry junior, and his cousin Henry Gerard (both of whom were made salaried Partners in 1865), and the high handed manner in which he took decisions without proper consultation. No doubt partly as a result of his dejection after his wife's death Peter Richard gave vent to a stream of complaints directed at Henry: '... it has been the custom for the Senior Partner not to attend. Your grandfather never did since I entered the House. He lived at Mitcham and came occasionally to the Banker's House adjoining the Bank. It would appear also ... as if you had supreme power here – whereas you may recollect that when we made fresh Articles of Partnership [1852] you thanked me for my liberality and kindness. I have sometimes been blamed by the family (not my immediate) for having given you the opportunity of buying the High Hoare's half of the freehold instead of buying for myself and my children – indeed you talk in a very grandiloquent style and I regret without any feeling for me ... if you were only here for half the year there would be no cause of complaint by anyone. Indeed it would appear but reasonable that you should take more than half – but the fact is you do not like to be tied down – and Convocation is your hobby. Notwithstanding all this I shall be heartily glad to give it up altogether and leave it as I have always said to Henry Hoare and Co.'

Whatever he may have wished, it was not Peter Richard who was to 'give it up altogether' and leave it to Henry Hoare, but exactly the other way round. Henry maintained a strong regard for his old college, St John's, and, on a trip to Cambridge, on 30 March 1865, Henry unwisely put his head out of the window as the train approached a tunnel and, failing to calculate the speed of the train, he was knocked out. He was taken back to Staplehurst Place and within a year he was dead. As a result, Peter Richard had to serve on alone as Senior Partner with the assistance initially of Henry junior and his cousin, Henry Gerard.

Watercolour of Turton in Lancashire, by Peter Richard senior, 1844. His wife, Arabella Greene, inherited two estates near Manchester from her father.

# CHAPTER SIX

# THE BLACK SHEEP: HENRY JUNIOR AND CHARLIE ARTHUR 1866–1885

Two years before Henry of Staplehurst fatally injured himself en route to Cambridge, Henry John Tilden joined the staff of the Bank as the junior clerk after a brief spell with the National Bank of Ireland in the City of London. Sixty years later he wrote down his recollections of his working life at the Bank, which were enlivened by descriptions of eccentric customers and scoundrels as well as frank assessments of the strengths and weaknesses of his fellow clerks and the Partners. His memoirs are especially valuable, as they cover the last years of the devout Henry and Peter Richard and the scandalous careers of their less conventional sons. Tilden's personal contact with 'old Mr Henry Hoare' was minimal but he remembered the impact of his physical presence as he was a tall man 'with a massive frame, majestic in his manners which made everyone keep their distance'. He spoke to everyone including his wife in the third person, and no clerk could ever address him without being spoken to first. When he was in the Bank there would be a constant traffic of clergymen in and out of the Partners' Room, but his popularity in church circles did not extend outside them. His death was not much mourned; his son Charles, who had been imprisoned in his bedroom for failing the 'Euclid test' as a youth, was heard to confide to one of the Brokers, 'I don't mind saying I hated my father.'

Henry Grabham, who became chief clerk in 1886, had his own tale to tell regarding Henry's tyrannical behaviour. It was 29 September, Michaelmas 1864, 'the great day of the year' when all the ledgers were balanced and the Partners dined together upstairs and arranged the division of the profits. This was one of the few occasions when the two cousins, Henry and Peter Richard, had to meet

*facing page*

*Lady Mary Hoare with her twelve children at Staplehurst, shortly after the death of her husband, Henry, in 1866.*

and discuss business directly with one another. Downstairs the Bank had closed for business at 5pm, dinner was finished, the oil lamps and candles had been lit and the clerks were applying themselves to taking out the balances from all the ledgers. Champagne flowed and the atmosphere was extremely convivial. At 10pm Henry came downstairs, not in an amiable frame of mind, and walked round each desk until he came to a closed ledger where Grabham had been working. Grabham had only been married a few months and he wanted to be sure he caught the last train home to East Molesey; so he had completed his work quickly and left the Bank. He didn't reckon on Henry who was already suspicious of this young man, whose speed was not always matched by accuracy, and was quick to find fault with him on any pretext. Expressing outrage that a clerk should leave on balance night without permission, whether or not he had finished his work, Henry ordered Billy Key, the senior porter, who was well over seventy, to pursue Grabham and bring him back to the Bank. At 1 am Key returned with Grabham, having got him out of bed, to find Henry sitting waiting in the Partners' Room. Without glancing at the reprobate clerk he observed, 'Oh he has come back has he? He won't go away on balance night again without permission. He may go now.' Dismissed without a hearing, Grabham was obliged to take himself off to Anderton's hotel in Fleet Street for what remained of the night.

In 1864 there were twenty-one clerks and two stockbrokers in the service of 'Messrs Hoare'. The arrangements for paying their salaries and other emoluments dated from the time of Harry of Mitcham, around 1800, when there had been only twelve clerks employed, and reform of the system was well overdue. Pensions were non-existent and it was customary therefore for clerks to remain in office for as long as they could, often dying in service. Henry junior, in addressing the problem of salary scales, calculated that the average length of service for a clerk was forty-six years (the senior clerk in 1863 was Thomas Lee who had joined the Bank in 1812 and occupied the post of chief cashier when he died in 1866 aged well over eighty). Taking into account those few who retired early or left to take up other posts,

*Letter of thanks for a pay rise from five porters to the Partners, dated 5 January 1878.*

vacancies occurred only once every two years. This meant that progress up the ladder from a junior to a senior level took a very long time: for example at the age of forty, after eighteen or twenty years' service, a clerk could only expect to be tenth from the bottom in terms of seniority.

As things were arranged this slow advancement had a particularly adverse effect on a group referred to as the 'middle men'. When there were only twelve clerks the senior six received, in addition to their salary of £120-£160, a division of the brokerage (commission on the purchase and sale of stocks and shares), and of the Christmas Fund, a staff account which was entirely funded by the customers. The six juniors received a salary of £100 and a fixed sum from the Christmas Fund which was paid to them before a division of the balance was made among the seniors. The brokerage and Christmas Fund increased over time and in consequence the senior men were very comfortably off and the juniors could reliably expect to receive twice their annual salary. As time went on more staff were taken on and there were those 'in the middle', neither seniors nor juniors, who didn't benefit from either of these additional sources of income.[1]

Henry junior, to his credit, advocated the introduction of a fairer principle and suggested that the clerks' remuneration should reflect their position in the Bank and that with every promotion there should be a corresponding increase in salary. Under his scheme the top ten men received a uniform salary of £160 and below that level salaries were graded by degrees. The four 'under the top six' were also given a small proportion of the brokerage (one eighth) between them and an increased share of the Christmas Fund which was distributed to all the clerks on a graduated scale from the bottom to the top. The seniors were compensated for their loss of some of the brokerage by an increased share of the Christmas Fund, which resulted from the abolition of the fixed contribution to the six juniors. In order to avert anxiety over the possible fluctuation in the two funds causing a fluctuation in income Henry also proposed that these increases should be guaranteed. In addition £60 was added to everyone's salary in cash compensation when the daily lunch and dinner was discontinued in 1867.

Lunch and dinner had been an important feature in the structure of the working day of the Bank. There was no 'going out'. Lunch was for half an hour only and dinner, described by Tilden as being 'of a very substantial character with four bottles of wine, two of port and two of sherry', was served promptly at 5 pm when the day's work was done except for checking the balances and copying letters by hand and delivering them to the post. The three clerks engaged on these tasks would be allowed to eat properly in the middle of the day. Once the balance was right the news would be brought to the senior clerk, who presided at the dinner table, and the porter, who brought the announcement, would be rewarded with a glass of wine. Board and lodging were provided in the Bank for the six juniors. With the demolition of the old Bank buildings in 1829, the juniors' sleeping

Henry junior, painted in
Paris after his marriage
to Beatrice Paley in
1865.

accommodation which had consisted of no more than a couple of truckle beds kept under the counter in the shop was replaced by six bedrooms in the attic where they slept comfortably enough but with no means of escape should there be a fire. A watchman kept vigil at night from his post in the back yard while the night porter slept on a structure in the middle of the counting house, known as 'the bed', which served as a desk during the day where all the registered letters were made up and sealed.

Customers calling at Fleet Street would be waited on by a junior clerk, who would take them through to the counting house or inner office (the outer office being the Shop) which contained four round tables, each positioned in front of a fire. Here they would sit to examine their accounts in the weighty morocco-bound ledgers. The system of inspection, whereby the customer would agree or 'allow' his account in person, led to the practice of entering the accounts in the ledgers non alphabetically. This was to ensure the privacy of individual members of a family who would be protected from the prying eyes or inadvertent gaze of their relations. In fact it was an inconvenient and time-consuming arrangement and necessitated maintaining an index to all the accounts. Customers would send the junior through to the Shop if they needed to withdraw money. Hoare's did not act as agents for any of the country banks, so that those customers in the country who wanted cash would have it dispatched to them by registered post.

Hoare's cheque books, mid 19th century. The engraved emblem of the Golden Bottle was added to the cheques in 1800.

Leading from the counting house was a small room facing the back courtyard where, behind a green baize curtain separating the two rooms, the daily ritual of 'calling over' was conducted by a Partner with the assistance of two juniors. Seated on a high stool the Partner would 'call out' the entries from the cash book while the clerks would check each one against the fair copy in the ledgers which were laid out on tables beneath him. Any discrepancy would be marked in the cash book by the Partner with a large red cross. As a new recruit Tilden was required to learn the ropes by attending at 'calling over' with 'old Mr Henry Hoare'. To his dismay he discovered this meant a very early start. He was woken by the night watchman at 6.30 and dressed hastily by candlelight. Downstairs the footman had laid out coffee and bread and butter for Tilden and his colleague. When Henry appeared he gave them permission to eat and drink and then business began punctually at 7 am. After Henry's accident, when it was clear he was never going to return to the Bank, many of the more onerous practices of his regime were abandoned and 'calling over' was moved back to the more civilized

hour of ten o' clock and was completed in time for lunch.

In January 1865, just before his accident, Henry had drafted a memorandum introducing two new names to the Partnership, his son Henry junior and his cousin Henry Gerard. Both were appointed as Partners on a salary of £2000 a year, an arrangement which he saw as uncontroversial as it would not undermine the existing agreement with Peter Richard over the division of the profits. The new Partners were expected to devote their full attention to the business but were given no access to the 'Private safe or closet or the Private Books of the Firm' nor were they permitted to have 'any voice as to loans or investments or granting of credit' without the permission of Peter Richard and Henry. The background to this memorandum was Peter Richard's self-styled 'affliction', his lapse into depression after his wife Sophia's death, and his consequent desire to leave Fleet Street, which had left Henry in sole charge of the Firm and feeling considerably overburdened as a result.[2]

Peter Richard cut rather a sad figure at the Bank. He worked in total seclusion in the half dark in a little back room at Fleet Street attended by David Moss, his factotum and only link to the rest of the establishment. At home he was looked after by his unmarried daughter Isabella who accompanied him on his frequent moves between Luscombe and his house in Beckenham, Kelsey Park. From there he travelled daily to London in a carriage with the blinds drawn; his arrival and departure from the Bank was announced ahead by Moss in order that the clerks could duck under the counter to avoid catching a glimpse of this strange nervous figure, with his long silver hair straggling over his shoulders, as he passed through the Shop. He felt aggrieved by what he saw as Henry's unfeeling manner towards his affliction.

Peter Richard had a further cause for concern: neither of his sons were appropriate contenders for partnership. The elder son, Peter Merrik, was born in 1843 and was thus eligible to start work in the Bank at roughly the same time as Henry junior entered from Cambridge. Merrik, as he was called by his relations, was a volatile young man with a propensity to spend. He suffered rather mysteriously from 'nerves' and by his own admission he never contemplated being able to undertake the workload assumed by his father. In February 1866 he wrote to his father stating categorically that he could not work at the Bank: 'You must know that my health or I should rather say my nerves would not stand work at Fleet Street or in fact my living in London at all. Of course I well know what a great difference it would make to me being in the Bank both now and probably in the future in point of wealth and therefore it is not likely that I should give up such a chance willingly … such being the case might I not rather be pitied than blamed.' Six months later he was writing again on the same subject but this time he proposed that he should be allowed to enter the Bank in the capacity of what he termed 'a working partner' his nerves being in 'dramatically better trim than they were'. He showed some sympathy for his father who must be 'extremely disappointed when you think that neither of your own sons would follow the profession which you have toiled in so long'. (Charlie Arthur, his younger brother by four years, was really only interested in horses and made a modest reputation for himself by championing the revival of coaching.)

Merrik's change of mind did not induce a change of heart on the part of his parent. Peter Richard in turning down his son was quite frank with him. 'I quite think that you are unsuited to the work … I trust that Charlie may in time become serviceable but he is very wild at present. The great thing for Fleet Street is efficient workers, those who will give up their time and talents to it which you well know has been the case with me.' This letter reached Merrik on his 23rd birthday and the compensation offered by the Bank of an annual allowance of £3000 did not do much to mollify him. He at once demanded to be reassured that he still could claim the right to nominate any son or sons he might have.

Relations between father and son had been strained for some time. Merrik's unpaid bills were mounting up and he and his wife Edith had fallen out with his sister Charlotte Strickland and her husband Algernon. His father's apparent favouritism towards the Stricklands lay at the heart of the problem. While Merrik had been refused entry at Fleet Street, Algernon Strickland had been asked to give up his life as a farmer in Devon for a career at the Bank. Merrik told his father plainly, 'I do not relish the idea (and what elder son would) of being supplanted by my brother-in-law.' In

*Kelsey Manor in Beckenham, Kent, bought by Peter Richard in 1835. It was within commuting distance of the Bank; so he favoured Kelsey over Luscombe after the death of his wife in 1863. Gilbert Scott added the chapel in 1869.*

a letter dated 25 October 1866 he elaborated on why he felt so wronged by the thought of Algernon being made a sharing Partner. It was not on account of any ill feeling towards his brother-in-law but, 'I do not like the idea of his taking away my birthright ... you always tried to impress upon me that the Bank was my birthright and by my efforts to enter the sacred portals of No 37 as a working partner I have shown most unmistakably that I also consider it as such. I think that my brother-in-law's good qualities (actually they are many) must form a mono-mania with you and that you are thus blinkered to the just calls of others. If you had no sons I could understand your placing your son-in-law in the Bank though in the annals of Fleet Street you would not find a precedent for such a course.' Peter Merrik was quite right in this. Nobody from outside the family, even linked by marriage, had been admitted to the Partnership since Christopher Arnold's pro-motion following the unexpected death of Good Henry in 1724.

Merrik was convinced there was a conspiracy to keep him out between Henry junior, 'who is enough to bewitch you with his many plans and cool assumptions', and Algernon, who was quite candid in his views that both Peter Richard's sons were wasting their time and his money. He urged his father not to forget 'Charley' in his arrangements for Fleet Street as it was evident that, 'it is to the interest of the same people to prejudice you against him as against me – if you would trust your own sons a little more I think it would be for your own com-fort as well as for theirs'.

Although Charlie Arthur did become a Partner in 1874, his father was right that neither of his sons were fit to be bankers. Peter Merrik took an interest in pol-itics, becoming a Conservative MP for Southampton from 1868 to 1874, but throughout his life remained reliant on his father to rescue him from his crippling debts. He claimed, in a letter to his father in 1866 that though his unpaid bills came to a very large amount they were 'composed of nothing more criminal than simple pieces of extravagance'. After being bailed out once for a sum of around £60,000, by the Spring of 1874 he had run up further bills for roughly the same amount. On this occasion it was agreed that he should be allowed to go bankrupt, the argument being that his creditors were well aware of his embarrassed circum-stances and were prepared to extend him almost limitless credit on the expectation that they would be paid off by his family. Some of the creditors' claims were deemed to be spurious but in order to relieve his son from his dishonourable position, Peter Richard agreed to meet a proportion of the creditors' demands by a payment of £10,000, which annulled the bankruptcy order in favour of liqui-dation, and thereafter Merrik's affairs were placed into the hands of trustees. The money was advanced to Merrik in anticipation of what would have come to him under his father's will, but in the short term Peter Richard had to take out a mort-gage on the Turton estates in Lancashire which he had inherited from his mother.

It was not a state of affairs that afforded Peter Richard much satisfaction but he did not hide the reality of the situation from himself or others. In a sardonic little note he wrote to Merrik from Kelsey in 1868 he tried to make light of the way things had turned out: 'My eldest son aspires to a seat in the Senate. My younger one to a seat behind four chestnut horses. The latter had rather guide a light barouche with four in hand than rule the land. He would I know humbly implore his elder brother to bring in a Bill in Parliament by which all taxes on stage coaches and horses employed in drawing them may for ever be abolished. I have both their printed notices [presumably an Election notice and a coaching timetable] in this Hall for the benefit of all visitors.'

Meanwhile Algernon had settled in comfortably to his new profession as banker. The immediate prospect of £5000 a year with an additional generous allowance from his father-in-law was, as he described, 'ample recompense to us for giving up country life'. He was well aware that his introduction into the business not only created tension with his brother-in-law but also aroused a certain amount of resentment from Henry junior. Following Henry of Staplehurst's death in April 1866 Peter Richard sent instructions to Fleet Street that there was to be 'no alteration in the mode of conducting the business without the sanction of PRH, no new Clerk or porter or servant of any description was to be engaged without the like sanction and no large advances to be made without his concurrence'. Algernon and the chief clerk, a Scotsman named Masson whom Tilden heartily disliked on account of his brutal treatment of the juniors, had to refer matters constantly to Peter Richard in his fastness at Luscombe or at Kelsey Park from where he could make occasional sallies to Fleet Street. He was still very much in control, which he made clear to young Henry: 'I imagine that it was understood between myself and your Father that on the death of either of us the business was to go to the survivor, not as might be said a good bargain for me as I was some years his senior both in point of age and more so in position in the Bank.' However, Algernon was concerned that Peter Richard should be fair to Henry and not run the risk of him leaving the Bank altogether in favour of one of his brothers, if he was not offered enough.

Some thought that the departure of Henry junior wouldn't be a bad thing. Although he was clever and knew the work of the Bank well, his manner towards the customers was not 'of the pleasantest'. By contrast Henry Gerard's qualities

*Algernon Strickland, c.1895. Dogged by ill health, but a guardian of the Bank's interests, he married Peter Richard's daughter Charlotte in 1863 and was the first outsider to be made a Partner since Christopher Arnold in 1725.*

endeared him to customers and staff alike. He was the son of Archdeacon Charles James Hoare and a grandson of Harry of Mitcham. He joined the Bank as a young man with no particular expectations and it was likely that he was only promoted to be a salaried Partner due to Henry's abrupt departure after his accident. He was often to be found taking snuff, especially before embarking on some arduous task such as 'calling over' or before sitting down to a batch of signatures. The porters were instructed to keep the horn snuff boxes, which lay on the counter in the Shop, well supplied for those customers who liked to call in for a pinch of snuff and a chat. When lunch and dinner ceased to be provided in house it was due to Henry Gerard that the convivial balance night dinners were continued for the clerks. He presided on these occasions with the help of a friend of his, a man of giant proportions called Tupwood Smith whom he had met out hunting. Tupwood Smith had nothing whatever to do with the Bank but kept the company amused on balance night by renditions of hunting songs delivered in his beautiful tenor voice.

Henry Gerard was joined by Henry junior's younger brother, Charles, as a fellow salaried Partner in 1867. The pair were as different from each other as chalk and cheese, Charles being described by Tilden as a 'chip off the old block' who 'hated the least opposition of any kind either from his partners or his clerks'. They were assisted by Hamilton Noel Hoare, a nephew of Henry of Staplehurst, who sacrificed his chances of ever becoming a Partner by what was described as his 'absurd self-conceit and indolence'. He was well aware of his reputation which he agreed was deserved to some extent since, 'casting books and the mass of examining that I had to do did not appear to me to be particularly interesting', and he admitted he didn't much like work. But he refuted any inference that he was neglectful, claiming that he always did the work which was allotted to him including, since he was a bachelor, more than his fair share of the sleeping duty although in this he was less than satisfactory, owing to his dangerous habits of smoking and reading by candlelight in bed.

After forty years working as an Agent, and having had no offers of preferment along the way, he abandoned any hope that he might be made a Partner but he nevertheless felt able to ask the Partners in 1897 for an increase in his allowance on the basis that he needed more money to fund his way of life as a man of property. He had a house in the country which needed alterations and several houses in Sloane Street which he had bought with a loan from the Bank, improved, and hoped to sell. His application was unsuccessful but his reasons for asking were typical of his generation within the family.

The wise words of Henry the Magnificent and Harry of Mitcham, which warned of the dangers of inattention to business and lack of caution in its conduct, had long been forgotten and the Bank was now regarded greedily by a clutch of their more privileged descendants as a self-perpetuating fund for their ease and enjoyment. Hamilton, not being a Partner, couldn't do much harm but some of those who came to power over him, namely Henry junior and Charlie Arthur and, to a certain extent, his cousin Charles, could and did.

However, the years immediately following the death of Henry of Staplehurst in 1866 went on quietly enough at Fleet Street. The profit division had been worked out to the satisfaction of all those concerned. Peter Richard took one half while the other was divided, giving one-third to Algernon and two-thirds to Henry. This arrangement gave due recognition to Henry as his father's heir, ensuring he had twice the stake and twice the profit share as that held by Algernon, the 'outsider', who was delighted to be admitted as a sharing Partner on any basis and was relieved that the main cause of friction between them had been removed. On 29 September 1867 the profits agreed by the Partnership were divided as follows; £19,200, £12,800 and £6400 plus a small contribution to the Sinking Fund.

Algernon reported regularly to Peter Richard supplying him with the necessary figures and reassuring him that all was running smoothly. Henry wrote to him on one occasion asking how they should deal with the problem of drunk clerks and Peter Richard was quite content to leave the decision to the judgement of the young Partnership. Although he quite agreed that it was undesirable that 'Messrs Hoare's clerks should have a reputation of being drunkards' and suggested various remedies such as requiring one junior, a Mr Parker, who was a particular offender, to be under a curfew every evening and not be 'allowed out with the Bills' during the day, it was an issue which didn't trouble him greatly. As he explained to Henry, 'Intoxication was much less thought of as a vice in my generation than it is now.' Generally speaking the absence of the senior Partner didn't appear to have any detrimental effect on the business although it inevitably caused inconvenience. An instance of this was Peter Richard's absolute insistence that all securities for advances should be transferred to his name alone and not to 'The House'. When the loan came to be paid off and the securities retransferred, the documents had to be sent down to Luscombe for his signature.

Every important decision was referred to him, such as an exceptionally large advance requested by the 12th Duke of Hamilton in 1867. A mortgage on the security of his Suffolk estates was proposed for the sum of £120,000 at 5 per cent, which Masson, as chief clerk, admitted was 'a large sum to be hooked up in one person', but the security, which had been approved by the Bank's solicitors, was considered ample since it yielded an annual income of £10,000. Henry indicated that he would like to make the advance on his own account, subject to Peter Richard's approval, and in forwarding this request Masson implied it would be a welcome offer as the Duke was already overdrawn £14,000 and 'his account is anything but remunerative to us'. However, the Bank owed the Duke's family more than ordinary consideration. It was the 12th Duke's father, also a customer of the Bank, who had alerted the partners to Henry Ainslie's gambling activities during his time in Paris, and had made it plain that had Ainslie been a Partner he would have closed his account at once.

Outside the walls of 37 Fleet Street the financial world was thrown into disarray by the collapse of the great discount house Overend, Gurney and Co., which for forty years had reigned supreme as 'the bankers' bank', dedicated entirely to trading bills of exchange. Following the legislation of the 1850s, which extended limited liability to banks, Overend Gurney, followed the example of hundreds of other companies and was floated on the Stock Exchange. Poor management led to unsound financing arrangements and the company soon ran into trouble. On Thursday 10 May 1866 it was forced to suspend payment with liabilities of £11 million.

This crisis prompted an immediate run on the Bank of England. After a day's hesitation the government responded by suspending the 1844 Bank Charter Act, by which note issue was tied to the gold reserve, and the Bank of England was able to issue a further £10 million and stem the panic of 'Black Friday'. For a short time money remained very scarce and the bank rate soared to 10 per cent, credit was virtually unobtainable and depositors rushed to withdraw their savings in cash. Within three months 200 companies, including some banks, had collapsed and the public were encouraged by a critical press to associate all manner of corrupt corporate behaviour with joint stock enterprises and to condemn the poor judgement of the unfortunate investors.

Private banking houses such as Hoare's were largely protected from the fallout of these calamitous events, and as far as public confidence was concerned they were positive beneficiaries. Mr Masson was able to write reassuringly to Peter Richard: 'The event has long been expected and altho' one cannot help regretting the ruin it will entail on many people, yet it will eventually bring things into a more healthy state. I think some of our clients are now aware of the danger they run in depositing their money simply upon the receipt of the Secretary or a Director of a Joint Stock Bank which is worth nothing and certainly no security … I think what has taken place will add strength to our, "Good Old House".' Yet, within a few years of the chief clerk signing off his letter on this note of confidence, Hoare's was plunged into a crisis which was entirely generated by the speculative behaviour of one of its own Partners.

Henry junior had the potential to be an excellent businessman. He was clever and bold and possessed the ability to think clearly and strategically. He was also an agnostic which caused distress to his family and in particular to his clergyman brother, Walter, who was fond of him and confessed that 'no one on God's earth would be more thankful [than me] if you could find reasonable grounds for belief'. At Cambridge Henry had made friends with the artist and writer, Samuel Butler, who was a few years his senior but, like Henry, had turned his back on his own ecclesiastical upbringing and indeed all the accepted conventions of Victorian society which he later satirized in his writing. Henry helped finance the publication of Butler's first novel *Erewhon*, which was published anonymously to great acclaim in 1870.

This absence of religious belief was a shocking thing in Henry's case, given his background and the extent to which religious conformity was expected of all those who worked at the Bank. George Whitely, who should have succeeded Thomas Lee as chief clerk, when he died in 1866, was passed over in favour of Francis Masson who was fourteen years his junior. It was discovered that Whitely was a Dissenter, something he did not disclose when he joined the Bank in 1825, knowing full well that had he done so he would never have been appointed. So too, although Peter Richard was a supporter of the Anglo-Catholic tradition within the Church of England, the Bank would not lend its name to any organization connected with Roman Catholicism although it was happy to accommodate individuals. One of their more distinguished Roman Catholic customers was Cardinal Edward Henry Howard who held a senior post in the Vatican. In March 1860 Viscount Feilding (later the 8th Earl of Denbigh), whose family had a longstanding connection with the Bank, had written to Messrs Hoare requesting that an account should be opened in the joint names of himself and Lord Campden for funds it was intended to raise for the Pope, whose revenues had been depleted in those European countries which had been in the grip of revolution in 1848. When he was refused, his answer was sharp and to the point: 'I had hoped you would have been above such narrow and sectarian feelings ... I regret however more than I can say to see that you make Business subservient to Bigotry and I feel it the more that Lord Campden and I ... have hereditary connexion with your House.'

Henry's agnoticism was regarded as a serious moral failing within the family to the extent that discussions took place suggesting that he should be disinherited on account of it. The story went that this opinion was only overrridden by the intervention of Henry's first cousin Agneta Bevan[3] who proposed an alternative view of his situation: 'We all know that Henry is damned in hell fire through all eternity and therefore it would probably be kinder to allow him to enjoy some of this world's goods.' Beatrice, Henry's widow, in reflecting on her husband's misfortunes in her old age, ascribed the beginning of them to his association with Samuel Butler. In 1859 Butler had left England for New Zealand and over a period of two years he had bought land and established a successful sheep station near Christchurch in the Canterbury district of South Island. In 1864 he returned home having doubled the capital he had invested in the enterprise. This was shortly before Henry went into the Bank. Once he was established there he took his new bride, Beatrice, out to New Zealand and following his friend's example he bought a house and some land near Christchurch called Meadowbank. He followed this up in 1873 with the purchase of a second, much larger estate of 20,000 acres called 'Raincliff' which had been established as a sheep run for several years. Henry had ambitious schemes for ploughing up thousands of acres to create fine English pasture which he assumed would then provide intensive grazing for years to come without requiring further attention. Henry kept these investments secret and for that reason did not borrow from the Bank, but whereas Butler stayed out in New Zealand to manage his affairs until he could turn in a profit, Henry had to leave the management in the hands of local agents, who ran it for their own benefit and transmitted a good deal of misinformation to England. The result was that Henry lost out considerably.[4]

Family control of the Red Lion Brewery continued, although it was not much of a paying concern. Henry, having inherited his father's stake in the business, was anxious to see it improve. Beatrice recalled her husband spending long evenings in East Smithfield working on the accounts after the sudden death of Charles Hugh in 1869. Charles Hugh's son, Charles Twysden, was only eighteen at the time but he was destined for the Brewery and Henry was working behind the scenes to get support for his brother William to join him. Although he managed this manoeuvre with success his interference over managing the business caused a breach with the young Charles Twysden. Henry wanted to expand the Brewery which would involve greater borrowings and interest payments. Charles Twysden raised objections and Henry, instead of getting what he wanted, which was raised interest of 6 per cent on his loan to the Brewery, found himself being paid off to the tune of £115,000.

According to Henry, as things turned out, the timing couldn't have been worse. He had begun investing speculatively, with his brother Charles, at the start of 1874, taking much of his advice from his clerk, George Whitley, 'whom we regarded as a god as he ought to have been considering his years and experience',

The original homestead at Raincliff, the 20,000 acre sheep station in South Island, New Zealand bought by Henry junior in 1873.

Henry and Beatrice
Hoare, c.1865-70.
After Henry was declared
bankrupt in 1891,
Beatrice is reputed to
have declared that
though she trusted her
husband with her body
she would never again
trust him with her
money.

and buying shares in a series of companies none of which made him any money. His major investment, after the pay off, was in Erie Railway Stocks but, regrettably, he allowed himself to become involved with a fellow-speculator called McEwen to whom he gave complete control. Henry virtually put his money at McEwen's disposal, until he found he had lent McEwen £100,000. In addition he had suffered a considerable loss on his original investment in Eries, as had his friend Samuel Butler.

Butler was shaken by Henry's behaviour. By his own admission he had been keen to invest the money he had brought home from New Zealand and Henry had no difficulty in persuading him to invest in a series of companies he had started. Butler described them as follows: a patent steam-engine company, a patent gas meter company, a company for pressing jute in India and one for treating hemlock bark in Canada, 'which was to pay at least sixty per cent and revolutionize the leather trade'. This enterprise also attracted a barrister, named Pauli, and he and Butler, both 'infatuated' with the project, were made Directors of the Canada Tanning Extract Co. Ltd.

'Pauli and I ought to have suspected something was wrong, but we had such confidence in him,' Butler wrote later, '... so little did we suspect, that on his asking us to hold shares for him with any amount of liability on them – many thousands of pounds – we had no hesitation in taking the liability on ourselves. His income was between £40,000 and £50,000 a year and in his position, the bare idea that he was gambling all this away never crossed our minds ... fancy wanting to treble £40,000 a year!'[5] Much later, in 1901, Butler reflected on his involvement with Henry's speculations and it is clear that he didn't know to what extent Henry had concealed his affairs from his Partners: 'I can plead no excuse for any of us but the confidence that Hoare's bank would not countenance any such schemes without having the best advice concerning them. We did not know that Hoare had been plunging [speculating heavily] for some time and we did not know that old family bankers ought to be and generally are the very last people in the world who should be able to advise on commercial undertakings. They and we were fools together.'

Algernon disapproved of what he knew of Henry's speculative adventures and warned him that he 'must set an example to the younger ones', in a reference to Charles and Charlie Arthur who started work at the Bank in 1873. But nobody in the Bank was aware of Henry's dealings with McEwen. It turned out that Henry was in debt to the Bank for £196,546. Since Henry's withdrawals had been unauthorized, this came as a total surprise to everyone at the Bank except Mr Rawlinson, one of the clerks. By chance he had earlier discov-

*Samuel Butler, c.1896. An old Cambridge friend of Henry junior and fellow agnostic, Butler lost heavily through Henry's speculations.*

ered that Henry was trying to raise money from another bank which made him suspect something was wrong. Mr Rawlinson's son, who followed his father into the Bank in 1888, judged the events of 1874 to be 'the most dramatic hour in the history of the Bank' and described the day of Henry's fall: 'Mr Henry Hoare had been speculating heavily and one day a cheque for £80,000 or so came in and was duly posted with some alarm to Red Ink, the partners' private ledger. Not long after a further cheque for the same amount came in and the other partners fairly got the wind up.'

Henry's debt was a sum he could not even begin to recoup so a deal had to be reached to cope with the emergency. Henry's half share of the freehold was valued at £50,000 and sold to the Partnership, £100,000 of the overdraft was converted into a loan secured by life policies, and the Sinking Fund was virtually exhausted in wiping off the balance of £46,546. Henry was to receive an allowance of £2000 but he had to leave the Bank at once. The partnership had to be dissolved and Peter Richard was hastily fetched from Kelsey to form a new one. An announcement duly appeared in the *London Gazette* which fortunately didn't provoke any unwelcome enquiries. Henry was angry about the terms, blaming Algernon; Walter tried to smooth over the disagreement by pointing out to his brother that nothing was to be gained by getting riled and that although the Partners 'may for certain reasons be glad to be rid of you,' they were not 'so glad that they rejoice in your having put yourself in their power'.

For Henry there was everything to regret and the years following his departure rolled by 'wearily and drearily'. Writing to Charles, who had also invested in Eries, in 1877, Henry attempted to minimize the blame that could be attached to him personally: 'I had not the slightest doubt but that if I had told you McEwen would sell a bear for you and recover the money you had lost by your purchase you would have accepted it and been thankful but I would not tell you because I did not wish to involve you in any risk in case anything went wrong and I thought if the result turned out as I expected, and I was positively assured by McEwen it would do so, I should have been able to recoup you myself.'

A brief visit to Raincliff in New Zealand confirmed Harry in his decision that he could never live there though he always retained an interest in the estate. Staplehurst was mortgaged to Lord Penrhyn who threatened to call his money in on more than one occasion and Henry knew that he and Beatrice could not afford to keep it even though Charles and William offered him £600 a year on condition that they did. The lawyers got paid but the paths remained unweeded. Henry could pay neither his builders' nor his brewers' bills and Mr Ediss, the artist, had his account outstanding for five years. His house in St James's Square was sold and he and Beatrice had to endure the constant humiliation of fielding embarrassing questions from their friends, such as where were the family going to spend their summer holidays and why didn't Henry provide Beatrice with a carriage. Henry had not a penny to call his own – something he could never explain to outsiders, 'who regard us as having a certain dependable income, reduced it is true but still sufficient for the way we live and to spare'.

Beatrice became ill with worry, but she was a practical woman. With no prospect of being able to pay for the education of their five small boys she paid little attention to the family view that they should try and remain at Staplehurst in order to maintain their 'position'. In her opinion this was something not worth having since they couldn't even afford to call on their next-door neighbour and, more importantly, as she wrote to William in 1876, 'if we live on here [Staplehurst] we cannot afford to send them to good schools. I don't think in after life people will think any better of them for having been brought up here compared with their having been to Eton and the University.' She confessed that she 'looked at money in a different light from any of you', and whereas Henry and Charles were content to keep things as they were in the expectation that 'something may turn up, one never knew', she was not prepared to risk her children's future on such a vague hope.

Staplehurst Place with its 3000 acres was finally sold to William and Laura Hoare for £20,000. They borrowed virtually the whole of the sale price from the Bank. But they were reluctant purchasers. They lived there for a trial year in 1879 during which time Laura became ill on account of the bad drains. Their inclination was to give it all up but 'the family urged us not to'. They 'gave in' but made it clear that if they were to move there permanently, a new house would have to be built on a more healthy site. Henry lowered his price but Laura nevertheless felt that they were being browbeaten into helping Henry, by Charles in particular. In Laura's opinion, by offering to come in on the purchase (on condition that William would buy him out once his capital in the Brewery had increased sufficiently) Charles was forcing their hand. William's financial position at the Brewery did not improve on account of being obliged to part with some of his shares to enable his brothers Walter and Tuppy to come in but Charles insisted on William keeping to the bargain nevertheless. William and Laura abandoned the old house at Staplehurst, which they reduced in size and let to William's unmarried sisters, and built themselves a rambling, extravagant mansion on the crown of the hill in Iden Park, using the architect William Anderson, well known for his designs for banks and breweries as well as country houses. They called the new house Iden Manor and it was said to have been designed with enough bedrooms to accommodate two cricket teams.

Henry persisted in his belief, notwithstanding the general depression in stocks, that he could restore his fortune by further speculative investment. The Bank increased his allowance to £5000 in 1877 and his brothers continued to lend him money after his disgrace. When Henry was finally declared bankrupt in November 1891, William again was the victim, having stood as guarantor for

Staplehurst Place, Iden, Kent. Previously a farmhouse, transformed by Henry of Staplehurst, in 1836, into an Italianate villa to house his twelve children.

him for £50,000 for the purchase of shares in the Neuchatel Asphalt Company which then had to be sold at a much reduced price. Charles Booth's view of William, when he interviewed him for his *Survey into Life and Labour in London 1886-1903*, was that he 'looked rather a weak man with no fixed views or policy' with regard to any of the questions he was asked.

By this stage in his life Henry had become rather confused about who had lent him what and still clung to the forlorn hope that one day he might be able to repay everyone's kindness.[6] In fact he was able to satisfy his major creditor though not in a way anyone would have chosen. On 5 August 1898 he died, the day before his sixtieth birthday. Each year since 1874 the Bank had kept up the annual premiums on his life policies which they had accepted as security for their loan to him of £100,000. Now it could be repaid. While the Bank got off the hook William continued to suffer as a result of Henry's activities. In 1901, only twelve years after it was completed, Iden Manor was let and the whole estate in Staplehurst was sold three years later. William had no choice. He was struggling to survive on £3000 a year from the Brewery, which was his only source of income, and amounted to less than the annual interest on his debt of £70,000. He confided in his eldest son Geoffrey, 'It is horrid isn't it but it's no good making the worst of it and at all events we have had a good try to keep the place in the family and it is not as if we had inherited it.'

One of Henry's younger sons, Edward, who became a Partner in 1910, always claimed that Henry had been unfairly criticized for his failures. He felt the Bank had been too tough in their dismissal of him in 1874 and that he had not been given sufficient credit for the wisdom of some of his later projects. In particular his large block of shares in the Neuchatel Asphalt Company would have been an excellent buy long term. The arrival of motorized transport revolutionized the Company's fortunes and Edward was convinced that without the bankruptcy order, which forced the sale of his shareholding, Henry would have recovered all his losses in his own lifetime by the rise in value of his shares. The other unfortunate consequence of ousting Henry was that it opened the way to giving Charlie Arthur a greater share of the profits.

In 1872 Henry Tilden was delighted to be offered an extra job. He was engaged as confidential clerk and private secretary to Charlie Arthur which 'provided an agreeable addition to my income and as he was constantly away from business my duties were not very arduous, consisting chiefly in paying his bills'. Charlie and his cousin Charles were both made Partners in 1873, with one share each, but their respective shareholdings increased after Henry's departure, with Charlie Arthur, as the son of the senior Partner, taking the greater part. All this was arranged despite the fact that nobody in the Bank was under any illusion that Charlie Arthur would be useful to the business, although they couldn't know quite how embarrassing he would prove to be. Peter Richard died in 1877 having become mentally incapacitated in the last two years of his life when he was only content when left alone in the care of Isabella. In his will he left his half share of the Bank's premises and the adjoining chambers in Fleet Street and Mitre Court to be divided equally between Charlie Arthur and his two sisters, Charlotte Strickland and Isabella, as tenants in common. His exclusion from a share of the Bank freehold provoked Peter Merrik into challenging the terms of the will on the grounds of his late father's lunacy and in 1878 he brought a suit against Algernon Strickland and Henry Gerard as the executors. The suit was unsuccessful but his action did have the effect of increasing his allowance from the Bank to £7000.

Charlie Arthur and his wife Margaret, whom he had married in 1867 when he was only twenty, had moved into Kelsey Park which Peter Richard had given to him hoping it would be a pleasant and convenient place for him to live and commute from to Fleet Street. Scarcely giving them time to settle in Peter Richard embarked on a campaign to persuade Charlie Arthur to come into the Bank: 'The sooner you come into Fleet Street the better it will be ... settle down to the business from whence you will mainly derive your income and with prudence make a good fortune for those that come after you if you are to be as prosperous as we have hitherto been for two hundred years.' In his old age Peter Richard knew he wasn't up to much any more and he was conscious that the descendants of 'Naughty Richard' were 'quite ready to slip into vacant places'. His only option to succeed him at the Bank was Charlie Arthur, who, in turn, had no other option

*Charlie Arthur Hoare as a young man with no interest in banking, c. 1867.*

but to accept this role, whatever his personal inclinations might be. Charlie Arthur had no particular objection to this but he disregarded any advice that went with it, particularly the unwelcome suggestion that it should involve any hard work. Peter Richard's warning that 'your success at the Bank depends entirely upon standing, no one will keep their money where they find the conductors of the Bank extravagant' also fell on deaf ears.

Charlie's Arthur's passion was horses. He never pretended to be interested in the family business and looked upon it simply 'as a means of subsistence and have always from my earliest infancy. Get the work done as safely and cheaply as we can and the more the profits the better pleased we ought to be.' He wanted to enjoy himself. One way of doing this was by running a seasonal 'coach' service between Beckenham and Sevenoaks, frequently taking the reins himself. He was a large stout man and when dressed for driving in his oversized box-cloth coat he looked every inch 'The Coachman', as he was nicknamed. Coaching had become a rather fashionable hobby for the rich and sporting who enjoyed competing with one another. It was enthusiastically promoted by the Duke of Beaufort, who started a joint stock company in 1866 for its supporters, and the start of the season was an occasion for great society gatherings. Most of the Duke's shareholders came from his own county, Gloucesteshire, and, when Peter Richard died, Charlie decided to give up coaching in Kent and moved his family to Cirencester in order to take up an invitation from the Beaufort hunt to become whipper in.

*Race card for the VWH steeplechases 1880. Charlie Arthur was MFH for the hunt to which he devoted most of his time in preference to his duties at Fleet Street.*

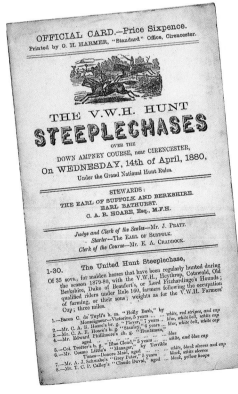

This decision changed his life. On the hunting field he met a young woman called Beatrice (Beatie) Sumner, whose striking looks and adventurous spirit completely captivated him and over the next few years they broke every rule in the book in order to be with each other. Beatie was no ordinary mistress, for although she was renowned for her precocious charm, which she exercised with great skill, she was in fact only fifteen when she first encountered Charlie. They conducted their affair with minimal discretion. Beatie's father was forced to confront Charlie after a particularly scandalous episode in 1879, when Beatie actually took up residence in Charlie and Margaret's house for four months after some trumped-up riding accident which she claimed necessitated her stay there.

The Sumners devised all kinds of stratagems to keep the lovers apart, none of which worked. Ultimately they were driven to make Beatie a ward of court in 1881. By this time Charlie Arthur had left the Beaufort and, with the backing of Lord Bathurst, had taken up the mastership of the Vale of White Horse – another Cotswold hunt. Despite the fact that he was now the senior Partner at Fleet Street drawing the major share of the profits, his entire working week was spent hunting. Charles remonstrated with him about his absence and total lack of concern for how the Bank was being managed but his efforts to rouse Charlie Arthur into feeling a sense of responsibility for the business were fruitless. Charlie Arthur was forbidden to see Beatie but his money gave them both an opportunity to keep in touch. Beatie's father was deeply in debt and her mother was persuaded by her masterful daughter to ask Charlie Arthur for help which he provided. Beatie was sent to Germany with her mother, escorted by a relation, Kingscote Fitzhardinge, who was also a friend of Charlie Arthur's and also in debt to him. In his letters asking for loans he smuggled messages from Beatie and she made every effort, using 'Fitz' as her go-between, to arrange a meeting with Charlie Arthur on her return to England in 1882.

While the injunction was in force Charlie Arthur was resolute in his determination to stick to the law and resisted her attempts to see him. The minute she became of age on 12 July 1883, however, Beatie consulted her solicitor to discover if there was anything in law to stop them living together and, having been satisfied that there wasn't, she and Charlie Arthur resumed their relationship. Within a year their first child, Sybil, was born. Charlie Arthur and Beatie moved their strange menage to a house in Faringdon while Margaret continued to live in Cirencester with their five legitimate children. The hunt was split between the landowners who supported their chairman Lord Bathurst (a relation of Beatie's) who withdrew the loan of his kennels from Charlie Arthur and informed him that 'we must be on different terms from those on which we have hitherto met', and the tenant farmers who readily supported their Master, 'Mr Hoare the Farmer's Friend', whose great liberality to them during the years of agricultural depression had bought their everlasting gratitude.

The decisive blow to Charlie Arthur's reputation came in March 1885 when, rather late in the day, an action was brought by Beatie's uncle, Colonel Kingscote, in the Chancery Court for the committal of Charlie Arthur to prison for breaking the Court Order of December 1881 which forbade any communication between him and Beatie. It was Charlie Arthur's money which was at the heart of the breach, but fortunately for him the judge took a lenient view. In his judgement the loans, which were given to Beatie's relations during the period of the injunction, and provided an opportunity for the two parties to communicate, invalidated the prosecution's case. If the parents and other relations of the ward had been in earnest to secure an end to the relationship between her and her married lover they should not have accepted money from him. However, the case was reported widely in the press and Charlie Arthur could no longer escape the consequences of his liaison. It was impossible for him to return to his previous life in Gloucestershire. The division in the hunt had led to a division of the country they hunted over and

Charlie had to set up new headquarters at Cricklade with his own hounds, but he resented being pushed out from the country around Cirencester, complaining that his private life had absolutely nothing to do with foxhunting and as long as he hunted the country properly there should be no need to attack his character.

He continued his vendetta against Bathurst for some years after he and Beatie had left Gloucestershire, finding the county to be an increasingly inhospitable place for them both, and moved to the Isle of Wight where they embarked on a new venture together. They bought a sailing ship and built a shore-based training school for boys entering the merchant navy, there making a life for themselves exiled from all society except their own. Margaret would not divorce him; so Charlie Arthur and Beatie never married. They were amply provided for by Charlie's profits from the Bank where his position as senior Partner had always been absurd but meant that nothing could be done without his cooperation. It was not until 1888 that he finally agreed to retire, and then only on the basis of a very generous settlement. He had borrowings from the Bank of over £150,000 but this overdraft was secured on the Kelsey estate, his house in Cirencester and various life policies. His terms to the Bank were that his entitlement to half profits would continue for his lifetime, that he would retain his interest in the Bank freehold and and all other privileges of Partnership such as the right to inspect the books, the right to nominate a son as a Partner, the right of veto over any other nomination and the right to approve any amalgamation or sale of the business. After his death a quarter of the profits would be paid into his estate for seven years. Surprisingly only one customer is known to have closed his account in protest at Charlie's behaviour.[7]

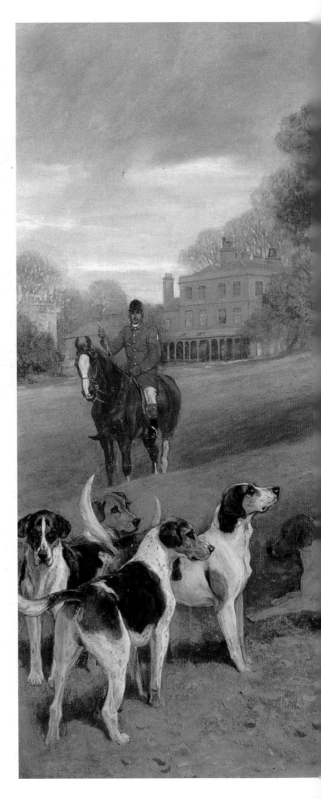

*Charlie Arthur Hoare and his hounds, by John Charlton. The picture is now hanging in the Bank after languishing in the vaults for a century. The partners had no wish to be reminded of Charlie Arthur's disastrous banking career.*

# CHAPTER SEVEN

# RECOVERY AND WAR
# 1885–1918

facing page

*Scaffolding at the front*

*of the Bank, with*

*balconies for customers*

*to view the procession*

*celebrating Queen*

*Victoria's Diamond*

*Jubilee in 1897.*

I n 1881 Charles had more or less compelled Charlie Arthur to accept Charles's younger brother Alfred as a 'probationer'. The Bank was short of Partners who were prepared to do much work. The cheapest solution to this problem, which didn't pose a threat to the profits, was to take on a new recruit from the family, 'if his manners suit our customers', at the lowest level possible. Alfred began his career at the Bank as a thirty-one-year-old married man with no promise of any kind regarding salary or partnership prospects. He had not expected to go to Fleet Street and after studying mathematics at Cambridge he went on to train as a doctor at Bart's Hospital. Henry and Beatrice lobbied hard for Alfred to be admitted to the Bank though it seems Alfred was hesitant to put himself forward at first on account of not wishing to gain by Henry's loss. Henry felt, quite to the contrary, that he didn't wish his misfortune to stand in the way of his younger brother's future in the Bank. Thus, with the endorsement of his two older brothers, Alfred was admitted as a salaried Partner in 1884, the last member of the seventh generation of the family to join the business.

When Alfred entered 37 Fleet Street it was certainly on the cheapest terms which the Partners could devise. Their most expensive Partner was making no contribution to the workload at the Bank and in engaging Alfred they were attempting to make up for this. For this reason they considered it fair that half of Alfred's salary should come out of Charlie Arthur's profits. Alfred's starting salary was gradually increased by increments to £2500 per annum in 1897 and it remained at that level for the next twenty-eight years. As it was also made clear to Alfred that he would be given no right of nomination should he have a son, it is hardly surprising that he carved out a career for himself which involved the minimum time spent on Bank business.

Alfred was not designed by nature to be ambitious. His strength lay in financial management, but his interest was in public service and philanthropic organizations rather than in his family's bank. He was given responsibility for the

audit department but, to the intense frustration of his Partners, he never extend-ed himself beyond that. Shortly after entering the Bank he was elected as the 'Progressive' member for Holborn of the first London County Council and became chairman of its Finance Committee. He took a keen interest in the provi-sion of housing for the metropolitan working classes and to this end founded 'The East End Dwelling Company' and 'The Tenement Dwellings Company' which occupied most of his time during banking hours. Although board meetings of these companies in the afternoons could just be tolerated, matters reached a head when he undertook the momentous task of compiling the first Italian-English dic-tionary and chose to work on it at Fleet Street. He began this at the age of fifty-six because, it is said, he was finding it impossible to read Dante in the original, unaided. The first edition of the dictionary was finally published in 1915, fol-lowed by a shorter version in 1919.

The creation of Alfred's dictionary took many years, during which time he slept several nights a week at the Bank, regularly rising at four, waking himself up by plunging into the small pool in the back courtyard, and then setting to work in his bedroom on the half of the alphabet he kept at the Bank. The other half was kept at his home in East Grinstead. The Partners pleaded with him to change his rou-tine: 'Could you not arrange to do your dictionary work down in the far back room and thus give us the benefit of more of your time when here? In practice when you are upstairs you are forgotten and it frequently happens that you come down at eleven only to go out to some board.' From time to time Alfred suggested that he should retire but he was valued for his judgement and wisdom, and given his lack of personal interest his views on matters regarding family succession were much respected. He was, as his daughter described, tolerant, broadminded, calm and well balanced, and someone who didn't know what it meant to feel anger.

None of these qualities could be said to define his elder brother Charles, under whose autocratic style of management, the Bank struggled through the clos-ing two decades of the nineteenth century. Charles's attitude to his Partners can best be described as defensive. He was acutely sensitive to any criticism of his financial management, and particularly to any hint of unflattering comparisons between his speculative behaviour and that of his brother Henry junior. He and Algernon Strickland had joint responsibility for the day-to-day management but Algernon was not robust and, although he didn't retire until 1909, he was absent from the Bank for long stretches of time during the 1880s and 1890s, laid low by attacks of neur-algia which he confessed rendered him fit for nothing but to 'lie on the sofa all day not even able to read a book'. During a particularly bad spell in December 1885, while he was convalescing in Bournemouth, he realized that if he didn't improve he would have to bid 'adieu to the Bank' which would have to look around for a more 'sturdy successor'. It was a great blessing that on this occasion he rallied as the chances of finding a worthy replacement for him, at that time, whether 'sturdy' or not, were not great. Despite recurring ill health he continued to work as an active Partner virtually until the end of his working life by which time his son Algy, who had joined him in 1894, had become well established.

Charles, with some justification, felt that he took by far the greater burden of the work and as a result was easily upset by the lack of endorsement he received from Algernon over some of the decisions he took, and in particular the implications that he ever acted otherwise than in the best interests of the firm. Charles was convinced that it was his contribution alone that was crucial in rescuing the Bank from the damage inflicted by Henry junior in 1874 and the undermining effect of Charlie Arthur. In fact Henry's departure had benefited Charles considerably in terms of his personal stake in the Bank since Henry's own son Harry was only eight years old at the time, so his shares went back into the Partnership and Charles's share was at once doubled. Although that didn't meet the problem of absentee Partners, it provided financial compensation and gave him the control he relished.

Algernon tended to take a back seat when it came to controversial matters relating to the family, but his and Charles's fundamental differences of opinion over how the Bank's money should be invested flared up into outright disagreement after the publication of the Bank's first Balance Sheet and the signing of the new Partnership Articles in 1892. The pressure of competition from the joint stock banks had persuaded Hoare's, following the example of other West End private banks, including Child's and Gosling's, to take the step of publishing their Balance Sheet for the first time in 1891. They undertook to continue to do this on an annual basis on the first Saturday 'convenient after the 5th of July'.

The timing in 1891 wasn't perfect. The Partners' had sizeable liabilities to members of the family in the form of pensions and allowances. In addition to their colossal obligation to Charlie Arthur they were paying out over £16,000 a year to meet their commitments to Peter Merrik, Sir Henry Ainslie, Henry junior and his wife Beatrice, and Henry Burney, Peter Richard's nephew (described by Charles as 'not a Partner not even a Hoare'); it was a figure in excess of half the sum divided for profits. Their securities were reduced in value in a depressed stock market which was reeling in the aftermath of a crisis which hit Barings Bank the previous year.[1] Nevertheless in 1891 they managed to produce a Statement of Assets and Liabilities which looked very respectable and could cause concern to no-one.

One of the most serious casualties of Henry junior's speculations was the Sinking Fund, which had been almost entirely depleted, and the Bank's reserves were generally a matter of some concern. In the Partnership Articles of 1892 it was agreed that, in the future, they should be increased to £500,000 and that the 'bonus on policies on the life of Henry Hoare be specifically hypothecated towards this'. But Henry was only fifty-four and it was the methods Charles adopted in the meantime to increase the return on capital that were to create such friction with Algernon.

In 1891 Charles was left in more or less sole charge of the Balance Sheet and, in his efforts to produce figures the Bank could be proud of, he took a very optimistic view of the value of some of the 'Miscellaneous Securities' held by the Bank. The auditors were Welton Jones and Co. but, as Henry Tilden observed, when he raised an objection to the prices that Mr Welton selected for the valuation of the securities for the Second Balance Sheet, 'I knew too much of Mr Welton's past career to think he was a very safe guide to Mr CH in compiling a Balance Sheet nor was his name at its foot any recommendation to business men in the City.' But Mr Welton was a personal friend of Charles and it later transpired the figures had been allowed to stand as they did by a 'special and individual guarantee' given to him by Charles. Charles felt entirely confident in doing this, as he explained to Algernon, having to his future credit the new Stourhead Mortgage worth £45,000 from Sir Henry Ainslie, who was now seventy, and life policies worth £35,000 at current value, apart from a number of other investments of a less predictable nature.

One of the innovations of the 1892 Partnership Articles was the introduction of new capital into the business by all four partners, including Henry Gerard and Alfred, and it was intended that the total sum should be increased further to a maximum of £240,000 after the death of Charlie Arthur. The capital could only be withdrawn as a result of death or incapacity. It was the use to which Charles put this capital which caused Algernon, uncharacteristically, to lose his temper with him one Saturday in November 1893. He at once apologized, but the effect of his outburst drove Charles to defend himself against charges of being 'a born speculator, obstinate, foolish and just like Henry'. He submitted to Algernon a summary of the facts and figures relating to the Bank's investments, and in the ensuing exchange of views it became clear that Charles's methods for running a profitable concern were in almost complete opposition to the tried and tested principles advocated by the 'Strickland' faction. Apart from Government stocks, a major part of the Bank's capital since the time of Harry of Mitcham had been invested in secure stock, principally New River Stock, and it was these copper-bottomed 'Bankers' investments which Algernon wished to see increased. Charles was forced to admit that the weak point on the Balance Sheet was the use of Partners' capital as part of the Bank's reserves, but on all other investment decisions, he justified himself by the fact that the results on the whole were good:

> You talk of my "specs" it is true I have had some. It is also true that many little ones amounting in a total to only a small sum have turned out not as I expected (Grand Trunks) ... but some have turned out well and the only large one (Oakley Slate Quarry) has been excellent. I claim no credit for this, except that if I have, as you say, "the same spirit of speculation in me as Henry did", I have kept the spirit under lock and key – it has never led me into extravagance or mischief. I feel I have had to initiate the whole of the finances. I can

facing page

*Charles Hoare, c.1874, made a sharing Partner when his eldest brother, Henry junior, had to retire. Described by his nephew, Harry, as always wanting 'more, more, more'.*

hardly remember you making an original suggestion of sale or investment. You have stated in general terms that you like liquid assets and dislike lock ups – I agree with you. If you will refer to the two accounts named (Miscellaneous Securities and Deposit Accounts) you will find they are liquid if Partners' capital is eliminated. All we have got to do qua the public is to show assets for the money deposited with us … in our Balance Sheet we show surplus assets of £400,000 … I therefore say qua public if the worst comes to the worst it is a sure thing they would be paid 20/- in the £ even if M/S [miscellaneous] securities = nil.

Having put his case Charles went on to say that for many years Algernon had left many important affairs for him to negotiate on his own. He cited the retirement of Charlie Arthur and his first cousin, Henry Burney, who had been a clerk at the Bank since 1865, all 'the bother' with Beatrice over an extra payment to her in addition to Henry junior's allowance and the internal arrangements in the Bank, especially sorting out the confusion following Henry junior's retirement and the work involved in the publication of the Balance Sheet. Why, he wondered, had Algernon given his agreement to so much if he had no faith in the way in which it was done? The Partnership Agreement had explicitly stated that no Partner was to speculate or invest in buying and selling stocks against written objections of the majority of other Partners except the 'purchase or mortgage of freehold hereditaments or the English Funds'. Charles received no written objections so he went ahead with his own ideas, his defence always being that Algernon was never there to ask and never had an opinion anyway.

There were other slightly dubious schemes such as the discounting of Trade Bills, 'a thing we had never done before confining our discounts to Bankers' and Government Bills' which Charles took on at the instigation of his chief clerk Grabham who wished to accommodate his own friends. Algernon found out and the practice stopped, but when an engineering firm, Easton Anderson and Co Ltd, ran up an overdraft of £60,000 'which every week was increased by a large cheque for wages and nothing came in by contra', Henry Tilden promptly showed the account to Algernon, 'who, poor man, knew nothing'. No more cheques were paid, the firm went into liquidation and the Bank was saddled with a very bad debt. Tilden, writing in 1924, reflected that, whatever Charles's intentions may have been, 'no single partner should ever be allowed to obtain sole control and every loan and investment should be explained to and adjudicated upon by the other partners' and 'having a true gentleman like Mr Algernon to deal with and a Chief Clerk to say ditto to him he almost invariably got his own way.'

The situation considerably improved for the future prospects of the Bank and the happiness of those who worked there when a group of three young men, from the next generation in the family, qualified, both in terms of age and 'fitness', to be admitted into the Partnership in 1894. Harry, who had been a small boy when his father, Henry junior, fell from grace, was twenty-eight; Peter Arthur Marsham, Peter Merrik's eldest son and Peter Richard's grandson, was twenty-five and Algy Strickland, a Hoare by birth but not in name, was twenty-nine. Charles reported to Charlie Arthur in his annual letter on the division of the profits, in September 1897, that he was 'particularly pleased with the harmonious and friendly feeling in the House ... no nasty jealousy or ill feeling ... this feeling is not confined to the Partners but persists throughout the House.' Charles's optimism about the Bank was certainly bolstered by the confidence he had in his junior Partners 'because they do their work thoroughly well and show their hearts and heads are interested in the continual success of the Leather Bottle ... The line and tone they adopt is very different from the more or less it doesn't matter kind of feeling shown by my late cousins HGH, HN and HH [Henry Gerard, Hamilton Noel and Henry].'

Henry Gerard, who had died in 1896, had also introduced a son, Philip, as a confidential clerk, but after his father's death the Partners showed no inclination to take him on as a salaried Partner. His indignant mother, Fanny, was much grieved; 'I cannot help writing to tell you how bitterly I and all who are interested in him are disappointed, when I remember that his father was in the Bank for over fifty years and how he devoted himself to its interests.' Charles felt the Bank were being more than generous. She, as Henry Gerard's widow, was to be paid half his salary for seven years following his death, and Philip, whom 'somehow or other we have not found indispensable ... and is not really wanted in the Bank' was nevertheless offered a promotion to Agent with an increase in salary and the unpopular sleeping duty.

Peter Merrik had pushed for his son to be taken on as partner at twenty-one, and to take priority over the other two, as part of his ongoing battle with the Bank to redress the injustice that he felt had been meted out to him. Algernon and Charles were at one in their opposition to this. Ideas concerning the Partnership were undergoing some radical rethinking and eligible candidates were being asked to deliver a little more than hitherto had been asked of them. As ever the interests of the Bank and its customers were to be the first consideration, and Partners were expected to be not only men of wealth but of the highest character. The Bank could not take the risk of carrying more debt and suffering further neglect if it was to prosper in the future.

A university education, which had never before been regarded as a prerequisite for entering the Bank, although it had become traditional in the senior branch of the family, was first mentioned as a positive advantage in a letter written from Algernon to Peter Merrik in 1889: 'The object of a University training as regards the Bank is not to learn Banking directly but to gain experience of life and knowledge of men.' He further explained that although they intended to treat 'young men now coming on' most fairly and more liberally 'than the late Mr Peter Richard Hoare or the late Mr Henry Hoare were', in view of the increased competition existing on all sides Messrs Hoare must have 'ample opportunity of satisfying themselves of the fitness of those to whom they will bequeath the management of the business', and the arrangements for Partnership were bound to become ever more important in the future than they had been hitherto.

With the bitter experience of Charlie Arthur's position still dominating their lives, they were ready to abandon the old principle of the senior Partner taking half the profits and the rest being divided up according to the shares held. The new young men were all treated equally in terms of salary and when the new Partnership Deed was drawn up in 1902, following Charles's death, each of them had two shares and each of them was paid a salary of £1500 before profits were divided. The only ranking was to be a natural order of seniority based on age and experience. Strictly speaking, Algernon was now the senior Partner but given his age and his natural reticence, it was not he but Harry who emerged as the commanding figure at Fleet Street.

Harry had grown up knowing at first hand the reality of living with debt and his father's fatal belief that he would strike lucky one day, but he had no affection for his uncle Charles. He strongly resented the way in which Charles had appropriated his own father's shares in 1874 and, having acquired an increased share for himself, had then done everything he could to bolster profits, disregarding the need to apply the money to writing down the securities in the Bank's reserve funds to their proper value. Moreover Charles had never offered these shares to Harry when the time came for his admission. Consequently Harry was not much disposed to welcome the arrival of Charles's eldest son, who was eleven years his junior, with a view to his becoming a Partner on the same terms as himself.

*Cover from Harry Hoare's* Spade Work, *published in 1902. Gardening was his passion; the grounds at his house, Ellisfield Manor, Hampshire, were renowned.*

Young Charles Hervey entered the Bank as an Agent in 1898, as did Harry's brother Frederick, who had been sent out earlier to Raincliff in New Zealand by Henry and Beatrice to try and make a living from the station. In 1889 the Raincliff Merino sheep had won many prizes at the Timaru Show but the estate, which at that time was carrying thirty thousand sheep, continued to swallow investment, which Beatrice later estimated amounted to £77,000 in the form of mortgages held by Charles and Alfred. Harper, the New Zealand agent, kept the improvement of the estate a secret from Beatrice knowing full well that it was contrary to her instructions that Raincliff should be made to pay its own way and no funds should be sent out from England. In the end Henry was compelled to put his £2000 annual allowance from the Bank into Raincliff to guarantee the interest charges to

his brothers, another transaction which all parties were careful to keep secret. In these circumstances Frederick's prospects were not hopeful. Although he appeared to be admirably suited to the life of a sheep farmer he was urged by his mother to return home in 1898 and take up a job in the Bank which had been offered him. In fact Frederick would not have had the option to stay in New Zealand. Charles's death, in the same year that he was recalled home, precipitated the sale of Raincliff to the New Zealand Trust and Loan Company and the old sheep run was cut up and sold off for farming.[2] The adventure for the Hoare family was over, but Frederick, who had spent more than ten years there, never lost his attachment to the place and when he retired to Cornwall in 1935 he named his house, 'Raincliffe'.

*above*

*Raincliff, New Zealand.*
*The avenue of limes,*
*planted during Harry*
*Hoare's time in New*
*Zealand, in the 1890s.*

*below*
*The avenue as it is today.*

In 1898 Harry's health was causing some alarm after he was refused a life insurance policy: his heart was operating like that of a man of sixty as a result of chain smoking. After a trip to Egypt in 1893 Harry had returned with an enthusiasm for drinking Turkish coffee and he encouraged Peter and Algy to join him every day after lunch for coffee and a cigarette in the ante room at the head of the stairs which ever after has been known as the Smoking Room. The walls were hung with framed photographs of cricketers and celebrity actresses, and the room was furnished with armchairs and adjustable footstools designed for the comfort of those who suffered from gout. It was a place where the Partners would gather to relax when not working and it was a not unusual sight to see Henry Gerard dressed in his hunting pink waiting to leave for a day's sport near his home in Godstone. Double doors led into the Billiard Room which had been converted out of the formal Drawing Room or Saloon. Their fun was partially spoilt when Charles put his head round the door one afternoon and told them, 'your cousin Algernon does not like you to smoke during banking hours.' Algernon was asthmatic. The restriction was lifted after four o' clock and to beat the ban before that time the young men perfected the art of blowing smoke up the chimney. After his doctor's warning Harry gave up smoking altogether and within a few years had been passed as fit. His father's short life caused Beatrice to worry continuously on Harry's account though her fears proved to be groundless.

Both she and her eldest son were remarkable for their longevity, Beatrice dying in 1945 at the age of a hundred and two and Harry living until he was ninety.

In 1896 Charlie Arthur's nominee, his son Reginald, known as Reggie, was welcomed as a probationer but on the understanding, repeated to his mother, Margaret, that he must 'take pains in everything given him, never think that he is put upon, on the contrary his aim should be how much he can do and how well he can do it'. Reggie was only eighteen when he arrived and made a poor first impression. He arrived late, idled his time away and infuriated the management by giving the idea of 'not caring a blow what any body thinks or wants'. Generally he was regarded as a 'young man that has never been licked into shape'. Time didn't do much to change things and it was agreed in 1904 that Reggie should be allowed to go out to New Zealand to give him 'a wide view of the world and a better knowledge of the value of debt'. It was hoped he might return a few years later with more to offer as a banker.

The Bank felt obliged, though not bound, to offer him a second chance but Reggie, who knew as well as they did that he was not cut out for Partnership, set his sights on extracting what he considered his due from the Bank. He wanted to take up sheep farming with his half-brother Robin, Charlie Arthur and Beatie's illegitimate son, and his idea was that he could finance this by 'selling' his father's right of nomination as an asset to the Partners. This was rejected outright and Reggie returned home with the express wish of re-entering the Bank. A compromise was reached whereby he was made a Partner for a year only and in return he sold his share of the Bank premises, which he had inherited from his father, to the Partners, for £14,000.

Meanwhile, Charles Hervey disqualified himself by his failure to manage his own money. He ran up a large overdraft which was partly incurred by the unauthorized purchase of stocks which, as Algernon told his mother, was quite out of order: 'We none of us make investments by overdraft without the consent of the firm.' When offered a Partnership, on condition that he could prove his ability to live within his income for one year, he felt the salary was not adequate to his needs and declined. When Charlie Arthur died in 1908, and the opportunity arose to take on more sharing Partners, it was evident that neither of these prospective candidates who had arrived at the Bank with every expectation of Partnership would be capable of carrying on the succession.

Harry's brother, Frederick, whose arrival from New Zealand coincided with that of his first cousin Charles Hervey, had been taken on to learn the business in order to assist Henry Gerard's son, Philip, and another first cousin, Vincent, the son of Walter, the Rector of Colkirk, but these three Agents were employed on the strict understanding that they were not to be considered for Partnership. The maximum salary they could expect would be £1000 a year and that would depend on a reduction in the charges on the business, in other words the death of one of the current recipients of an allowance from the Bank. In Philip and Vincent's case their reward came with the death of Hamilton Noel in 1908. Their only 'privilege' as family members, apart from a more generous holiday allowance, was the possession of the Bank's keys. Between them they were responsible for locking up at 11.30 at night, sleeping overnight and unlocking the doors at 8 and the closet at 9 o' clock the following morning. After Charles

George Ottley, night watchman at the Bank, as Sergeant in the Queen's Royal Lancers at Ladysmith 1897.

Hervey and Reggie joined the Bank and were obliged to undertake some of the sleeping duties themselves, the restrictions on the Agents' social lives were slightly relaxed. They were now allowed to ask one friend in to dine once a week when on duty, and the married men were allowed to bring their wives with them on duty nights and as a couple they were further permitted to invite one other couple to dine with them on one occasion during the week.

Altogether there were ten members of the family working in the business at the turn of the centur, Arthur Hervey as Charles's second son joined in 1900, while his elder brother Charles Hervey, Frederick and Vincent were away for eighteen months, fighting as volunteers in the South African War. The Bank staff then comprised thirty-three clerks, five porters and household servants which included a footman, assisted by a 'boy', to attend to the family's valeting needs. Staff rates of pay had improved under the scheme introduced in 1875 and Hoare's were well known for their generous holiday allowance which entitled even the most junior men to a month's annual leave. In 1899 a new salary scheme was drawn up which introduced, for the first time, a compulsory retirement age and a pension provision anticipating, by some years, the principle of the non-contributory pension introduced by Lloyd George in his 'People's Budget' of 1909.

This new arrangement removed a major source of aggravation. Under the old rules several of the senior men, who were anxious not to retire, continued to work unhindered and consequently blocked the chances of promotion for those junior to them. George Whitely, whose investment advice Henry junior had mistakenly relied upon, carried on as Head of Correspondence until he was well over eighty and made an extremely good living for himself, being one of six who shared the brokerage, and in addition acting as an unofficial agent for Lord Spencer. He was rumoured to have made a fortune of £100,000, although half of it came from a legacy left him by a Bank customer.

Under the new rules everyone entered the Bank as a probationer and if found satisfactory was paid a starting salary, as a 'third class' clerk, of £60 for his first two years. The salary would rise by annual increments to a maximum of

£200 after twelve years, promotion to 'second class' would raise his salary to a top level of £400 and if moved into 'first class' he could expect to receive £600 once he had qualified for a senior post. Those seniors who occupied the five chief posts of Head Clerk, Head of Books and Correspondence, Chief Cashier and Deputy Broker were paid a premium in addition to the top salary. All 'first class' clerks received a proportion of the brokerage contingent on it reaching a figure above £7350 and all clerks were eligible to receive half commission on each brokerage transaction entered into by any new customer they had personally introduced to the House. Clerks could retire at the age of sixty if they chose and were required to do so at sixty-five unless the Bank specifically required them to stay. Pensions were only payable after forty years' service and were calculated on the basis that they should equal as many sixtieths as years of service but should never exceed two thirds of his salary at retirement. In 1912 Henry Tilden retired as Deputy Broker at the age of sixty-nine. He told the Partners that when he came to the Bank in 1863 Thomas Lee was Chief Cashier, having entered the Bank in 1812, the year that Napoleon reached Moscow, and therefore their two lives at the Bank had spanned a hundred years.

The ownership of the Bank's premises and the freeholds comprising 33 and 40-43 Fleet Street and 5 Mitre Court had now gradually been transformed from individual Partners to the Partnership as a whole. Henry's half share had been bought in 1874 and by the end of the First World War the remaining half share had been purchased in stages from the various owners: Reggie, Algy, Isabella and Peter Arthur, all of whom had inherited a proportion of Peter Richard's moiety or half share. After half a century of uncertainty the Partnership was now the sole proprietor of the business and its buildings.

*Anna Pavlova, c.1920. The illegitimate daughter of a Russian laundry maid, she was the best known ballerina in the world during her lifetime. She and her partner, Victor Dandre, whom she never married, opened accounts at Hoare's after they settled in England in 1912.*

The Bank had been rescued from disaster by the insurance paid on the early deaths of Henry and Charles but the turn of the century was not marked by any increase in prosperity at 37 Fleet Street. Charlie Arthur communicated through his solicitors that, given the fall in his profit share, he assumed that the Partners must be putting unduly large amounts into reserve. The profit dividend had sunk to £15,000 in 1900, in a year when there had been exceptional provision for bad debt, chiefly on account of the liquidation of Easton Anderson and the problems at the Brewery. Although this was reduced in the following two years, by 1903 the outlook continued to be unpromising and there followed another two years of poor profits. The truth of the matter was that Charles had left them in a difficult position, with overvalued securities in a stock market which had not yet recovered. As Harry explained to Charlie

Algernon Swinburne, by Dante Gabriel Rossetti, 1861. The poet introduced his cousin Robert to the Bank. Robert drank an entire legacy of £4000 at the Green Dragon public house in Shaftesbury Avenue and, having decided that 'his life's work was accomplished', then died.

Arthur, 'we have not added a shilling to reserve for some years past nor are we likely to be able to do so for several years to come … I regret to say that Charles took an over sanguine view of the profits and divided some that were not earned leaving behind a large accumulation of bad debts and stocks and shares at very inflated prices quite unprovided for. I may also mention that by a mistake the last Michaelmas he was here (1897) he wrote up Consols £10,000 and divided that as additional profit. You will remember that that was the year divided profit came to £48,000.' Consols – consolidated government stocks carrying a fixed rate of interest or annuity – had been the first casualties of the financial depression and, since the Bank had a large holding of them, their loss on this and other securities meant the publication of the Balance Sheet in 1899 had been something of a challenge. It had only been possible, as Harry explained, ' by using all our hidden reserves'.

There was no falling off in the number of accounts but the amount in them was certainly dwindling. Algernon had voiced his concern on the subject: 'I wish we could get new accounts – many of the good old fashioned ones disappear from death and other causes and the new ones are not so profitable. The deposits are down but I suppose that is the case with all Banks.' Richard Rawlinson, who came into the House as a junior clerk in 1888, well remembered some of the more remarkable private accounts of his early career. The best was the Welsh slate baron, Sir Charles Assheton Smith, who regularly kept a balance of nearly £80,000, and old Lord Roberts who 'if he came to look at his account and found the balance had fallen below £5000 he would borrow another £5000 to make it look respectable.' Such men as these were 'a joy to a banker's heart' as were 'the string of old ladies in Ledger 7' with sizeable private incomes which they allowed to accumulate. Arabella North was 'the prize old lady of the early nineties' with an income of £2000 a year and a regular balance of £20,000 in her account.

Letter to Algernon Swinburne, confirming the purchase of consols, 1907.

When Rawlinson first arrived at 37 Fleet Street it was in the days when there was no electric light, no hot water on tap, no telephone and of course no women. The smell of oil lamps still permeated the atmosphere since Hoare's never used gas. During the 1890s they attempted to provide an electricity supply for the Bank using power supplied from their own generator which they installed in the garden in a small building near the plunge bath, engaging an engineer to maintain it. This experiment led to the Bank being threatened with an injunction from their neighbour, the Master of the Temple, who was disturbed day and night by constant noise. The generator was abandoned, the engineer dismissed and the Bank was linked up to the supply from the street. Hot water pipes were not installed until 1918. Clerks and Partners wore white ties and black frock coats and top hats outside the House except for Harry's father, Henry, who always wore a felt hat, and was accused of 'pure swagger' by a disapproving customer for so doing. This remained required dress until the First World War when the arrival of female clerks, to replace the men who had been called up, prompted a reassessment of the rules. Black ties as well as white ones were allowed on account of the increase in the cost of laundry in wartime.

At the same time as the eighth generation of the Hoare family were taking up their positions as junior Partners in the Bank their relations at the Red Lion Brewery in East Smithfield continued to make heavy weather of their business. The 1880s and 1890s were highly competitive times for the brewers who, for the first time, were faced with rival attractions to their public houses. The development of suburban London, the availability of alternative amusement to be found at football matches, music halls and day excursions on the railways and the sales of cheaper bottled beer bought 'off licence' from the grocer's shop threatened the survival of the metropolitan tied houses. In order to attract custom the breweries had invested a great deal of money in the purchase and refurbishment of good houses and when the licensees were unable to make them as profitable as they needed to be, and began to default on the repayment of loans, the owners were in trouble.

To meet the costs of expanding their public house trade Hoare and Co were formed into a limited liability company with capital of £1,600,000. The Bank, under Charles's management, handled the share issue. Three family members, William, Tuppy and their nephew Walter Robertson, remained on the board although in William's case it was not for long. In 1904 his near bankruptcy forced his retirement as Chairman and, though he ascribed his downfall largely to his support of his brother, Henry, the effect of his own insolvency was to wipe thousands of pounds off the value of the Brewery shares at a time when his fellow-directors wished to sell. One or two of his relations who were badly affected went so far as to accuse him of fraud.

The slump in the brewing trade went from bad to worse between 1900-10. Beer consumption fell progressively each year and the Liberal Government, encouraged by the Temperance lobby and driven by the economic legacy of the Boer War, took every opportunity to limit trade and raise taxes through increases in duty and the introduction of licensing laws. The Bank lent considerable sums both to the Brewery and to the individual Directors. In William's case his loans were almost entirely secured by Hoare and Co 'A' Preference and Preference shares, and in making terms with him in 1904 the Bank insisted on retaining control of them, and calling in all Preference stock owned by the other Directors to meet the Brewery's liability to the Bank. By 1908 nearly £2 million had been written off the capital of the Company. The Bank gave up hope that they would ever be repaid and wrote off the remaining £35,050 owed to them as a bad debt. The Brewery continued to keep an account at Fleet Street, but relations between the two family firms were not very cordial and the Bank insisted that a minimum of £5000 should be kept in their account at all times.

During the First World War all breweries suffered from the restrictions on output imposed by Lloyd George, and when normal trading conditions resumed Hoare and Co became one of the players in the merger activity which characterized the brewing industry during the 1920s and 1930s. In 1924 Hoare and Co purchased the Lion Brewery whose principal shareholder and Chairman was Sir John Ellerman. He joined the board of Hoare and Co and devoted his considerable resources to its expansion. With his backing several smaller companies were absorbed until Hoare and Co Ltd grew to a size which, in 1934, attracted the attention of Messrs Charrington of the Anchor Brewery in Mile End. In the subsequent merger the Red Lion Brewery was closed down and all production ceased at East Smithfield. The name of Hoare and Co Ltd passed into history and with it five generations of family management.

The family's connection with Clapham, which dated back to Henry the Magnificent's residence there and William Henry's close friendship with the members of the 'Clapham Sect', was renewed by his brewer grandson William who launched an Appeal in 1891 for the establishment of a home for the dying on the north side of Clapham Common. His wife Laura whose health was not good encouraged him in this endeavour. The home was to be accommodated in one of the large houses built for the gentry in the eighteenth century, similar to the grand villa which Henry had built for himself in the 1750s, when Clapham was a salubrious rural retreat from the smoke and filth of London. By the late nineteenth century the wealthy householders had retreated deeper into the countryside and Clapham was being absorbed by the spreading city with all its attendant problems of overcrowding and ill health. William made clear that there was a desperate need for the establishment of a home to care for those who were dying: 'Hospitals exist for the cure of disease, and if a patient is not curable he must vacate his bed in favour of his more hopeful brother; it must be so. In many cases those who leave hospital with the doom of death ringing in their ears have neither home, nor money nor friend.' For them there was no alternative but the workhouse and the stigma of being labelled a pauper.

In keeping with the charitable tradition established by Good Henry's foundation of Westminster Hospital, the provision of care for the dying was to be free. An Appeal was made for £2000 which was sufficient to meet the cost of buying and refurbishing a suitable house. The home was to be run by an order of Anglican nuns who would provide free nursing services. William, who had some spare money at that time, launched the Appeal with a personal donation of half the required amount. The 'Free Home for the Dying' or 'Hostel of God', as it was better known, soon outgrew its original premises and within a few years of opening it had moved round the corner to its present building on Clapham Common Northside where, renamed as Trinity Hospice, its palliative care for the dying carries on the original purpose of the 1891 Appeal.

From the time of their founder the family had shown an impressive record of commitment and generosity in support of

*Trinity Hospice, Clapham, formerly known as the Hostel of God, founded with an Appeal chaired by William Hoare in 1891.*

philanthropic causes. After his departure from the Bank in 1888 Charlie Arthur's life underwent a complete change, as touched on in the previous chapter. His days of reckless hedonism were behind him and although, from the Bank's point of view he was milking them dry, the profits that he was so anxious to see maximized were entirely devoted to his own good cause, the nautical school HMS Mercury.[3] After seven years' exile on the Isle of Wight, he and Beatie moved the whole enterprise to Hamble, near Southampton, where a safe anchorage and more space on shore allowed for further development of the school. The original intake of boys had been described as 'street arabs of fourteen or fifteen years of age who have vouched for themselves that they are willing to enter the Royal Navy'. They were picked up from the slums of London and quarantined in a cottage in Tooting before being sent to the ship. Their training was free and as well as the rigorous discipline of learning about life on board ship the boys were introduced to gentler skills they had never dreamt of acquiring. Music became an important part of their daily life with every boy given the opportunity to play an instrument, sing in the choir and

Charlie Arthur Hoare's training ship Mercury, c.1888-90, which he converted from a barque into a replica of an early 19th century warship.

even to learn to dance. Under Charlie Arthur's guiding hand the place grew in size and importance and a full tribute was paid to his life's work in his obituary in the *Hants Independent* on 23 May 1908:

> It was as founder of the Mercury that his memory will remain green. The Mercury was his life work, built up bit by bit, plank by plank, if not with his own hands at least at his inspiration. He knew every stone in the place, and every plank in the ship, every animal which roamed the contiguous grounds, the name and note of every bird which sang in the trees. The name and life story of every one of the thousand odd boys who owe more than they know to him were graven on his heart and his memory in turn will never pass from the recollection of those whose first steps in life he directed with such loving care … The value of the Mercury from a national point of view is quite incalculable … 565 Mercury boys have joined the navy, 227 have obtained situations ashore, 141 are helping to push the commercial well-being of England to the front in the Mercantile Marine, 93 have gone into army bands, 11 into the army and 57 into employment on yachts.

Charlie Arthur Hoare, c.1900. After his death his collection of naval artefacts and ship models was acquired as one of the foundation collections of the National Maritime Museum in Greenwich.

Charlie Arthur, who once said, 'If I could see only a single boy out of all the numbers who have passed through here going straight I shall be satisfied,' was more than amply rewarded for his dedication to his boys. But the sacrifice he made in his loyalty to Beatie did not have such a happy outcome. In 1898 C B Fry, one of the greatest all-round sportsmen of his day, arrived to take up the post of

secretary to *HMS Mercury*. Within months he and Beatie, who was ten years his senior, were married. Charlie Arthur removed himself from the scene and went to live at Hall Place in West Meon where he spent the last decade of his life alone. Beatie's defection was not enough to deter him from continuing the work he loved. He never gave up his control of *Mercury* and installed Reggie's younger brother, Wilfred, to manage the ship on his behalf in conjunction with Beatie.

In January 1902 Charlie Arthur and Algernon corresponded over the matter of the Bank's arrangements for viewing Edward VII's Coronation procession as it passed down Fleet Street. In 1897 tiered seating had been provided along the front of the Bank for customers to watch Queen Victoria's Diamond Jubilee procession, but it had caused such worry and expense that the Partners were disinclined to do more for the Coronation than they did for the annual Lord Mayor's Day, which was, allow customers to view events from inside the Bank, with perhaps a 'show of flags and the odd illumination at night'. Charlie Arthur on the other hand thought they should set up seats and charge for them: 'If it worked it would be very

*Two cheques signed and designed by a Bank customer, A Campbell Colquhoun, 1912-1913, one as an oil painting, the other as an embellishment of the Bank's printed form. Stamp duty was charged at one penny; it was abolished in 1971.*

Counterfeit one-pound note 1914–1918. The first small denomination notes in Britain, known as 'Treasury' notes or 'Bradburys', replaced gold sovereigns and were introduced at the outbreak of war to protect the Bank of England's stock of bullion. Wartime inflation led to a great increase in the number of notes including forgeries.

remunerative and I think as times are we can hardly forgo taking such a chance.' If it was necessary to give a reason for the charge to the customer the Bank could say the proceeds were to go to support Mercury which he described as 'our only attempt' at real philanthropic work. Algernon replied most indignantly. No other bank in London would stoop to letting out seating and as for the suggestion that Mercury was 'the only philanthropic institution that we are interested in, we all of us here have some Hospitals or Schools or 'Dwellings' etc in which we individually take an interest'. When Charlie Arthur died, Beatie and C B Fry took charge of his project and even after Beatie's death in 1946, Fry and Sybil Hoare tried to keep Mercury going along the lines Beatie had established. They retired in 1950 but Mercury continued as an ordinary school, with a much reduced nautical element in its curriculum, until, unable to compete in an era of large comprehensives, it was forced to close in 1968.

Arthur was made a sharing Partner in 1908 in place of his elder brother, Charles Hervey. Algernon then retired. The share paid after Charlie Arthur's death to his executors was only half the sum the Bank had been liable for during his lifetime and the profits for 1909 were a satisfactory £36,000. At this point Peter Arthur announced that he wished to be relieved of his duties at Fleet Street and devote his time to his own interests based at Luscombe. He did not wish to retire: he simply did not want to work at the Bank any more. What might have been very unwelcome news for his fellow Partners fortunately did not cause much disquiet on this occasion. Harry's younger brother Edward, who was a qualified solicitor, was invited to take his place at the Bank. Edward had been working in the City since 1890 and his considerable experience was regarded as a great asset. Since all Partners were now paid a salary in addition to their profit share Edward would receive Peter

Arthur's salary and no further expense to the Bank would be incurred.

The difficulty of making decisions when a sharing Partner was absent, which had been a cause of such a trouble in Peter Richard's day, was resolved by a clause in the Partnership Agreement of 1904 which allowed any difference of opinion with regard to the conduct of business to be settled by a majority vote within twenty-four hours. Peter Arthur was entirely happy with the arrangement and wrote cheerfully to Harry on 9 June 1912, 'I hope you are going strong and coining money by the million. Things down here go on very peacefully and no regrets are expressed by yours truly at his arrangement whereby he is not a regular attendant in London weekly.' In September 1912 a third member of the Strickland family entered the firm. Under the new rules each sharing Partner was given the right to nominate one son, to be admitted into the Bank at the age of eighteen, with a view to succeeding him on his death or retirement. Algy who had inherited Algernon's share in 1909, thus nominated his own son, another Algernon conveniently known as 'Tom' who, on his father's retirement in 1923 became the last representative of his family to have a share in his grandmother's family's business.

The new Partnership arrangements had scarcely time to get established before war with Germany was declared on 4 August 1914. Business at the Bank was transformed. Days before war was declared the financial markets had been hit by a rapid selling of securities on the continent. On 30 July the Stock Exchange closed at 10.30 am and there then followed a run on all the banks as people tried to gather in as much gold as they could lay their hands on. The Bank Rate shot up to 10 per cent and the Bank Holiday of Monday 3 August was extended for a period of four days to try and stem the panic. The issue of Treasury notes in one pound and ten shilling denominations, designed to replace gold sovereigns as currency, which was combined with a press campaign to warn the public that hoarding of gold was regarded as unpatriotic, had the effect of restoring confidence and resulted in people returning gold to the banks. According to the Partners' Memorandum Book only two customers, who were not named, made any unusual demands on them and they received, on the contrary, many offers of help should they require it.

*Adding Machine, early 20th century. Tilden recalled 'how the old Duke of Northumberland (the 7th) came behind the counter where Jock Noel showed him how the adding machine worked'.*

Extra demands were made on the Bank as a result of the government issues of War Loan which in addition to National War Bonds, Treasury Bonds and War Savings Certificates put more pressure on the staff of the stock department than they could cope with. To deal with the increased load the Partners' wives and daughters were commandeered to help. Once an effective advertising campaign was under-way the support for the government was impressive and the Bank could report by the end of 1916 that 95 per cent of its total deposits were invested in five per cent War Loan. Each year that passed saw an increasing investment in the war effort: in 1917 customers put over £2 million into War Bonds alone.

The staffing of the Bank changed dramatically during the war. In 1914 Parliament voted an immediate increase in the Army of 500,000 men, and the Territorials were asked to volunteer for service abroad. In September Arthur, Vincent and Tom Strickland joined their regiments and among the clerks, Messrs Charles, Pennington, Mobberley, Humby (who had changed his name from Stoltenhoff), Cockerell, Sparrow and North left for active service.

In February 1915 Vincent was killed in action near Ypres. During the year Harry rejoined his Yeomanry regiment and five more clerks, Messrs Bennett, Newton, Fleming, Vidler and Williams, and a porter, Mr Blackshaw, volunteered. In 1917 Mr Charles, who had been granted a Commission and was mentioned in Dispatches, was killed in action. Mobberley, Fleming and Vidler all lost their lives in 1918. After Harry's departure Frederick was taken into the Partner's Room to assist but the responsibility for keeping things going rested with Edward and Alfred with help from Philip and from Algy, though less from him since he was ill for most of 1915.

From February 1916 there was conscription for men of military age who were fit for service; the age was raised to fifty-one in March 1918 to counter the final German offensive in France. Consequently the process of recruiting lady clerks, to replace those who were fighting overseas, which had begun in 1914, was carried on until 1918. It was always intended that their positions were to be tem-porary. Those clerks who were in the armed forces had their military pay supplemented by the Bank in their absence. In 1917 Tom Strickland was taken pris-oner by the Turks in Egypt. At about the same time, Harry was transferred to the Territorial Free Reserve and was able to return to business until he was appointed as Milk Controller to the Ministry of Food in April 1918. Arthur, having been invalided home in 1917, took up several posts, first with the Financial Censor, then as Range Officer on Salisbury Plain and finally as 'Instructor of Yeomanry to Heavy Batteries'. In November 1918 Philip died in a hunting accident.

Peter's 'little arrangement' with Edward managed to survive the pressures of wartime, although Peter was asked to come to London to help out on occasion. Edward's contribution to the business throughout the war was exceptional. If it hadn't been for his constant presence, in Algy's words, 'it would have been impos-sible for Messrs Hoare to give either HH [Harry] or AHH [Arthur] leave of absence to join the forces.' In 1915 he was rewarded with a special grant of £400 for his extra work, 'notwithstanding our previous resolution that his admission should not in any event put the Bank to expense'. It was given to him at a time when there was virtually nothing to spare. The sharp fall in the value of all securities reduced profits to an all-time low. The sums to be divided for 1914 and 1915 were £8400 and £7800 which, after the deductions paid to the executors of Charlie Arthur and Algernon who had died in January 1914, left only £1346 each for Peter, Harry, Arthur and Algy. In these circumstances Peter Arthur was faced with the difficulty of keeping Luscombe open and, as he explained to Edward, his dilemma had important implications for the Bank:

> Of course it may not appear of importance to any of you at the Bank whether I sack all the servants and shut this place entirely or not, and if I did this I should try and find some small place out of the district where I should try to live as cheaply as possible until things improve, but the point is if I do it would be absolutely certain to cause a great deal of gossip connecting my name with the Bank which in these times would probably grow into entirely foolish rumours with regard to the position of the Bank which would be the particular thing I wish to avoid … if only people around here didn't jaw so much about other people's affairs and I was not connected with the old family bank it would be far simpler to cut down wages etc.

It was not only a shortage of money that was causing difficulty; human resources were likewise stretched to the limit. After Vincent's death the Partners decided, without hesitation, to pay a pension of £1000 to his widow who was left with five children. They forgot to consult Peter over this and he complained to Edward, 'I was only a post away and a 1d stamp would have at least advised me of an important proposal such as that. Under yours and my excellent arrangement you will remember that though I gave up my salary I did not give up my rights as a Partner in the Bank.' Edward took the blame entirely upon himself but asked for a little understanding: 'The only thing that I can plead is that owing to Algy's continued illness and Harry and Arthur away fighting yours very truly with his uncle (Alfred) have been kept with their noses to the proverbial grindstone with very little time to call their souls their own.'

At the end of the war Tom returned unharmed and, after demobilization, the majority of those clerks who had survived returned to their posts. Although the ladies were still needed, the Partners remained committed to their original intention of gradually replacing them with men.

The experience of the First World War had shut the door on the old world order. The Bank had been forced to adapt and innovate to meet the demands of a country in crisis, and, although the return to peacetime conditions facilitated the return to many of the pre-war routines at Fleet Street, it had to come to terms with its own losses. The testing financial circumstances of a high-tax post-war economy combined with an active labour movement would increase its sense of vulnerability. Ways had to be found to maintain its position.

CHAPTER EIGHT

# KEEPING INDEPENDENT; SURVIVING THE BLITZ 1919–1945

The return of peace encouraged a period of short-lived economic prosperity in the country and a high level of welfare spending by Lloyd George's coalition government, largely financed by an increase in direct taxation. Income tax had increased fivefold from the rate of six per cent at the beginning of the war and a super tax had been introduced on incomes over £2000. When the boom quickly turned to slump the country was faced with a sharp increase in the cost of living. Higher prices and rates of taxation meant that the Partners had to address the issue of financial hardship among the staff and with it the inevitable realization that employment costs were likely to escalate rapidly in the near future.

To meet any immediate need they granted a one-off 'war bonus' to all staff, calculated on the price of certain commodities and the size of the employee's family, but in October 1919 a new salary scheme, affecting all staff, including the separate category of 'Ladies', was introduced. The structure remained the same as the one introduced in 1899 and, as before, promotion from one grade to the next still depended on a vacancy rather than on merit alone, and longevity of service continued to be the norm. However, each of the three clerical grades was awarded a further annual increment and an increase in the top rate for each class. Ladies (of whom there were fourteen employed in the Bank) were officially graded as 'Class II' but paid at the rate of a Class III clerk, a grade which paid a maximum of £200 per annum. Promotion to Class I was possible and it was recommended that Miss E Smith should, by special arrangement pass into this category automatically, but the salary would be paid at the rate of a Class II clerk and thus her entitlement, at the top level, would have been £400, £200 less than her male colleagues in Class I. Pensions for ladies were also introduced in 1919 but in most cases this was rather an academic benefit. The Bank did not undertake to pay them

facing page

*The lantern tower of St Dunstan's lit up by fire during an air raid on Fleet Street in 1944.*

*Edward Hoare,*
*by T C Dugdale.*

to anyone who had been in their service for less than forty years and, since none of the lady clerks had managed more than five years and, in any case, had to retire on marriage, the prospect of there being a significant number of female pensioners was remote. This anomaly was not corrected until fifteen years later when the pensionable age for women was reduced to fifty.

On the whole ladies were encouraged to leave as a matter of policy, to create vacancies for ex-officers who were seeking a job after demobilization, and they were disbarred from jobs which involved close association with the public such as Cashiers, which were reserved for the senior men. Whatever the rules regarding pensions there was always room for exceptions to be made, as with Miss Pratt who had virtually run the Income Tax department throughout the war. In 1921 her health broke down and she felt obliged to resign. Harry was genuinely sad to see her depart: 'Not only shall we all miss you very much but so I feel will many of our customers who I think had got to look upon you as their special friend.' He offered her a 'special annuity' of £200 per annum 'for as long as you are unable to obtain and undertake work again'.

Pay remained an issue after the 1919 award. Edward wrote to Peter Arthur at Luscombe in April 1921 informing him that the Partners had received a signed application, 'from all the men clerks for a rise in salary to bring them up nearer to the scale now paid to clerks in Joint Stock Banks', despite a cost-of-living bonus of 30 per cent having been paid in June 1920. (Single ladies without a household to maintain were presumably considered to be unaffected by inflation.) A further 23 per cent on their 1919 salaries was agreed to, which Edward informed Peter Arthur would cost the Bank precisely £2900 6s 0. In addition the Porters were given a bonus and Fred and Tom an increase in salaries to £1250 and £1000. In reply Peter Arthur made the point that these extra charges on the business would be largely offset by the amount which had been paid to the executors of Algernon out of the profits and which would now cease, seven years after his death in January 1914. Peter Arthur added the gloomy forecast that he was unlikely to see any reduction in taxation in his lifetime, which proved to be correct and, even though a slow economic recovery halted the progress of inflation, the Partners continued to grant annual bonuses to the staff throughout the 1920s to ease the burden of income tax.

Profits had recovered from the alarmingly low figures of the early war years but for the decade 1917-1927 they remained more or less static at the pre-war level of a division of around £36,000, except for a dip in 1921. Arthur, Harry and Edward continued to run the Bank in partnership with Tom, Alfred and Algy, whose delicate health kept him away from Fleet Street more than he would have chosen.

In 1920 Peter Arthur proposed that his son, Peter William, should enter the Bank which at once revived an old argument among the Partners as to whether they considered him eligible to come as a raw recruit, in his case straight out of the army, without first obtaining a university education. Arthur was quite clear in his mind that he didn't regard the young man as educated and recommended that his father should be told that 'fit and willing', as pre-conditions for Partnership, meant rather more than willingness to stick to business and being 'punctual and regular and reasonably sensible about his personal expenditure'. But Peter Arthur's contention that his son had much more experience of life, acquired in the trenches during the last two or three years, 'than men ten years older than him would have had the chance of getting previous to the war', coupled with Peter William's evident enthusiasm to get down to work straightaway, won the argument; so he came to the Bank as a probationer aged twenty-two. Three years later he was joined by Harry's eldest son, Rennie, on his graduation from Cambridge. These young men were, as Harry put it, 'left to themselves to work out their own salvation', and it was during this period when they were learning the business that the senior generation were giving serious thought to the wisdom of carrying on the Bank as an independent concern.

For nearly three decades following the retirement of Charlie Arthur in 1888 the Bank had been handicapped by the financial arrangements they were compelled to make with him at the time of his 'dismissal'. As late as 1915, at the end of the seven-year period following his death, when they expected to be clear of all financial obligations to his estate, Beatie and her two children by Charlie Arthur brought a claim against the Bank for further payment which, largely to avoid more trouble and expense, was settled in her favour.[1]

In 1920 a proposal was made to Algy by Vesey Holt of Holt's Bank. He outlined a scheme whereby Child's, Drummond's, Hoare's and Holt's private banks should amalgamate and between them maintain offices at Charing Cross, Fleet Street and possibly the City. Holt's idea was not greeted with much enthusiasm by Lord Jersey at Child's, nor by Algy who reported to Holt: 'Harry Hoare does not feel at all attracted by a scheme of amalgamation. His view with which I agree is that our business is very largely a personal one and this personal influence would be to an extent lost by an amalgamation which loss would only be compensated for by a very large increase of capital and this would not occur in such an amalgamation as is suggested ... We should be losing our independence without acquiring any real additional strength'.

MESSRS HOARE BANKERS

*Bearer Bond, 1919, with dividend coupons and coupon cutter. All stock certificates and bearer bonds were held by the 'Coupon Room', staffed by the family. Their main job was lending the Bank's money on the money markets.*

Although Holt's particular scheme did not develop, the idea of amalgamation was not buried for long. In 1923 Holt's joined Glyn Mills to whom Hoare's soon afterwards transferred their clearing business, being dissatisfied with the over-lent position of their previous bankers, William Deacon's. Lesley Hine of Glyn's wrote to Harry to ask if Hoare's would care to come in with them but received the same reply, that Hoare's preferred to remain as they were. Drummond's were acquired by the Royal Bank of Scotland the following year. Child's were undecided and it was rumoured that they would be bought by Lloyds, although Hoare's were perceived by many in private banking circles, as well as by themselves, as being the natural partners for Child's and indeed came very close to settling with them. In 1924 Mr Fane, the General Manager at Child's, approached the Partners with the suggestion that Hoare's should absorb their business. He met with a very favourable response and the two Banks were preparing for definite negotiations. But then came the unwelcome news that the executors of Lord Jersey had amalgamated Child's with Glyn Mills without letting Mr Fane know that they had even thought of doing so.[2] After the approach by Child's came to nothing, Hoare's remained as the only private bank in London. It was a position which was not particularly advantageous to them in the uncertain economic climate of the 1920s, but in 1923 it had given them the distinction of achieving 250 years of continuous operation as an independent family-run business.

The anniversary prompted unprecedented press coverage, which brought it to the attention of the King. A letter of congratulation arrived from York Cottage, Sandringham, addressed to the Partners and written by the Royal Equerry, conveying a message from King George V: 'His Majesty feels that this record must be unique among the great banking houses in the City of London and desires me to convey to you his congratulation on the past history of the Bank and his sincere good wishes for its continued prosperity in the future.' The occasion was modestly commemorated at Fleet Street by the purchase of cases to display the Bank's collection of old coins and paper money. Several years later Lancelot Bennet began to create the first museum. He had retired as Head of Books in 1931 and, having married late in life, was given this post-retirement job at the age of sixty-five to help pay for his children's school fees. His main task was to catalogue all the customer names from the Bank's old ledgers but he was also charged with rationalizing the coin collection by arranging suitable exchanges and purchases with Spinks, principally in order to achieve a complete set of gold coins going back to 1673, the year of Sir Richard Hoare's foundation. The scheme was partially sabotaged by the abdication of Edward VIII in 1937 when it was noted by the Partners, with some disappointment, that there would be an interruption in the sequence of the collection since no coins were issued during his brief reign, other than some 'colonial coins of small value of which we were fortunately able to secure a few specimens'.

In 1925 Alfred left the Bank, at the age of seventy-five, in circumstances which must have been acutely embarrassing for his family if not, it seems, for him. He was caught by a policeman with a prostitute in Hyde Park and was charged under the Sexual Offences Act. The following day he had to appear before the Magistrate. In the light of the adverse publicity which was bound to follow Harry felt obliged to ask for his resignation, and recorded for posterity Alfred's explanation to him for his behaviour: 'Well it was just a perfect summer's evening and just the perfect place to do it.' Until then he had been working four days a week at the Bank, which nevertheless left him time for his voluntary work and the study of economic theory which replaced Italian as his intellectual hobby once the Dictionary was completed. He was elected to the council of the Royal Economic Society where he met J M Keynes with whom he corresponded until his death in 1938. His last letter to him, at the age of eighty-seven, was on the subject of Keynes's 'General theory of Employment'. Keynes wrote Alfred's obituary for The Economic Journal and in it he made reference to Hoare's Bank, 'now run by the ninth generation' as 'uncomplicated by branches, unseduced by amalgamations, undisturbed by any process of change, unshaken by financial crises of two and a half centuries, being put to no hazard by excessive ambitions or too much guessing'. He mourned the passing of Alfred as representing the departure of an 'old and beloved civilization' and warned that now could be heard 'the barbarians at the gate'.

The return to the gold standard in 1925, ordered by the Conservative Chancellor of the Exchequer, Winston Churchill, which at once overvalued the pound and prompted a rapid downturn in Britain's export trade, marked the begin-

*The Bank's first museum in the Saloon at 37 Fleet Street, c.1935. It had been used as a billiard room until after the First World War.*

ning of the nation's slide into Depression. The lowering of wages led to a nine-day General Strike in May 1926 when members of the Bank staff joined thousands of volunteers who took over running London's key services, working as tram drivers, 'motor constables', 'gate men on the Tube railways', and production workers on the government newspaper.[3] Meanwhile both the Bank and its customers were locked into a system of falling markets and low bank rates and found that very little return could be made on their money.

Tom Strickland had been a Partner for five years when the sad news came in 1928 that his father, Algy, had died in Jamaica while on a cruise to the West Indies, which he had undertaken in an effort to restore his strength. By then, Rennie and Peter William, having served their time learning the business, had qualified themselves to become Sharing Partners and their simultaneous arrival in the Partners Room on 5 April 1928 was an event which was particularly pleasing for their fathers. Harry and Peter Arthur had become great friends during their early days at the Bank and they were gratified to see that their sons enjoyed a similar relationship with one another. Peter Arthur wrote to Harry on this point on 3 January 1928 from Luscombe: 'I fully agree with your remark that our respective sons have the same real friendship for each other as did their two parents, and if our Co-partners will agree to this entering of our two sons at the same time and upon the same terms, I think it will be an excellent thing for the future amicable working of the Partnership and the business.'

In September, to the great relief of his widowed mother, Vincent's son Quintin was taken on as an Agent. His arrival was particularly welcomed by Frederick who, hitherto, had been fully responsible for the sleeping duty, which included weekends, unlocking and locking up each day and the opening of the morning post. The probationer Partners took a share of these duties, as would any one of the Partners who happened to be sleeping at the Bank, but only if specifically asked to do so; 'otherwise, not knowing, he might change his plans'. For the junior member of the family 'taking the keys' involved a curfew, and 2 am was set as the latest time he could return to the Bank after a night out. For all other staff sleeping in, the Bank's doors were locked at 11 pm.[4]

The two new Partners had scarcely been installed a year before a change in the organization of the firm brought an end to the Bank as a Partnership. For thirty years the possibility of forming themselves into a Company to keep in line with their joint stock competitors had been, unofficially, on the Partners' agenda, but they were prevented from taking action until they were rid of the incubus of Charlie Arthur's

claim on the profits and his half ownership of the freehold. His death and the ensuing seven-year commitment to his estate coincided with the First World War which further postponed the issue. The first formal mention of the possibility of making new arrangements had appeared in the Partnership Agreement of 1904, when reference was made to amalgamating or winding up the business and this particular clause was amplified in the subsequent Agreement of 1925 when specific mention was made of the fact that there was nothing to prevent the Sharing Partners from selling, or converting the business into a limited or unlimited liability company. The real impetus for incorporation was taxation and, since the introduction of Estate Duty in 1894, the Partners had been increasingly concerned to see that their capital in the Bank was protected. Once super tax was introduced, which was payable on the income from money placed to reserve, conversion from a Partnership to a Company became even more of an imperative.

On 5 July 1929 C. Hoare and Co was registered as a Private Company with unlimited liability. The Partners made over a part of their previously owned private capital to the Company, to form part of its reserves, and retained for themselves merely the shares in the Company to the value of £120,000 between them. Published paid up 'Capital and Reserves' amounted to £500,000. The Partners then became the sole Shareholders and Directors of the new Company, but in the Articles of Association they retained the description of themselves as Partners (or, more specifically, Managing Partners) and continued to be referred to as such in the interests of minimizing unnecessary changes and maintaining the manner in which they had always run the business.

In addition to the transfer of capital, a few important alterations were made to the existing Partnership Deed, such as the formal abandonment of the provision that the estates of deceased partners were entitled to receive a half share of their profits and salary for seven years after death. This practice had lapsed in 1921 after the obligation to Algernon's estate had been discharged and it was now replaced by a fixed annuity, based on the number of shares held, and paid as an 'honourable undertaking' and not as a legal liability. A deceased Partner's shares were sold at par to his nominee or failing that to the other Partners, and succession within the family was secured by the continuation of the tradition that the rights of nomination were restricted to 'one son or other male relative being a

*Algernon W Strickland, known as 'Tom'. The third and last member of his family to be made a Partner, he died in 1938 aged forty-seven. Posthumous portrait by Colin Corfield.*

descendant of any then or former Sharing Partner'. The style of the firm, C. Hoare and Co, remained the same. A circular letter was sent out to customers in which they were reassured that there would be no alteration whatever in the management or conduct of the Bank and that all the existing Partners will 'continue to give their personal attention to the Business', their liability for its engagements being, as at present, unlimited'. Shortly afterwards the Bank published its first Balance Sheet in its new form and its altered status was said to have been 'kindly and sympathetically noticed by the Public Press'.

The new Company set about celebrating its quiet achievement in ways designed to appeal to its customers. Plans were started to open a branch in Park Lane for the convenience of their West End residential customers. Another grandson of Henry of Staplehurst, William and Laura's son, Geoffrey Lennard, who already had a number of other business interests, was taken on specifically as 'Local Managing Partner' in charge of the new enterprise. In 1932, Rennie, who had taken a very active role in supervising Mr Bennet's work in the Bank archives, produced the first history of Hoare's Bank which was sent to all customers, many of whom, in their letters of thanks, were able to shed further light on the history of the relationships between the Bank and their families.

After nearly a hundred years some work was needed in the 'new' premises to bring them up to date and certain alterations were pressing. Among them was the need for a larger and more secure Strong Room and more space for staff dealing with Income Tax. The principal requirement, however, was for a separate department to house the newly fledged Company, 'Messrs Hoare Trustees', whose business, acting as trustees and executors for customers, had begun during the War at a time when the Partners couldn't cope with such demands being made on them personally, and had then increased considerably throughout the 1920s. These changes involved the Partners. Rather reluctantly they had to vacate their old room leading off the Shop.

In 1929 Sir Herbert Baker, recently knighted for his services to architecture and currently engaged on the rebuilding of Soane's Bank of England in Threadneedle Street, was commissioned to produce designs for the new Strong Room and Partners' Room. The latter was a splendid and spacious oak panelled room built as a single story extension to Charles Parker's building and tucked discreetly away at the back of the premises overlooking the courtyard, away from the bustle of the daily traffic in and out of the Bank and the telephone box which stood in the middle of the Shop feet away from the entrance to their old room. A new passage leading from the foot of the main staircase connected the new Room with the front door onto Fleet Street, and thus there was no longer any necessity for the Partners to pass through the public area of the Bank once they were inside the lobby. The old 'Back Room', which Peter Richard had occupied in his reclusive old age, and which his grandson described as the Partners' 'holy of holies',

was replaced with another, which served the same purpose and led directly out of the new Room. A new 'Coupon Room' (which derived its name from the arcane custom of tearing off coupons from bearer bonds for the payment of dividends) was constructed, again leading directly out of the Partners' Room, on the side opposite to the Back Room. The Coupon Room was connected by a staircase to the Strong Room below to which the Agents held the keys.

Sleeping accommodation still occupied two floors of the Bank with seven bedrooms on the second floor, used by the family, and eleven staff bedrooms carved out of the space on the attic floor. The kitchens, storerooms, wine cellar, porters' room and steward's office and all the service areas were in the basement along with the clerks' sitting room and canteen. This left the Bank's office accommodation confined to the ground floor and three floors in the Warehouse, a rather makeshift building on the western side of the courtyard opposite the new Partners' Room. After the Second World War major refurbishment was necessary which provided the opportunity to dispense with the pre-Victorian domestic arrangements. The Warehouse was demolished and was replaced by a permanent block of offices which also contained a staff canteen, a recreation room and the kitchens, which were now, more conveniently, on the same level as the Partners' Dining Room.

The year 1929 was also the year that a minority Labour Government came into office, followed six months later by the collapse of the American economy, which had a profound effect worldwide. The Partners reported that the Stock Exchange was practically at a standstill for six months following the Wall Street crash, and the fall in trade and reduction in prices sent the unemployment figures soaring. Having failed to deal with the crisis, the Labour Prime Minister, Ramsay MacDonald, was obliged to form a coalition with the Opposition, and in 1931 the voters returned a Conservative-dominated National Government to power with a remit to reduce the enormous budget deficit. Cuts in public spending and wages and an increase in the rates of income tax only succeeded in contributing to further unemployment, and it was not until the Government finally sanctioned the abandonment of the gold standard that the value of the pound dropped and conditions improved enough to allow for a revival in export trade.

Inevitably the crisis was accompanied by a heavy fall in the value of British Government securities and

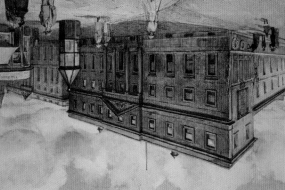

top
*The actress Mrs Patrick Campbell, c.1895, a customer of the Bank.*

below
*The Royal Mineral Hospital, Bath – watercolour by Samuel Poole. The hospital opened its account at Hoare's on its foundation in 1737 and maintained it until it became a National Health hospital in 1948.*

in the year ending 1932 most of the Bank's profits were utilized in making good the losses on their investments. This left them with only a few thousand pounds to carry forward and they had to 'trust that such a thing would never happen again'. It gave them a certain bleak satisfaction to note that the joint stock banks were in an even worse position since, in order to pay a dividend to their shareholders, they had to dig deep into their hidden and published reserves. Although measures introduced by the National Government restored confidence generally and the Bank was able to take advantage of the steady appreciation in the value of British Securities, the whole experience contributed further to the lingering unease they felt about continuing as an independent business.

The Partners were convinced that it was only a matter of time before another Labour Government was elected and with it, presumably, would come a fulfilment of its manifesto promise to nationalize the banks. If this was going to happen, the argument ran, a sale now would pre-empt any forced purchase and pay the Partners a better price than they were likely to get from the Government. In 1931 approaches were made by two large joint stock banks, the Union Bank of Scotland and the Royal Bank of Scotland, who were keen to expand their business-es in London. But neither made anything approaching an offer. One of the conditions that the Partners felt very strongly about was that the name, C. Hoare and Co, should be retained after a sale or amalgamation, and in the case of the Union Bank of Scotland it was this insistence on preserving the family name that Harry judged to be the reason their interest in the Bank evaporated.

The Partners were not of one mind over the best course to take. Harry did not wish to do anything that might give the impression that the Bank was asking to be 'gobbled up'. He really didn't see that amalgamation was a way to attract more accounts in the short term and, given that the Banks under consideration had their head offices in Glasgow and Edinburgh, he couldn't imagine the attraction of spending two nights in the train every week to attend board meetings at which they were likely to be treated as 'insignificant offspring and told we mustn't do this and mustn't do that'. If anyone was a natural partner it would be Glyn's but there were important implications regarding death duties which would have to be addressed and, as he wrote to Peter Arthur, amalgamation should only be considered 'when we have had a normal or good year not when the year has been one of the worst on record'. He lamented mistakes made in the past, especially during the Charles Algernon Strickland regime' when they divided 'too lavishly' rather than paying themselves a modest dividend in year out, which would have given them another '40,000 or 50,000 in the box' now. On a rough calculation he valued the Bank at just over a million pounds, and in his judgement the Partners should wait and see how profitable the new branch at Park Lane proved to be over the next few years. However, should it come to negotiating an amalgamation,' we must abandon all hope of perpetuating our name ... other than as Hoare's branch

of so and so … for our figures are too insignificant'.

By 1934 the Bank's assets had recovered their value and were showing a marked surplus over their liabilities. Arthur was convinced that it was a propitious moment to sell and strongly argued his case in an open letter to his Partners. He didn't believe that it was in their best interests to allow the Bank to continue as it was. They had just recovered from a severe financial crisis but the inevitable return to power of the Labour Party would be sure to trigger another fall in the value of investments and, whatever figure the Partners managed to accumulate as hidden reserves over the next few years, it could not possibly be enough to make good any shortfall. Moreover,' with an absolute majority over all other parties one must contemplate that they will endeavour, without doubt, to nationalize the banks'. It would be inconceivable that Hoare's Bank would be allowed to continue as the only bank in England not under a Government department, but should the inconceivable happen, they could not possibly compete with the rates which the Labour Party had indicated the Government would offer once in control of banking countrywide. He was sure that any bank to whom they sold their business would take on at least two of the Partners as directors and this would be a great advantage with regard to his main proposal.

His idea was to form an investment trust company constituted along the same lines as C. Hoare and Co,' with regard to Capital, Dividends, Directors' Fees, Management and appointment of new Directors', and then sell the Banking and Trustee businesses, for which they would be paid partly in shares by the purchasing bank which would enable at least two of the Partners to take up Directorships. The new trust company would be domiciled in the Channel Islands or anywhere where income tax was low and death duties could be avoided. Without the need to publish a balance sheet there would be no necessity to make provision for a depreciation in securities. If the Bank stayed as it was, it would be effectively ruined by a Labour Government who would pay a rock-bottom price for its assets. But if those assets were safely transferred to a trust company, set up as he described, then the family business could continue and he urged his cousins to see that it was 'our duty and privilege to take this decisive step not only in our own interest but in the interest of our family and of our descendants born and unborn'. Harry remained firmly against touting around for a purchaser. As he con-

top
Deed boxes in the vaults of Hoare's Bank photographed by Country Life in 1956.

above
Searching the shelves of ledgers, dating back to 1673, which were kept in the 'Books' department. Press photograph taken in 1938.

fided to Peter Arthur, who had shown some interest in the trust company scheme,' putting out feelers … would do irreparable harm to the growth of our business which is already showing signs of popularity in several directions and we should certainly have to put an end to trying to push our Trust business which would come to an end ipso facto by a sale of the business. … These actions always leak out and if they did we might at once lose some of our more important accounts at the present time.' Harry had no wish to live the life of a tax exile, and would rather stay in England, pay his taxes and do his job. He was not easy with the idea of 'a hole and corner arrangement to dodge taxes'. In his opinion if there was to be a sale it must be a straightforward affair with the recognition that all liabilities for death duties for this and successive generations must be faced. The sale of the Bank would in itself be the end of the Hoare family,' for death duties and bad investments without the necessity of having to make good Capital loss-es out of income will very soon wipe out everything'.

He was supported by Rennie who agreed that they would be far better off in the job at which their family had proved they could excel. Rennie was uncon-vinced by Arthur's apocalyptic vision of the future Socialist state and by his suggested measures designed to protect the family's capital. He replied to Arthur's proposal in great detail concluding with the thought: 'I would say that in my opinion the heritage which has been handed down to us by our predecessors is not simply so many thousands a year income, [but rather] the privilege of having a job whereby we can be of service to other people which at the same time is pleasant to perform and not poorly rewarded in this world's goods.' No agreement was reached in 1934 but Arthur did not let the matter rest for long. The possibi-lity of making an approach to the Royal Bank of Scotland, through a friend of his, was revived in 1938, with Tom Strickland, Peter Arthur and Peter William all expressing their support. Harry's position, however, remained the same; the dis-turbing events in Germany, effectively put all speculation about the future of the Bank into abeyance.

Meanwhile at Stourhead Sir Henry Hoare and his wife Lady Alda had also been struggling to come to terms with an equally uncertain future. Henry Hugh Arthur Hoare, born in 1865, had inherited both the baronetcy and Stourhead on the death of his first cousin Henry Ainslie, the 5th baronet, in 1894. Although the Bank and Stourhead had been formally separated under the will of Henry the Magnificent, family relationships between the Banker Hoares and their Wiltshire cousins remained strong. While the Partners might enjoy the hunting and shooting, for the incumbent at Stourhead there were obvious benefits in the readily available finan-cial facilities. The 'old mortgage' of £25,000 raised on Stourhead, which was set up by Colt Hoare with his half brother Henry Hugh, had changed hands several times within the family. After Henry Hugh's death it passed to his executors (his four co-Partners: two brothers and two sons) and thence to his nephew Peter Richard.

During the difficult times of the agricultural depression in the 1870s and 1880s the 5th baronet sold off many of the great treasures of Stourhead. Notable losses were: Turner's *Lake Avernus* and his watercolours of Salisbury, Poussin's *Rape of the Sabines*, Francis Nicholson's paintings of the gardens at Stourhead, and Richard Colt Hoare's magnificent library of British topography. The proceeds from these heirloom sales were sufficient to reduce the 'old mortgage' substantially, but there still remained a shortfall in the income of the estate, aggravated by the difficulties of letting and by falling rents, and the Bank was ready to assist further. In 1887 Charles took on a new mortgage of £45,000, secured on the extensive disentailed estates, and as a result, when Sir Henry and Lady Hoare arrived to take up residence at Stourhead in 1895 they found the estate in reasonable shape, although the house and pleasure grounds had suffered from being virtually abandoned for nearly a decade while Sir Henry Ainslie chose to live his last years shuttling between France and London. There was much work to be done and the young couple resolutely embarked on a lifetime of improvement. On the outbreak of war in 1914 their only son and heir, Henry Colt, who had been born at Wavendon in 1888 and on whom so much depended, enlisted in the Dorset Yeomanry. He fought at Gallipoli in 1915 but became critically ill with typhoid and double pneumonia the following year. He pulled through, only to be fatally wounded in Palestine in 1917 where he died just before Christmas and was buried in the military cemetery in Alexandria.

Stourhead then took on a new significance for his grief-stricken parents who now regarded their work there as a memorial to him, and its preservation became a cause as dear to them as had been the life of their only child. In his anxiety to find a solution which would give him an absolute assurance that Stourhead would survive unaltered, Sir Henry's first thought was to bequeath it to the Bank, to be used by the Partners as a country retreat and sporting estate. His particular wish was that it should be occupied by an individual Partner at any one time. A principal consideration in any scheme was the avoidance of death duties, which had recently been increased in scale, and it seemed inevitable that the estate, if it remained in the family in the way Sir Henry suggested, would be whittled away to virtually nothing by charges levied on the estates of any of the individual Partners who had taken up occupation of Stourhead. Since Sir Henry was determined that his gift should not carry with it any power of disposal, Harry's opinion, that the whole idea was impractical from the Bank's point of view, was shared by his Partners, with one exception.

Arthur, characteristically, took a different line. He particularly liked the idea of Stourhead coming into the Partnership, telling Sir Henry: 'I am very nearly as keen as you are to preserve Stourhead in its integrity ... and if it can be found possible to keep it as a family possession it would be a greater matter than if it became the possession of the National Trust.' He devised a scheme which would drastically

reduce Sir Henry's liability for Estate Duty and guarantee him an adequate income. He proposed that Sir Henry should hand over his investment capital to Harry, Algy and himself who would undertake to pay him and Alda an annuity for their lives. In order to avoid death duties Sir Henry would have no legal right to recover his capital although of course he would have the word of the Partners that they would return it on his request. The agreement had to remain 'an honourable undertaking' only. As he explained in a letter written, on 5 May 1925: 'all that you would have would be our absolute promise, this is all any of us have among ourselves and all there has ever been in the history of the Bank, these promises have always been carried out both in the letter and the spirit. But Sir Henry was not prepared to surrender his capital and his independence. He had been 'told by his friends

*Sir Henry Hoare, 6th Bt., in his electric wheelchair at Stourhead, c.1940. After his death in 1946 the house and the pleasure grounds passed to the National Trust.*

that he would be a fool to do so' and he was worried that Alda (who was five years older than him) might be left in a difficult situation should he predecease her. He was disappointed with the Bank's demurring over terms and conditions; he thought that they were looking a gift horse in the mouth.

On his sixtieth birthday Sir Henry took Alda on a visit to Bryanston in Dorset, which was being sold by the Portman family, and he was much moved by what he saw. The whole contents was being offered for sale by auction and he told Arthur that the visit had impressed on him the absolute necessity of reaching a definite conclusion: 'In [the Sale] are included family portraits, photos of the family and most of the late man's intimate personal effects. It brought home to me what may happen when we are gone.' He now made one last attempt at a settlement whereby he should give Stourhead to the Bank, absolutely, and if they decided to sell it, the proceeds should go to a particular hospital (Edward VII's was suggested) or a list of hospitals of his choice. Sir Henry's view of this being a great gift of his lifetime's work to the Partners was regarded in a rather different light by them. They saw themselves as being made mere custodians of a property over which they had no control and, while it might provide a very pleasurable existence for those concerned while the going was good, it could equally end up being an encumbrance.

Both sides were thoroughly disheartened that discussions had ended in failure. Algy, not being in the heart of the family, was less involved, but Arthur, who was himself childless, always had an intense interest in maintaining family succession, and he minded a great deal, not least because his own scheme had been rejected. Harry took a broader view and recognized that they were all facing impossible odds in trying to keep Stourhead in private hands 'in these days when you have the whole legislative force of the nation, Conservative,

*The young Henry Hoare looking down at Fleet Street, c.1935. He became a Partner in 1959, and has spent more than fifty years working for the Bank.*

Liberals and Socialists alike, conspiring to make it impossible to continue in the ownership of valuable properties'. He suggested that the only possible way Sir Henry would get what he wanted would be to leave it to the nation though he didn't think they would keep it for very long 'on account of its distance from any big town'.

Sir Henry's other considered option was that he should leave the property to the National Trust, but he had not given up his wish that at least some part of the great estate should be retained for the family. By 1938 he had reached a compromise which satisfied him. He decided to give the house and grounds, with 3000 acres to support them, to the National Trust. At that time the Trust owned half-a-dozen historic houses and 75,000 acres. Their historic buildings secretary, James Lees-Milne, who had been invalided out of the army, visited Stourhead on 12 October 1942 in order to talk over Sir Henry's offer. He left an unforgettable description of the twenty-four hours he spent with the eccentric, elderly couple in his diaries, *Ancestral Voices*, which he published in 1975.

Sir Henry is an astonishing nineteenth-century John Bull, hobbling on two sticks. He was wearing a pepper and salt suit and a frayed billycock over his purple face ... Lady Hoare is an absolute treasure, and unique. She is tall, ugly and eighty-two ... She has a protruding square coif of frizzly grey hair in the style of the late nineties, black eyebrows and the thickest spectacles I have ever seen ... [they] took me round the house, which is packed to the brim with good things, and some ghastly things like cheap bamboo cake stands and thin silver vases filled with peacock's feathers ... [at dinner] he spoke very little, and that little addressed to himself. She kept up a lively and not entirely coherent prattle ... [the following morning] Sir Henry gets into his electric chair, and I accompany him to the lakes and temples; or rather I gallop at break neck speed behind him. He keeps saying "Where are you? Why don't you say something?" When I do catch up I am so out of breath I can't get the words out. All he says (to himself) is, "I don't understand what has come over the boy" ... They are the dearest old couple. I am quite in love with her out-spoken ways and funny old-fashioned dress.

To retain an element of family ownership Sir Henry left the remaining 2215 acres to the relation in the Bank whom he considered to be his most suitable heir.

His choice fell on Rennie who had a young son, Henry, born in 1931. The transfer of ownership was finally made in 1946 and on Lady Day, the following year, Sir Henry and Lady Alda both died, extraordinarily within hours of one another, and Rennie brought his growing family to live in the house at Stourhead. Although he had inherited a portion of his cousin's estate the entitlement to the baronetcy passed to Sir Henry's next of kin, Peter William, whose ownership of Luscombe had precluded him from being considered as a candidate for inheriting any further property at Stourhead.

Meanwhile, the Bank continued unaltered in the conduct of its business. The opening of the new branch in Aldford House, Park Lane, was a well-judged move. From the outset it was a profitable concern, and the recovery of the stock market in 1933-34 enabled the Bank to meet all the outstanding costs involved in its installation, and the building works at Fleet Street, from annual profits. Encouraged by the success of setting up temporary stands outside the Bank, for customers to view the Silver Jubilee procession of George V in 1935, the following year the Partners erected two handsome

*A 'customer' of Hoare's Bank, posing for a press photograph using a quill pen, c.1938.*

wrought iron balconies at first-floor level, which incorporated gilded replicas of the 'Golden Bottle' and commemorative plaques bearing the initials of all the Partners, whose number was brought up to eight by the recent admission of Quintin. Harry's brother Frederick had retired and the two vacancies for Agents were taken by his son, Derick, who had arrived as a school leaver in 1931, and a great-grandson of Henry of Staplehurst, Bertram, who had been offered a place in the Bank when he lost his job working as an engineer in India as a result of the earthquake in Bihar in 1934.

The Bank sold £500,000 of its holding in War Loan in 1936, and the uncertain situation on the Continent did not encourage the Partners to reinvest. With Germany's annexation of Austria in March 1938, and its subsequent threatened occupation of part of Czechoslovakia, war seemed inevitable by September and Britain geared itself up into a state of alert. At the beginning of the month the Partners resolved on steps to take to protect the Bank. Instructions were drawn up which were to be acted on in the case of an emergency and many precautions were carried out immediately. The space under the roof was rendered with fire-proof material, a gas and bomb-proof shelter was constructed on the ground floor of the Warehouse, sand buckets and other fire-fighting appliances were placed in all the passages and individual members of staff were trained in fire-fighting and first aid. The courtyard was lined with rows of sandbags and the ceiling of the Strong Room was reinforced with concrete. Large supplies of preserved food were laid in, staff were issued with a list of basic essentials to have ready in case of sudden evacuation, including an instruction to bring with them 'ample spare cash – five pounds', and extra help was called in to list and photograph all important documents. Wives of Hoare family members were called upon, as in the First World War, to volunteer their services to list all the securities held by the Bank and its customers, which Wallace Heaton was employed to photograph the ledgers from Hoare's Trustees.

The expected crisis did not arrive for another year, by which time the arrangements for keeping the Bank operating during a state of emergency were fully developed. The week before war was declared on 3 September 1939 the major part of the Bank's business and most of the staff had been transferred down to Arthur's house, Ovington Park, on the River Itchen in Hampshire. The move was in line with steps taken by other banks to move out of London. The details of the Bank's move had been worked out with utmost precision and the process had begun six months earlier with the transfer to Ovington of 'The Diary', containing standing orders, and its keeper George Cotterell, accompanied by the Bank's cumbersome printing machine known as 'The Elephant'. Arthur caused much amusement to his fellow travellers and railway staff as he commuted backwards and forwards between Waterloo and Winchester laden with suitcases of documents. All was ready by the Friday afternoon of 25 August when Arthur caught the one-thirty train to the country. Over the next two days he had the whole of the ground floor of his house dismantled and trestle tables set up in readiness for the arrival of the staff on Sunday afternoon in time for the start of business at 9am on Monday morning, six days before war was declared. He reported with satisfaction that within that short space of time, 'three-quarters of the Bank was functioning at Ovington and one quarter at Fleet Street as if it had always done so'.

Work was now essentially carried out in triplicate. All daily business at Fleet Street and Park Lane was copied and the copy sheets were exchanged at the end of the day between the two offices; the totals of all credits and debits were posted fortnightly in the ledgers at Ovington. A loose-leaf system was introduced to facilitate the arrangements, not only for the daily debit and credit sheets and the ledgers, but also as a replacement for the old cus-

*Hoare's first printed advertisement published in The Times on the occasion of the 150th anniversary of the newspaper in 1935.*

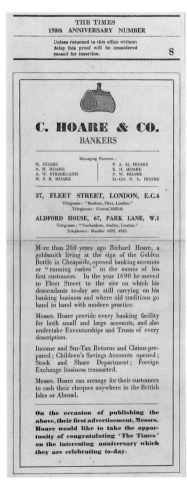

tomer pass books which had been used for the past 150 years. Customers hence-forth were to receive single-sheet statements of their accounts which was, in fact, a return, in printed form, to a practice which had been in use before pass books were introduced. The Books Department, Correspondence, Statements, Drafts, Tax and Trustees, transferred to the country while the Brokers Department, which took charge of safe custody, remained, under the watchful eye of the Agents. Cashier facilities carried on as normal in London.

A list of the names and addresses of all the clerical staff had been drawn up, with notes attached to each name indicating whether they intended to volunteer to fight – banking was classed as a 'Reserved Occupation' – if they were married, and had children or dependent parents, and, if they did, which members of their fam-ily would accompany them when they were evacuated. Finding billets for the staff was not difficult as Arthur owned most of Ovington and, in addition to the hous-es and cottages in the village, the Bank received offers of accommodation from the owners of several of the large houses in the vicinity. Every member of staff was asked if they could drive a car or ride a bicycle; surprising numbers said they

*Evacuated Bank clerks at Ovington Park. Three quarters of the Bank's work was done in the country during the War.*

*Evacuated Partners at Ovington Park. Harry, Sir Peter William and Arthur Hoare in their makeshift Partners' Room.*

couldn't do either. These were important considerations when it came to arranging the actual transport out of London, and where they were billeted in the country, since petrol was rationed. Any member of staff, aged under thirty, who wanted to volunteer for the Territorials was not discouraged from doing so, provided that he decided within a month of the outbreak of war. Seven of the clerks signed up.

When the partial evacuation of the Bank was under discussion Edward had offered his house in Ascot but the fact that both Harry and Peter William had houses in Hampshire and could commute to Ovington (for Harry, who lived at Ellisfield, this was a twelve-mile journey which he did on horseback) predisposed them to accept Arthur's offer. Edward's house provided sanctuary for the Bank's oldest ledgers, a billet they shared, appropriately, with Westminster Hospital. Fleet Street was kept open by a skeleton clerical staff with Rennie as the Partner in charge assisted by Quintin, Derick and Bertram, who was put in charge of the premises. They were looked after by the steward Mr Cheeseman, a cook, two boys classed as 'footmen', and half-a-dozen maids. They were joined a year later by the police force from Snow Hill. Their station had been completely destroyed by bombing and so they had been invited to set up a new sub station in the Warehouse at the Bank. At Park Lane three people kept the branch open. They lived in the flat above the office and the wife of the senior clerk, Mr Howlett, took on the task of housekeeping.

Life in the country for those who had lived all their lives in London had its drawbacks. There were cricket matches and dances in the Village Hall and weekends off, but the main complaint was that the clear division between office hours and free time, which was what they had been used to, was now gone and couldn't be easily remedied in the circumstances. Two enterprising members of staff, Stan Dean and Jim Kenney, started a monthly newsletter called *The Leather Bottle* which, beyond the usual notices, carried an eclectic collection of articles including book reviews, lengthy pieces on film music, reports on the Ovington platoon of the Home Guard, a knitting column, crosswords compiled by Arthur and a serialized history on aspects of Income tax, submitted by Harry. The editors lamented the fact that they couldn't raise the slightest interest in their venture from their colleagues in London.

In notes he made in December 1939 Arthur felt it was worth recording that the evacuation of Fleet Street was not due primarily to fears of the effect of air raids on the lives of people when they were in the Bank, but to the difficulties and dangers that the staff would face in travelling to and from their homes, which would make work nearly impossible for anyone who didn't live on the premises. As events turned out it was the Bank building which was very nearly lost during the heavy air raid on London on Saturday 10 May 1941, a night that the House of Commons, Inns of Court and the British Museum were all hit and 1436 killed. The fire-fighting team at 37 Fleet Street was on full alert. Incendiary bombs were dropping all around them but any fires that developed were quickly put out. The real threat came when a bomb landed on the roof of the Temple Church, which caught fire. Due to a complete failure of the Temple's fire-fighting team to deal with the blaze, including refusing the Bank's offer to run a hose to the church from their own water supply, the whole Church was soon engulfed and the flames which then largely destroyed the magnificent building spread alarmingly in the direction of the Bank.

*A Forces' Christmas card sent from Iceland to Ovington by George Macleod, a Bank porter, in 1941.*

With bombs continuing to fall all around, the Bank was quickly trapped by a ring of flames. That it didn't succumb was largely due to the great competence shown by Bertram, who was ably assisted by a gallant team of helpers from the Bank, nearly half of them housemaids. Equipped with three garden hoses and five stirrup pumps the fire-fighting force of sixteen was able, by means of the Bank's own deep well pump, to draw water from an artesian well deep underground. Without it the Bank would have burned down as the City of London's main water supply had failed. With wet rags plastered over their faces the fire fighters faced appalling danger as they tried to quench the flames which licked through

*Daphne Dorrymeade, a maid at 37 Fleet Street, whose bravery in fighting the flames during the Blitz in 1941 left her injured but the Bank standing. Photographed in the Bank's garden after the War.*

adjacent structures at frightening speed. They leapt from roof to roof as the fire spread around them and not surprisingly there were serious injuries. As part of the Master of the Inner Temple's house collapsed over the boundary wall and into the Bank, two of the maids, Marjorie Miller and Daphne Dorrymeade, were badly hurt as they fell off a roof while attempting to hose down the burning rubble.

Official fire watchers, including the City's Fire Chief, who came and went during the night considered the situation to be hopeless and were unable to offer Bertram any further manpower. In desperation he called on a colleague from his own ARP post in Paddington for assistance. The battle went on and the situation continued to deteriorate until, long after the 'All Clear' had been sounded at 5.25 am, the wind miraculously changed direction. The weary crew watched the flames turn and the smoke float off in the opposite direction and for the first time that night they could see that they were winning.

Their extraordinary commitment to saving the Bank from destruction was given due recognition. Immediately the Partners gave a reward of £100 each to all the staff who had helped on the night. Writing to thank the Partners for their present and letter of personal congratulations, Bertram also thanked them for 'so freely providing whatever equipment has been asked for', before paying tribute to his colleagues: 'All the kind things that have been said to me personally leave me feeling rather humbled at receiving so much credit for a success resting upon the achievements of others and the attentiveness of the Bank's Guardian Angel.' Mr Cheeseman, in writing to the Partners on behalf of the staff, made particular mention of their leader: 'I want to tell you how much we owe to Mr Bertram for his leadership and bravery. He was an example to us all and without him we should never have seen it through.'

The Home Secretary, Herbert Morrison, also wrote to Bertram, having had brought to his attention such 'a remarkable story of courage and endurance'. Bertram in reply took the opportunity to comment that much had been lost due to the poor organization of the various fire-watching groups and, in the case of the City, 'the losses have been out of all proportion to the number of fires started by enemy action due to a shortage of water'. Three years later, when another heavy air raid hit Fleet Street and caused great damage to St Dunstan's Church, the Bank again escaped and with fewer injuries than before. On this occasion, Bertram was pleased to report to Herbert Morrison, there was a plentiful water supply and rapid assistance from the National Fire Service: 'It is only because you found time to write me a friendly note when we fought fires under adversity that I think you may be interested to know that we have had a very different experience this time and that, in the eyes of the local inhabitants, the fire fighting services have won their spurs.'

When peace came in May 1945, 37 Fleet Street was left battered but unbowed. Nearly every pane of glass in the building and in Mitre Court Chambers was shattered; the stone work, which already bore the odd scar from the occasional air raids of the First World War, was pockmarked by pieces of flying shrapnel; inside, most of the plasterwork was seamed with cracks. To bring duplication of work to an end, the Bank returned to full functioning at Fleet Street as soon as it could. In July 1945 twenty-one members of staff came back to their desks in London from Ovington. Among them, arriving for the first time, was Mike Wilson. He had been taken on in the country as an orphaned fifteen-year-old evacuee, who had outgrown the local village school. The headmaster, having no further use for him, had asked Arthur and Harry if they would give him work. He had nothing to offer save decent manners. He was instructed at the beginning of his interview to draw up a chair and, at the end of it, he put it back in its place without being asked. He feels sure that it was this unconscious gesture which got him a job at £90 per annum. Mike Wilson stayed at the Bank for his entire working career, save a brief spell as a national serviceman. Since he had no home to got to in 1945 he lived in the Bank, the last member of staff of Messrs Hoare to do so.

At the end of the war there seems to have been a consensus among the Partners that the question of a sale was now off the agenda, and attention was focused on a post-war policy for the Bank. With Arthur's death in 1954, followed by Harry's in 1956, the ghosts of the old feuds of the inter-war years were laid to rest. Arthur's shares were inherited by Quintin who returned to the Bank with a commendable war record in 1945. He and Rennie, now the ninth generation in direct descent from Sir Richard Hoare, effectively took charge of the Bank and through their efforts it was ensured that the Bank could provide for the generations to come both an inheritance and a future.

Rennie had inherited his father's determination that C. Hoare and Co should continue as a bank, not as an investment trust company, and regarded its proper business as 'dealing in money payable on demand'. Arthur was known to 'loathe loans', but Rennie was convinced that all the serious bad debts of the pre-war years were simply the result of bad management and that to do their job properly the Partners must take an interest in loans and not merely make them and then trust to luck: 'Provided when we make a loan we are certain we can be repaid in due course and that the loan is properly reviewed I see no reason why our bad debts should be more than infinitesimal.' These could have been the words of advice offered in a different generation by his forbears Henry the Magnificent and Henry of Mitcham.

*Shrapnel found in the courtyard at 37 Fleet Street. Scars left on the doors leading into the present-day garden are a reminder of the heavy assault made on the Bank by the air raid on 10 May 1941.*

# CHAPTER NINE

# THE SHOW GOES ON
# 1945–2005

*Three generations of Partners; Henry, Harry, and Rennie (left to right). Photographed soon after Henry joined the Bank in 1953.*

W hen Rennie's eldest son, Henry, arrived at the Bank as a twenty-one-year-old history graduate from Trinity College, Cambridge, in 1953 his father was effectively the senior Partner, although his grandfather, Harry, still commuted regularly between Fleet Street and Ellisfield. In 1951 the Partners had formally relieved Harry and Alfred of their duty of 'constant attendance to the business of the Company', but Harry still managed to travel to the Bank two days a week until the age of eighty-eight; his only concession to his advanced years was an agreement that a car would meet him at Waterloo station, in order to carry his briefcase while he walked most of the way. Henry described his grandfather as a 'highly civilised and charming man who especially enjoyed female company and through such friendships brought many customer and Hoare Trustee accounts to the Bank'. He continued to write out the daily balance well into his eighties but the management of the business and the real work of getting the Bank on its feet after the war was under the direction of Rennie and his second cousin Quintin who, in modern parlance, would be described as the Bank's chief executive. Sir Peter Hoare was Chairman, 'a post he filled with quiet efficiency', but he was not much involved in the routine work of the Partners' room.

Rennie, who tended to be shy of lending, took the view that 'banks exist by looking after lots and lots of small accounts, which, when added together amount to large sums [and] the Partners' job is to see that as many accounts as possible are kept with CH & Co.' This approach was partly a reflection of the fact that during the 1950s, long before the era of minimum balances and other 'net worth' criteria, many of the Bank's customers were employees from local businesses, who kept modest balances. The Partners were also genuinely apprehensive that the tax

facing page
Sir Peter William Hoare
7th Bt., painted against
the backdrop of
Luscombe Castle by
David Jagger in 1953.

burdens – income tax, surtax and death duties – imposed on their traditional 'landed' customers would eventually lead to the erosion of their wealth and therefore they must look elsewhere for new business. Quintin saw diversification in terms of extending the customer base to include several smallish trading and manufacturing companies, which was a policy departure for the Bank that did not, in the end, help profitability. However, he and his generation of Partners who had been running the business during difficult wartime conditions, followed by a decade and more of lending restrictions, were not seeking to make their customers a principal source of the Bank's income. For this purpose they were more interested in investments where they were generally very successful, deriving good profits from dealing in gilt-edged securities, and, in particular, from the dividends retained during the buying and selling process, a practice known as bond washing, which was made illegal in 1960.

The Bank's buildings had been badly damaged by air raids during the war. The architects Messrs Devereux and Davies were commissioned in 1950 to repair and rebuild the premises where necessary, and to reorganize the staff facilities within the building, which were still basically Victorian in layout. The major change was the replacement of the warehouse with a permanent building on the west side of the garden, and this was fitted out internally with oak panelling to match the panelling Charles Parker had used for the Shop and the Counting House in 1829. The Bank's complete set of ledgers dating from 1672, which had previously been housed in the warehouse, were moved into purpose-built oak-framed cases which lined the corridors of the new block, and the clerks' canteen, the 'servants hall', the steward's room and the kitchens were all moved up to the first floor from their previous location in the basement. Across the south end of the garden the Partners' Room and the Bank offices in Mitre Court Chambers were connected to the new building by a two-storey wing which contained a new 'back room' for the Partners, now known as the Garden Room, as well as further office space. Arrangements in the Private House remained much the same. Although the Partners had to sacrifice their billiard room in the old Saloon for a new museum, they retained their bedrooms on the second floor. (In time the pressure for more office space would drive the family to use the bedroom accommodation on the attic floor and, in 1979, this was converted into a comfortable flat which managers could also use, during the day, to host informal lunches.) To celebrate the Bank's physical renewal, the Golden Bottle fixed above the front door facing Fleet Street was re-gilded for the first time since it was placed there in 1829, and, inside, a magnificent sculpture of a double-headed eagle by Jonathan Kenworthy was put on display at the end of the ledger-lined corridor on the ground floor of the new west wing.

The Partners continued the family tradition of maintaining a serious commitment to their outside interests. Sir Peter was a Director of the Eagle Star Insurance Company and was a member of the syndicate that financed the yacht

left

*Quintin Hoare, by Middleton Todd, 1956. Quintin was effectively the Chief Executive of the Bank in the 1950s.*

right

*Rennie Hoare, by Edward Seago. He led the Bank as the Senior Partner after the War, although titles and jobs were not allocated within the Partnership.*

*Sceptre* in 1958, as a challenge to the United States in the first America's Cup race to be held after the war. Quintin was less of a 'private' and more of a 'merchant' banker by nature, and his skill and interest in investment was matched outside the Bank by his enthusiasm for playing bridge and golf for high stakes. Rennie was dedicated to his estate at Stourhead, and to the care of the woodland in particular, but it was not a commutable distance from the Bank. It suited him to spend much of his spare time in London on the research and development of the Bank as a family treasure. Henry's assessment of his father is that he was not a natural banker, but that his devotion to the Bank, as evidenced by his defence of it against Arthur's scheme in the 1930s, was unmatched. Following his work on the revision of *Hoare's Bank: A Record* in 1955, he co-opted several members of staff to continue his research. Their main task was to write out the individual details of all the customer accounts dating from 1672 until 1919 on over 90,000 cards. This was achieved but only at the cost of irritating his fellow Partners, who would have preferred the staff to have been more usefully engaged elsewhere in the Bank at a time when profits were thin.

The Bank continued to be actively managed by the family alone. Sleeping duty remained the responsibility of the Partners and Agents, on the basis that, as proprietors, they themselves must be responsible for opening and shutting the shop every day. The keys were kept in a small canvas bag which the member of the family on duty would take to his bedroom when he retired. The theory was that if a customer called at the Bank during the night – perhaps to withdraw money to pay a gambling debt – a proper check could be kept on the caller and the purpose of the visit. In practice the nightwatchman would usually deal with the situation himself, quietly removing and replacing the keys without disturbing anyone's night's sleep. Bream, the butler, and Louie Cook, who ran the Pantry, looked after any member of the family who was in residence, bringing tea and newspapers to them in the early morning and pressing and sponging their suits. Sleeping on the premises, as a duty, was gradually phased out until it was finally abolished in 1996.

Only the family held the keys to the strong room and, when the new external auditor to the Bank, Philip Willoughby, arrived in 1976, he was much impressed by the fact that there was no requirement then, and for some years after, for there to be two keys to unlock the safe, such was the complete trust that the family had in one another. Frederick, known as 'Derick', who was made a Partner in 1947, had a talent for story telling and gave his explanation to *Interiors Magazine* in 1983 as to why 'there was always a Hoare on the premises'. He claimed that well over two hundred years previously, 'one of the Partners had the axle of

*The Partnership in 1982. From left to right: Henry, Michael, David, Richard, Dick, Quintin and Sir Frederick (Derick) Hoare.*

his coach break on the way to London. He had the key of the strong room with him so next morning they could not open the Bank which is the equivalent to the Bank closing. It was vowed that this would never happen again.' True or false (and many of Derick's stories, however appealing, are acknowledged to be apocryphal) there is no denying that this crucial element of trust defined the Partners' relationship with one another, a confidence which was made evident by their traditional practice of working together in one room which discouraged any secrecy in matters affecting their daily business.

Willoughby admitted that as an outsider he had to get used to the Partners all working in one room: 'It was a very strange feeling walking into a room and no heads moved. You went to stand by the side of the partner that you wished to talk to and when he was ready he would do just that.' The Partners took all the decisions and signed all the letters leaving the Bank. Quintin, who took on the task of overhauling the staffing arrangements and pay scales (and maintained the handwritten list of staff salaries himself), introduced the concept of heads of department in 1957, but in practice the Partners continued to give instructions to individual members of staff directly. Officially, staff were encouraged to take the Institute of Bankers' examinations, and a contribution towards expenses was paid with a one-off bonus for passing, but there was not much incentive to work for them. The lectures were tedious and Quintin, who was in charge of staff 'appraisals', seemed unfussed if clerks failed. The principle of promotion through seniority alone remained unchanged.

Nevertheless the Bank's paternalistic care of its staff created a culture of respect and confidence. Once the clerks had passed their probationary period they had a job for life, unless they committed a serious misdemeanour, and the Partners could rely on their loyalty and long service. They could also rely on their clerks' family contacts. In the case of the Cottrell, Ennis, Breakspear and Pollentine families, one generation followed another into the Bank and, in the case of the Ennis family, further recruitment occurred through marriage! In the days before advertising – John Mabberley believed he was the first clerk to be recruited by an advertisement in 1968 – staff came from a few well-known sources. Many had been pupils at Christ's Hospital (the Bluecoats School), a connection that had been formed originally by the founder Sir Richard Hoare. Others – including Peter Stevens, Peter Colin, John Kenney, Neville Page and Alan Towler – came from the Regent's Street Polytechnic school, which was renamed the Quintin school,[1] on its move to St John's Wood in the mid-fifties, after its founder Quintin Hogg, Quintin Hoare's grandfather. One of the more unusual sources of supply for the female staff was the Orpington Junior Singers. The wife of the head of the Tax Department, Mr Brown, ran the choir, and through her recommendations 'a string of suitable young ladies' was recruited to the staff. The Civil Service and the Bank of England lifted their ban on employing married women after the war and, although there was no compulsion before the sex discrimination legislation of the early seventies, Hoares followed suit by the mid-sixties when staff numbers were just short of a hundred and nearly half those employed were women. By the early seventies, when an increase in business had seen the payroll rise to 135, women outnumbered the men.

Much of the work was repetitive and undemanding. All ledger entries and customer statements were handwritten until 1962, and any printing (cheque books, debit and credit slips etc.) was done in-house on the Bank's antiquated printing machine known as 'the Elephant'. This lived in the 'Elephant Room' along with the 'Diary' and the Drafts team who sorted all the cheques. The cheques, which came in from Metropolitan Clearing every morning, were processed by a system known as 'machining down the Met', before being distributed to the cashiers who, in turn, handed them to Books, where each individual item was posted. 'Machining down the Met' was acknowledged to be one of the most boring of the routine jobs, although tedium was relieved by a rota system which ensured staff moved around from one task to another and also by recourse to a table tennis room, situated above the staff canteen, which had been moved from the basement up to the first floor of the new block built to replace the old warehouse in 1958.

With all this paper in circulation, in an era when those who smoked outnumbered those who did not, it was remarkable that nothing was ever lost by fire. Alan Towler described the routine for the smokers in the Books Department: 'Regularly at about 3 o' clock in the afternoon individuals lit up … normally the first used to be Peter Dare closely followed by Vera Pearmund and then Charles Beverley. That gave the green light to the pipe smokers, Bill Inman, Neville Page, Bernard Pollentine and John Parsons. The department within

*The garden of Hoare's Bank today. It was redesigned by Georgia Langton in the early 1990s.*

about 20 minutes resembled the days of London smogs, or Paddington railway station at about 9 am on a 1950s summer Saturday morning with steam trains awaiting to take hoards of families on their annual holiday to the West Country.'

The interview process for new clerks was a gentle affair, apparently designed to make the candidate feel comfortable rather than tested. Alan Towler was interviewed by the Head Clerk, Henry Grove, in 1959. He was asked to add up a column of about four numbers and, having done so, he was then told about the Bank's cricket team. Nearly a decade later John Mabberley was given similar treatment by Mr Ware, Head of Books, who, having explained the system of posting the twenty alphabetical ledgers currently in use (each clerk being responsible for two) moved the conversation on to a discussion of sailing. The dress code was more rigorous, insisting on stiff white collars for the male clerks, which were supplied by 'Collars of Wembley' and delivered to the Bank at a cost of five shillings a month for each clerk, and rather disastrous thin blue synthetic overalls for the ladies, which were soon abandoned after protest. The porters wore tailcoats, and in 1951 were provided with brown gaberdine raincoats if needed when out on Bank business. They were reminded to wear their top hats on all occasions when out. The top hats disappeared in the 1970s, but tailcoats remained as winter uniform until the end of the century. Banking hours included Saturday mornings until 1969, but the daily hours were not onerous and staff were only required to work one Saturday in four.

Staff perquisites were exceptionally generous. Salary increases were given on marriage with subsequent allowances for all dependent children. Full housing

*The Partners' Dining Room at the Bank. Hung with portraits of Partners from the 18th and 19th centuries, it is still used by the family on a daily basis.*

loans were available at two per cent, and fuel bonuses were issued, irrespective of age, to everyone after a hard winter. Hoare Trustees offered their services as executors to the staff, more or less free of charge, and staff overdrafts were never referred to as such but rather as 'small loans'. However, the most significant long-term benefit was the introduction of a non-contributory pension scheme in April 1956. It was inaugurated with a sum of £32,428 14s, which was paid to Hoare Trustees who managed the scheme; members of staff over the age of twenty-one were eligible to join, and any years they had served in the Bank, prior to reaching their majority, counted towards their qualifying years of service. The Bank lowered the retirement age of men to sixty in 1989.

At that time Hoare Trustees was one of the largest departments in the Bank, with more than a dozen staff. It had an efficient accounts department and was also of direct benefit to the Bank since the Company kept large balances and most of the trust income was paid into C. Hoare and Co accounts. Its growth resulted from taking over a large number of trusteeships from individual Partners as well as acting as trustees and executors for numerous members of the family. This job alone more or less occupied one full-time member of staff, who became, in essence, 'a skilled and helpful family servant to the Partners'. The senior staff, the secretary,

James Bell, and the other trust officers were all men of 'considerable education and intelligence', and it was Bell's ambition to build up the trustee business so that it became larger than the Bank. He had a similar goal for the pension fund. Henry remembers being told by him that he fully expected that one day it would be worth more than the Bank. His prediction came close to being true in the case of the pension fund but his efforts on behalf of expanding Hoare Trustees were less successful in the long run.

Insofar as the Partners had a strategy it was based on a commitment to deal competently with any business that walked through the door without engaging in any active marketing to attract it. It was, in Henry's words, designed 'to encourage our friends to join the club' and it was hoped that the standard of service offered would be a sufficient marketing tool. This approach worked for banking, at that time, but it did not bring in new trustee business. Furthermore, the most important group of customers recruited in the decades after the war were the lawyers in and around Fleet Street and the City, in

The Drawing Room at 37 Fleet Street. The latest decorative scheme by Tom Helme, dating from the early 1990s. The room was designed as 'Mr Charles's sitting room' when the new Bank was built in 1829.

particular firms of solicitors, several of whom had longstanding relationships with the Bank. Solicitors were an excellent source of introductions for new banking business, but they naturally wished to keep the trusteeship work for themselves. In addition, Hoare Trustees, which had its origins in the Partners' paternalistic care of customers (described by Henry as 'the very essence of private banking'), became less popular as bank trust corporations in general were regarded as both expensive and inflexible. In time the Bank lost out to its legal rivals and the staff working in Trustees dwindled to a handful.

Lending, as a source of profit for the Bank, took a back seat for many years. Government controls on lending introduced after the war made it difficult. When the President of the Institute of Bankers and Vice-Chairman of Barclays Bank, Sir Cecil Ellerton, was asked, in 1952, what banks did, he never even mentioned loans: 'The main work done by banks is the payment and collection of cheques and the provision of cash.' Hoare's Statement of Assets and Liabilities for 1953 certainly shows that very little 'active' banking was being done. From a balance sheet worth nearly £8.5 million, less than a quarter represented advances to customers, whereas the value of investments was nearly double the figure for loans and overdrafts. Customer accounts had increased by nearly 1000 to just over 8000 in the decade following the war (when there were only 8 million bank accounts in the whole country, or one third of the working population) but the work being done on these accounts was largely restricted to calculating the interest on deposits and overdrafts. The proportion of loans to deposits, which historically the Partners had maintained at very conservative levels, continued to be much lower than their competitors' but, after the lifting of credit restrictions by the Government in 1958, demand for loans began to increase and it was agreed at the Board meeting of 15 July of that year that: 'We should not be too perturbed if our advances increase to at least 30 per cent of the Deposits ... [but] we must still be very cautious with regard to any long-term loans and there should be no slackening in our scrutiny of every application.'

*The Lord Mayor's coach passing in front of 37 Fleet Street in November 1961.*

Geoffrey Lennard's son, Dick, arrived at the Bank, as an Agent, in 1947 and was made a Partner in 1954. Five years later Henry also became a Partner and between them they can be credited with reviving profitable banking at 37 Fleet Street. Dick's major contribution was to restore banking as a key element in the Bank's business. He was extremely clever – described by his cousin, Christopher, as a 'cork in a champagne bottle – stubborn and lumbering in business, but a really super chap'.

(Christopher Hoare, a great-grandson of the snuff-taking Partner, Henry Gerard, had joined the Bank as an Agent in 1959 at the age of twenty-five. He had previously been in the army but his lack of any relevant experience was no handicap to him and he was assured by Quintin that he possessed the only two qualifications that were needed – the right name and the right age.)

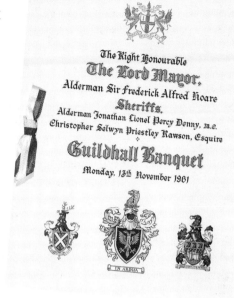

*Menu from the Guildhall Banquet, 1961. After an interval of over 200 years, Sir Frederick Hoare was the third Partner in the history of the Bank to be elected Lord Mayor.*

Dick worked indefatigably, shrouded in cigarette smoke. He was as cautious, if not more so, than his fellow Partners with regard to lending, but from his basic belief that all customers were out to rob the Bank stemmed his excellent loan and overdraft control system, which is still in place today. He also introduced the revolutionary concept of bank charges but, although he set up a workable system (the basis of the system currently in use), his fellow Partners at first refused to operate it. With income tax soaring to 95 per cent under the 1964 Labour Government, and surtax charged on their profits as a Private Company at the same rate, trying to make a profit was a discouraging business. The Partner's attitude was summed up by Henry: 'Why charge your friends bank charges when 95 per cent would go to the Revenue and perhaps out of gratitude they might ask you out to dinner?'

The situation changed as the Bank was challenged from outside and within. Competition from other banks, finance houses and building societies, which had emerged with the opening up of the credit market, compelled the Bank to review its position and Henry succeeded in his wish to increase Bank lending and to implement bank charges. In this he was ably assisted by Peter Stevens who, after the retirement of Henry Grove in 1972, was given the title of head of banking, a move which underlined Henry's desire to see less interference by the Partners in the day-to-day administration of the Bank's departments. Peter Stevens formed excellent relationships with the larger firms of solicitors who brought a great deal of business to the Bank – through their firms' business accounts, partners' private accounts and healthy sums of money held on deposit in their client accounts. He was, in Henry's words, 'a natural banker' and a 'sympathetic and constructive lender'.

The Tax and Trustee Departments continued to use up disproportionate staff resources when compared to the income they generated from their fixed fees, and this reinforced the argument for imposing bank charges. Resistance to them could no longer be sustained and, with great reluctance, they were introduced. Nobody relished informing the customers of this break with tradition and it also produced the uneasy feeling that charges would mean an increased responsibility on the part of the Bank to be absolutely faultless in the service it offered.

Sir Frederick Hoare in his mayoral robes 1961-62. A great chess player, ornithologist and raconteur, with a fund of stories about the Bank, the strict accuracy of which will never be known.

The Coupon Room was now staffed entirely by the family. Bertram was in charge of the building he had helped save from destruction and Sir Peter William's son, David, who arrived at the same time as Christopher, conveniently filled the gap left by Henry's promotion to Partnership in 1959, until he too became a Partner five years later. Derick's wife, Mary, and Quintin's brothers Malcolm and Graham were all part of the Coupon Room family team. Lunch in the Partners' Dining Room with the three brothers, all of whom had formidable wit and intellect, is remembered by those who were present as being a wonderful spectator sport.

Mary remained in the Bank until 1961 when Derick ran for election as Lord Mayor of London. A suggestion had been put to the Partners, by the City fathers, that it was time another member of the Hoare family stood for office. The idea did not appeal to them greatly but Derick was persuaded to take it on and was duly elected. The Partners solemnly recorded their pleasure at his success noting that, at his installation by the Lord Chief Justice of England, he wore 'the world-famous gold collar of esses which was presented to the City in 1544 and which both previous Lord Mayors in our family can be seen to be wearing in their portraits'. At the Lord Mayor's Banquet on 13 November the Lord Chancellor, Lord Kilmuir, paid tribute 'to the unique position of our Bank and the fact that Sir Derick was the third Partner to have been elected Lord Mayor of London'.

The Partners kept control of all security matters through their Agents. In the words of Edward, Rennie's second son, 'The Partners did the thinking and the Agents did the doing' and moreover, if 'an attempt was made on a Partner's life you as Agent were expected to "stand in the way of the bullet" if necessary'.[2] As custodians of the strong room, Agents kept control of customers' valuables placed in safe custody,[3] cash and stock certificates. Connected to this role was their management of the 'City Walk', the procedure that kept control on all money entering and leaving, ensuring that the Bank was always liquid. The 'City Walk' had a physical presence in the Shop, a glazed cubicle adjacent to the cashiers, from which the Agent could keep an eye on everything that was happening and be aware immediately if large sums of money were coming in or going out. It dealt with all overnight loans on the money markets and, traditionally, the Agents could sign all such cheques with a sole signature. Its name derived from the practice of 'walking' the cheques and surplus money to the City every day for deposit before the closing of the money markets at 3 pm. By the early 1990s automation and regulation had made the 'City Walk' redundant, the glazed cubicle was dismantled and the space given over to the porters as a reception desk. Another job for Agents was reading all the mail first thing in the morning. The porters would open the letters in their presence in the Coupon Room and then move with the Agents to the centre table in the Partners Room where the 'reading' would take place. The point of this arrangement was that everything would have to be dealt with and cleared up before the Partners began their working day. The Agents on duty were rewarded for their early start with breakfast in the Partners' Dining Room.

Staff in 'Brokers' worked closely with the Coupon Room. Hours were spent every day removing and returning stock certificates from and to the strong room, in the presence of an Agent or a Partner, in order to deliver them to the customers' brokers for sale purposes or receive them after purchase. Posting these 'Ins' and 'Outs' was one of the more laborious jobs in the Bank and it was one where Christopher admitted he 'nearly died of boredom'. The system of applying the dividend income to individual accounts was a more complicated but no less tedious task in terms of manual labour. The Bank's brokers were not qualified to give investment advice to customers – although, in the days before financial services regulations, this did not preclude the giving and receiving of 'tips' – and they confined their services to taking custody of investments, collecting and applying dividend income and taking instructions to arrange purchases and sales through outside firms of stockbrokers. Two firms did most of the Bank's work: James Capel and Co, and D A Bevan, Simpson and Co, where Rennie's brother Rollo was a partner. He would call in at Fleet Street every Friday asking if there was 'anything to take through – any questions?'

The Park Lane branch had flourished under the charge of Geoffrey Lennard, who was 'pushy and effective', but contrary to the original hope that it would attract the rich and fashionable from the neighbourhood, in the event it had had to take in some business of a 'lesser quality', including casual 'walk-ins' who chose to make an approach to the branch rather than the head office. It had an added advantage, however, in being managed later by Mr Brunswick, whom Henry had worked with during a spell spent at the branch and regarded as one of the 'most astute and intelligent men our Bank has ever had the privilege to employ'. In 1975 the owners of the building, Aldford House, wanted to redevelop it and the Bank found new premises in the heart of London's clubland in Waterloo Place. This location was not their first choice, and the new manager, Mr Dracup, met with a mixed reception when he wrote out of courtesy to introduce himself to the managers of other banks in the vicinity. He received a rebuff from Barclays, who were well represented in the area, and who did not feel that it would be in their interest 'to assist a rival Bank and its Manager in establishing itself in competiton with [our] local branches'. Within a few years the branch was on the move again and in 1983 opened in a modern block in Lowndes Street, which has proved to be most convenient for the Knightsbridge and Chelsea dwellers the Bank hoped to attract.

*Silver sweetmeat dish issued to Bank customers on the tercentenary of the Bank in 1972.*

In the 1980s, never having developed a branch network, at a time when the 'Big Four' were represented in practically every town and village in the country,[4] Hoare's could have been at a distinct disadvantage, long-term, with regard to their country customers. Although arrangements for drawing cheques were made with local branches of other banks for their customers' convenience, it was the advent of the credit card and the system of automated cash withdrawals that came to their rescue. In 1987 selected customers were offered a plastic Visa card, which doubled up with their previously issued cheque guarantee card, and enabled them to make cash withdrawals at any bank or cash dispenser displaying the Visa sign. As automation took hold and employment costs soared, the major banking groups were faced with the necessity of restructuring and closing down much of their branch network. Hoare's, however, unencumbered by this 'legacy effect', were net beneficiaries of the card scheme which, in Henry's words, was 'of fantastic value to our customers world-wide', while removing '95 per cent of the disadvantage of us not having a branch network'.

In July 1972 the Bank celebrated its tercentenary as a business owned and run, exclusively, by the Hoare family. In anticipation of this great event, the Partners resolved 'that a commemorative object is to be sent to every customer of the Bank, these objects to be identical regardless of the status of the recipient'. It was decided that this object should be a silver sweetmeat dish embellished with the double-headed eagle, made of 'Britannia' rather than ordinary sterling silver, and bearing the Bank's own maker's mark which was registered at Goldsmiths Hall.

As with the distribution of *Hoare's Bank: A Record*, in 1932, this gesture prompted a good deal of correspondence and, owing to Rennie's indexing of the ledgers, on this occasion the Bank was able to inform many of their longstanding customers of the history of their relationship with the Bank. Felix Calvert, the Bank's first customer, was still represented in the Bank's books by his direct descendants, as was Richard Michell, whose account was opened in 1695, and whose family have maintained an unbroken relationship with the Bank ever since. William Hale, who is distinguished in the Bank's history as the signatory of their oldest known cheque, dated 1676, is represented today by a customer who is his tenth-generation direct descendant.

However the prize for the longest unbroken record of banking with Hoare's, in 1972 and now, goes to the direct descendants of the 3rd Baron Alington (of the 1st creation) who opened his account with Richard Hoare on 23 June 1675. Shortly after the new millennium Henry wrote to Alington's many times great-granddaughter on a banking matter, prefacing the business contents of the letter to her with the words: 'I am so pleased that our fourth century as banker and customer should get off to such a good start ...' In 1975 the tercentenary of this special relationship was marked by the customer who, having first enquired what they would like, presented a pair of silver mustard pots to the Partners each engraved with the crest of both the banker and the customer.

Another present for the Partners came from the staff who, through the joint general managers Mr Stevens and Mr Wood, presented them with a set of table silver. In writing to thank them, the Partners took the opportunity to say, 'how deeply grateful and appreciative we are ... for the prompt and kind care and attention which you always give to our customers about which our customers are continually reminding us'. The depth of their appreciation can be measured by the extraordinarily generous bonus which all staff received in the tercentenary year. It was calculated on the basis of a month's salary for every year worked and therefore, for those who had worked for the Bank for over forty years, and there were a few, this bonus amounted to three and a half times their annual salary. The Partners were also prepared to stagger the payment of large bonuses to avoid heavy tax obligations.

*Pair of mustard pots, given to the Partners in 1972 by a customer, whose family now holds the longest record (330 years) for continuous banking at Hoare's.*

Staff numbers have now increased to nearly two hundred and fifty, and many of the 'old-fashioned' aspects of paternalism have disappeared. However, staff welfare is still a priority for the Partners and the flourishing 'Hoare's Bank Sports and Social Club' which grew out of the post-war cricket and football teams, is a testament to this. The Partners subsidize its activities and Richard Hoare is its President; for many years he hosted cricket matches at his house in Hampshire. With a few exceptions every member of staff has joined the Club, which now offers subsidized tickets to cultural as well as sporting events, interdepartmental quiz evenings and subsidized gym membership. Its longtime secretary, Barry Pollentine, wrote in the Club's annual report for the year 1999-2000: 'The climate out in the big bad city is one where we see employers no longer supporting their sports and social clubs ... this is very alien to us ... [and] is not the case at

C. Hoare and Co as our Partners take a great interest in the Club and realize it is a vital ingredient to the well-being of the Bank and give it generous financial support.'

A modern management structure, in fledgling form, first appeared at Fleet Street in 1971, with the appointment of Reg Wood and Peter Stevens as joint general managers. Reg Wood took over the job of running the Bank from Quintin and Henry Grove, and put into operation a more devolved system of administration, encouraging the Partners to work through their heads of department. A succession of general managers followed Mr Wood but real change only occurred after Alexander, Bertram's grandson, came into the Bank in 1987 three years after Dick's premature death. After serving his probation, Alexander was made a Partner in 1991. Regulation had been introduced into the Bank with the passing of the 1979 Banking Act, which gave the Bank of England power to license and supervise banks; further control and changes followed the Financial Services Act, which came into force in 1988 and was designed to prevent abuses arising from the deregulation of the stock exchange or 'Big Bang' of 1986. Alexander identified the need for the Bank to reorganize its internal operations and, under his direction, as Chief Executive, a formal written strategy was produced in 2001, the first of its kind in the whole history of the Bank. Concerned that the staff should have a bigger role to play, and work with the kind of incentives which had hitherto been unavailable to them, he instituted wide-ranging staff training programmes, covering all areas from man-management to customer relations and technical skills, and geared up the Bank's recruitment to attract professionally qualified 'advisors' from other City institutions. Although the need to overhaul the Bank's internal organization was partially driven by external regulation, the changes have had an invigorating effect on working practices throughout the Bank.

Perhaps the most radical change was the departure from the family's time-honoured practice of managing their business entirely themselves, and the introduction of a new regime whereby the Partnership as a whole was formally relieved of the obligations of day-to-day management. A new non-executive Board, composed of all the Partners and Consultants, including non-family members, was formed with a specifically supervisory role. Executive responsibility was delegated by the Board to a group of Partners who, with the heads of department, were formed into an Executive Group with the job of running the Bank. In recognition of these distinct roles within the Partnership, the three senior members Henry, David (Chairman) and Richard relocated to the Garden Room, leaving the young Partners, the eleventh generation, free to use the Partners' Room for the conduct of daily business. Of the four Executive Managing Partners, as they are known, two are women. Rollo Hoare's son Michael was the Bank's first compliance officer, appointed in 1987, and it is his elder daughter Venetia who became the first female Partner in 1994. She was joined by Henry's daughter, Arabella, and David's son, Simon in 2001.

For all the readjustment of important relationships within the Bank none of the things that fundamentally distinguish the Bank from its competitors has changed. Hoare's remains the only private bank in the country. It is private, in the literal sense that it is privately owned with no non-working or outside shareholders. Its system of appointing Partners, though restricted to the family, enables the net to be cast widely within it, increasing the chances that those most suitable are likely to be chosen. All aspiring Partners are expected to have had previous working experience and must serve a probationary term, and nobody is appointed without the full agreement of the Partnership. C. Hoare and Co's unlimited liability status has imposed on the Partners what the *Economist* described in 1989 as 'a peculiarly disciplined kind of banking, for when such a bank lends money the partners are lending their own money'. It is a very small bank (roughly 10,000 accounts) in a world where generally there are only big ones but, as Henry told *Accountancy Age* in 1994, 'we aren't under pressure to maximize growth and we don't need more profit than is necessary to keep up reserves ... There are no shareholders clamouring for dividends.'

The recently completed computerized banking system has the capacity for expansion,[5] but the Partners are deliberately keeping the Bank at its present size, which allows them personally to manage their business and to know their customers. It has also meant that they have been able to stay in their banking house, following historical precedent by expanding into adjacent buildings in Fleet Street only as the need arises. As well as being a distinguished and highly unusual building for a modern bank, 37 Fleet Street has also been in exactly the right location to attract both private and professional customers, and is now equally well placed to benefit from London's top position as a global financial centre.

Private banking has also developed a more colloquial meaning as specialist banking for the rich or, in the words of the *Economist*, 'what Americans – in a clumsy attempt to avoid the word – call high net-worth individuals'. This has been Hoare's expertise for centuries, though it has always had competitors in the same field: these are now private bank offshoots of the large banking groups. What distinguishes Hoare's, beyond its independent status, and perhaps as a consequence of it, is the quality of the service it can offer.

A memorandum entitled 'Customer Complaints' was circulated to staff in 1982, outlining the benefits customers enjoyed by banking at Hoare's. It was to act as an aide-memoire for staff when dealing with customers who complained about high bank charges. Of the nine 'benefits' listed, three or four could be described as characteristics unique to Hoare's Bank. The staff, in particular the senior staff, rarely changed, 'enabling a considerable saving of customer time since their affairs are intimately known over many years by the staff with whom they deal'. Lines of communication (manager to proprietor by telephone) 'are the shortest possible': 'We are very much more flexible in bending ourselves to a customer's requirements rather than insisting that they slot into a standard package.' In addition the Bank provided (and still does) full narrative statements. Above all (and it is unlikely that this was ever said directly) the Bank wished to emphasize: 'We remain, in an increasingly competitive industry where disturbingly unscrupulous practices appear to be developing … gentlemen.'

In recent years the Bank has put particular emphasis on developing a range of financial services to offer its customers in addition to banking. Trustee services are once more in demand while investment management and financial planning advice are seen as two important growth areas. In line with the other 'private banks', this takes the nature of the business closer to the Swiss model of private banking which is the provision of investment banking services for wealthy individuals.

These developments have not detracted from the underlying principle governing the Bank's strategy which is its focus on the long term, a lesson learned from its own history. For all that he cared deeply about his new bank, and worried about his successors, the founder, Sir Richard Hoare, could have had no conception that he was establishing a dynasty of bankers who would continue his business, on the site he had moved to in 1690, for hundreds of years to come. No doubt it would have delighted him to see, in an age so different from his own and so conspicuous for its lack of personal attention in business relationships, his family continue that close connection with their customers that he had taken such pains to establish in his lifetime. He would have applauded the philanthropic efforts of every generation – not least the present one for establishing the grant-giving Golden Bottle Trust in 1985 – and it would have warmed his heart, given the trials and tribulations he suffered with his own children, to see the young generation taking on the responsibility of running the Bank with such enthusiasm and dedication. Every generation of Partners has been indebted to its predecessors for their guardianship of the Bank and especially to those who defended the Bank from Partners who had little interest in its future.

It is firmly indoctrinated in each new Partner that his or her position is one of a life trustee of the Bank, a concept first articulated by Henry the Magnificent and given new vigour as a result of the arguments within the Partnership over the issues of sale and amalgamation in the 1930s. In 1972, in a letter to a customer, Sir Peter William allowed himself to speculate on the future: 'Rennie, Quintin and I each have boys now junior Partners. We go back direct on Rennie's side ten generations but none of us here expect to see the 400th anniversary of Hoare's Bank. Could it happen?' Given its unmatched record of survival, the odds are that the Bank could still be there.

*The present day Partnership, from left to right: Simon, Sir David (Chairman), Alexander (Chief Executive), Richard, Arabella, Venetia and Henry.*

**RICHARD** (Naughty), a merchant of London and Bury St. Edmunds trading in Europe & Levant. b. 1673, m. Mary dau. of William Bolton. d. 1721.

**HENRY** (Good) of Stourhead, Wilts, b. 1677. **Partner** 1698. m. Jane dau. of Sir William Benson, Kt, d. 1725.

**JOHN** b.1682, d.1721.

**JAMES** (Jimmy), b.1686, d.1712.

**WILLIAM** a merchant of London and Bury St. Edmunds, b. 1673, m. his cousin Martha Cornelison. = d. 1753.

**JANE** m. Henry Cornelison. d. 1762

**MARTHA** m. her cousin William. d.1777

**HENRY** (Magnificent) of Stourhead, Wilts, b. 1705, **Partner**, m. 1. Anne dau. of Lord Masham, 2. Susanna dau. of Stephen Colt, Esq., d. 1785.

**HENRY** (Harry), of London and Mitcham Grove, Surrey, b. 1750, Partner 1777, m. Lydia Henriette dau. of Isaac Malortie Esq., d. 1828.

**SUSANNA** (Sukey), m. 1. 1753 Charles Viscount Dungarven, 2. 1761 Thomas 1st earl of Ailesbury, d. 1783 leaving issue.

2 other sons who died young.

**HENRY** b. 1730, **Partner** 1750, d. unmarried 1752.

**WILLIAM HENRY** of Broomfield House, Battersea, b. 1776, **Partner** 1798, m. Hon. Louisa Elizabeth dau. of Sir Gerard Noel 2nd Bart, and Baroness Barham, d. 1819.

**GEORGE MATTHEW** a brewer, b.1779 m. Angelina Greene sister of Peter Richard's wife. d. 1852.

**THE REV. CHARLES JAMES** Rector of Godstone, Surrey, b. 1781, m. Jane Isabella, dau. of Richard Holden, Esq., d. 1865.

**SIR RICHARD COLT** 2nd Bart., F.R.S., F.S.A., F.L.S., well-known archaeologist, **Agent** 1782-3, b. 1758, m. Ho. Hester dau. of Sir William Henry 1st Baron Lyttleton, d. 1838 leaving no surviving issue.

**SIR HENRY HUGH** 3rd Bart. of Adelphi Terrace & Stourhead, b. 1762, **Partner** 1785, m. Maria Palmer dau. of Arthur Acland Esq., d. 1841.

**HENRY** of Staplehurst, Kent, b. 1807, Partner 1845, m. Lady Mary Marsham, dau. of Charles 2nd Earl of Romney, d. 1866.

**THE REV. WILLIAM HENRY** b. 1809, m. Araminta Anne, dau. of Lt. Gen. Sir John Hamilton, d. 1888.

**HENRY JAMES** brewer, b. 1812, d. 1859.

**CHARLES HUGH** brewer, b. 1819 d. 1869

**HENRY GERARD** of Stansted House Surrey, b. 1827, **Partner** 1865, m. Jane Frances dau. of Rev. Samuel Hurry Alderson, d. 1896.

**HUGH EDWARD** (Tuppy) b. 1854, brewer, d. 1919 leaving issue

**ALFRED** b. 1850, **Partner** 1881–1925, retired, m. Beatrix Pollard, dau. of Edward Bond Esq., d. 1938

**WILLIAM** (Willie) of Staplehurst, Kent, and Hoare & Co, Brewers, b. 1847, m. Laura, dau. of Sir John Lennard Bart., d. 1925

**CHARLES**, of Hackwood, b. 1844, **Partner** 1867, m. Patience Georgiana dau. of The Rev. Lord Arthur Charles Hervey, d. 1898.

**REV. WALTER MARSHAM** Rector of Colkirk, Norfolk, b. 1840, m. Jessie Mary dau. of Richard Robertson Esq., d. 1912.

**HENRY** Junior of Iden (Staplehurst), Kent, b. 1838, **Partner** 1862, m. Beatrice Anne dau. of the Rev. George Paley, retired 1874 d. 1898.

**HAMILTON NOEL** b. 1837, **Agent** 1859, d. 1908.

**CHARLES TWYSDEN** brewer, b. 1851.

**HENRY GERARD PHILIP** b. 1862, **Agent** 1885, m. Margaret dau. of Henry Gosthen Esq., d. 1918 leaving issue.

**JOHN EDWARD ALFRED** b. 1895, **Agent** 1926–1939, m. 1. 1918 Gwendoline dau. of Samuel P. Trounce Esq., 2. 1942 Beryl Evelyn Blanche dau. of Capt. Spencer Thornton Treffrey, d. 1974 leaving issue.

**GEOFFREY LENNARD**, b. 1879, **Partner** 1932, m. Lady Ann Stopford dau. of 6th Earl of Courtown, d. 1960.

**SIR REGINALD HERVEY KCMG** b. 1882, **Partner** 1944, m. Lucy dau. of William George Cavendish-Bentinck Esq., d. 1954.

**ARTHUR HERVEY** of Ovington Park, Alresford, Hants., b. 1877, **Partner** 1908, m. Anna Margaret dau. of Rear Admiral Samuel Long, d. 1953 without issue.

**CHARLES HERVEY GREY** b. 1875, **Agent** 1898–1908, m. 1. 1909 Elizabeth widow of Sir Lepel Griffin & had issue Iris Marie b. 1911, 2. 1919 Cecily dau. of Arthur Grey DLJP, d. 1955, Lady Griffin had issue.

**WALTER ROBERTSON** b. 1867, m. Constance Gertrude dau. of Sir Edward Hill, d. 1941.

**VINCENT ROBERTSON** of Devonshire Terrace, London, b. 1873, **Agent** 1890, m. Elsie Florence dau. of Quintin Hogg Esq., killed in action 1915.

**RICHARD GEOFFREY STOPFORD** (Dick) b. 1923, **Partner** 1954, m. 1952 Gillian Mary dau. of Gilbert Vivian Esq., d. 1984 leaving issue.

**JOSEPH ANDREW CHRISTOPHER** b. 1925, **Agent** 1954–5, m. Lady Christine Alice Mc. Donnell dau. of 5th Earl of Antrim. d. 2002 leaving issue

**RONALD LEPEL GRIFFIN** b. 1898, **Agent** 1947, d. 1955.

**BERTRAM EDWARD WALTER** b. 1901, **Agent** 1934–66, m. Elsie Margaret dau. of Capt. Charles Edward Crane, d. 1994.

**QUINTIN VINCENT** b. 1907, **Partner** 1935, m. 1. Lucy Florence dau. of the very Rev. Gordon Selwyn, 2. 1952 Mia Rosemary dau. of Lt. Col. Charles Heslet, d. 1992.

**MALCOLM VINCENT** b. 1912, **Agent** 1961–79, m. 1. Judy dau. of Odon Ujvars Csell, 2. Margot Carol dau. of Arthur Blout Esq., d. 1991.

**GRAHAM MARTIN VINCENT** b. 1913, **Agent** 1958, m. Elizabeth Louise dau. of Dr. Sebastian Gilbert Scott, d. 1991 leaving issue.

**HENRY PEREGRINE RENNIE** of Stourhead, Wilts b. 1901, **Partner** 1928, m. 1. Lady Beatrix dau. of 6th Earl Cadogan, 3. 1947 Dorothy Margaret dau. of John Duncan Hairs Esq., d. 1981.

**CHRISTOPHER EDWARD BERTRAM** b. 1931, m. Sylvia Margaret dau. of Godfrey Bremridge.

**RICHARD QUINTIN** b. 1943, **Partner** 1969, m. 1970 Hon Frances Evelyn dau. of Lord Hailsham of St. Marylebone, Lord Chancellor.

**ANTHONY MALCOLM** b. 1946, **Agent** 1973, m. 1969 Elizabeth Mary Gay dau. of Cdr. Frederick C. Burge OBE, **Partner** 1986. Retired 2001.

**MICHAEL GRAHAM** b. 1943, m. Beatrice dau. of Comte Bernard de Monts de Savasse. Consultant to the board.

**HENRY CADOGAN** b. 1931, **Partner** 1959, m. 1. Pamela Saxon dau. of George Francis Bunbury, 2. Caromy dau. of Robert Jenkins Esq.

**EDWARD ANTHONY** b. 1949, **Agent** 1978, m. 1981 Susan Elizabeth dau. of Brig. T.S. Dobree.

**ALEXANDER SIMON** b. 1963. **Partner** 1990

**ALEXANDER RICHARD QUINTIN** b. 1973.

**ARABELLA SAXON** b. 1968, **Partner** 2001, m. 1995 Richard Alexi Prince Hopewell.

**HENRY HOARE** of Walton, Bucks, d. 1655, a yeoman farmer

**HENRY HOARE** of St. Botolph, a horse dealer.
m. Sicilia (surname not known). d. 1669.

**SIR RICHARD HOARE** Kt., Lord Mayor of London 1712–1713. b. 1648,
m. Susanna dau. of John Austen. **Opened his own ledgers** in 1672. d. 1719.

**THOMAS**
b.1683, d.1712 Lisbon.

**BENJAMIN** of Boreham, Essex,
b. 1693. **Partner** 1718.
m. Ellen dau. of Benjamin Richards Esq. d.1750.

Oher issue;
5 sons, 6 daughters.

**SIR RICHARD** Kt, Lord Mayor of London 1745–6,
b. 1709, **Partner** 1731, m. 1. Sarah dau. of James Tully Esq,
2. Elizabeth dau. of Edward Rust Esq., d. 1754.

**RICHARD** of Boreham, **Partner** 1758,
m. Susannah dau. of Robert Dingley,
d. 1777.

**ANNE** (Nanny),
m. her cousin Richard, =
d. 1759.

**SIR RICHARD** 1st Bart., of Barn Elms, b. 1735, **Partner** 1754, m.
1. Anne dau. of Henry Hoare, Esq. of Stourhead,
2. Frances Anne dau. of Richard Acland Esq., d. 1787.

**HENRY** (Fat Harry), b. 1744, **Partner** 1770, m.
Mary dau. of William Hoare R.A., Esq, of
Bath, the painter, d. 1785 leaving issue.

**CHARLES** of Luscombe, Devon & Adelphi
Terrace, b. 1767, **Partner** 1787,
m. Frances Dorothea dau. of Sir George
Robinson Bart., d. 1844 without issue.

**HENRY MERRIK** of Adelphi Terrace,
b. 1770, **Partner** 1791,
m. Sophia dau. of HenryThrale Esq.,
d. 1856 without issue.

**PETER RICHARD**
a barrister, b. 1772, m.
Arabella Penelope Eliza dau.
of James Greene Esq., d. 1849.

**HENRIETTA ANNE**
m. 1. Sir Thomas Dyke,
Acland 9th Bt.
2. The Hon. Matthew
Fortescue.

Henry Hugh, Charles of Luscombe & Henry Merrick known as "The Adelphi".

**SIR HUGH RICHARD** 4th Bart. of
Stourhead, b. 1787, **Partner** 1828,
m. Anne dau. of ThomasTyrwhia
Drake Esq., retired 1845, d. 1857
without issue.

**HENRY CHARLES** b. 1790,
**Partner** 1828, m. Anne Penelope
widow of Capt. John Prince & dau.
of Gen. George Ainslie, d. 1852.

**HENRY ARTHUR** b. 1804,
**Agent** 1837–45, m. Julia
Lucy dau. of Thomas Veale
Lane Esq. , d. 1873.

**PETER RICHARD**
b. 1803, **Partner** 1841,
m. Lady Sophia Marsham dau.
of 2nd Earl of Romsey, d. 1877.

**SOPHIA** b. 1814,
m. Rev. Henry
Burney of
Wavendon, d. 1872.

**REV. GEORGE EDWARD
GERARD** b. 1863,
m. Winifred Mary dau.
of Walter M. de Žoote
Esq., d. 1950 Rector of
Godstone.

**SIR HENRY AINSLIE**
5th Bart., b. 1824, **Agent**
1845–8, m. Augusta
dau. of Sir George
Clayton East Bart.,
d. 1894 leaving issue.

**SIR HENRY HUGH
ARTHUR** 6th Bart. of
Stourhead, b. 1865,
m. Alda dau. of
Henry Purcell Weston,
d. 1947 on the same
day as his wife.

**PETER MERRIK** of
Luscombe, Devon,
b. 1843, m. 1. Edith
Augusta dau. of Rev.
Edmund Strong
2. Marguerite Johanna
dau. of John Bell Esq.,
d. 1894.

**CHARLES A.R.**
b. 1847, **Partner**
1873 m. Margaret
dau. of Francis
Baring Short Esq.,
retired 1888, d. 1908.

**ISABELLA**
b. 1840,
unmarried

**CHARLOTTE**
b. 1841,
m. 1863 Algernon
de Lille Strickland
of Apperley Court
Gloucester, b. 1837,
**Partner** 1866, retired
1909, Charlotte d. 1890.

**HENRY E.
BURNEY**
**Agent**
1867,
d. 1924

**HENRY** (Harry) of
Ellisfield Manor,
Basingtoke, b. 1866,
**Partner** 1894,
m. Lady Geraldine
Mariana dau. of
Lord Augustus H.G.
Hervey, d. 1956.

**EDWARD HENRY**
b. 1872, **Partner** 1910,
m. Eleanor Mary
widow of John
Thompson of Clare
Hall, Raheny, Ireland &
dau. of M.J. Crean Esq.,
d. 1949 without issue.

**FREDERICK
HENRY** b. 1871,
**Agent** 1915–1936,
m. Dorothy dau. of
George
Christopher
Burley, d. 1955.

**REV. KENNETH
GERARD** b. 1903,
m. Joyce Aylwyne
dau. of Frederick
C. Palmer Esq.,
Rector of
Godstone, d. 1987.

**HENRY
COLT
ARTHUR**
b. 1888,
d. 1917 of
wounds
received in
action.

**PETER A.M.** of
Luscombe, Devon,
b. 1888, **Partner**
1894, m. Norah
Alicia Beresford
dau. of Dr. N.
Stewart Falls,
M.D., d. 1939.

**REGINALD ARTHUR**
b. 1878, **Partner** 1909,
m. Una Mildred dau.
of Thomas C.
Williams of
Wellington, New
Zealand, killed in
action 1918.

**ALGERNON H.P.
STRICKLAND** (Algy),
of Apperley Court,
Gloucester, b. 1863,
**Partner** 1894, m.
Mary Selina dau. of
Walter Drummond
Esq., d. 1928.

**ROLLO** b. 1903,
m. Elizabeth
Nancy dau. of
Brig. Harold
Vincent S.
Charrington
DSO MC,
d. 1983.

**ANGELA BERYL**
b. 1903, m. 1 Lt.
Col. Lionel C.
Frisby DSO
MC, 2. Eustace
J Guinness DSC
RM.
d.1990.

**SIR FREDERICK ALFRED BART.**
(Derick), Lord Mayor of London
1961–2 b. 1913, **Partner** 1947,
m. 1. Nora Mary dau. of Addison
James Wheeler Esq., d. 1973,
2. 1974 Oonah Alice dau. of Brig. Gen.
Ramsey Sladen CMG DSO d. 1980.
He died 1986 leaving issue.
(N. Mary **Agen**t 1945–57)

**CHRISTOPHER
KENNETH GERARD**
b. 1934, **Agent** 1960,
m. Caroline Mary
dau. of Charles
Gustav Westendarp
Esq., retired 1993.

**SIR PETER WILLIAM**
7th Bart. of
Luscombe,Devon,
b. 1898, **Partner** 1928,
m. 1929 Laura Ray
dau. of Sir John
Esplen 1st Bart.,
d. 1973.

**REGINALD
MERRICK**
b. 1918, **Agent**
1945–48, m.
Barbara Jean
dau. of Francis
Buckland Esq.,
d. 1984.

**ALGERNON WALTER
STRICKLAND** (Tom),
of Apperley Court,
Gloucester, b. 1891,
**Partner** 1928, m.
Lady Mary Charteris
dau. of 11th Earl of
Wemyss, d. 1938.

**MICHAEL ROLLO** b. 1944, **Partner** 1982,
m. 1. Penelope Anne Mander dau. of
Sir Charles Mander Bart.
2. Caroline Jane Abele dau. of Derek
Abele Esq. d. 2001.

**SIMON ROLLO
FRISBY** b. 1933,
**Agent** 1956–7,
m. Sara Belinda dau.
of Capt. W.H. Fox.

**SIR PETER RICHARD**
8th Bart. b. 1932, **Agent**
1956–8, m. 1. Jane dau.
of Daniel Orme Esq.
2. Katrin Alexa dau. of
late Erwin Bernstiel Esq.
3. Angela Francesca de
la Sierra dau. of Fidel
Fernando Ayarza.
d. 2004

**DAVID JOHN** 9th Bt. b. 1935,
**Partner** 1964, m. 1965 1. Vanessa
dau. of Peter Cardew Esq.
2. Virginia Victoria Graham dau.
of Michael Menzies.

**ALGERNON
GUY
STRICKLAND**
b. 1919, killed
in action 1942.

**PAMELA SABINA**
b. 1921, m. Major
Henry M. Vander
Gucht M.C.,
**Agent** 1949–57,
d. 1983 leaving
issue.

**VENETIA ELIZABETH** b. 1965, **Partner** 1996,
m. 1996 Hamish Julian Peter son of Gen. Sir Peter Leng.

**SIMON MERRIK** b. 1967, **Partner** 2001,
m. 1999 Aurélie dau. of Jean-François Catoire.

# END NOTES

## Chapter 1: Sir Richard and the Golden Bottle 1672–1719

1     Robert Tempest had taken over his business from his predecessor, the prominent gold-smith John Perryn, who had occupied premises, also known as the Golden Bottle, on or near the same site in Cheapside since 1637. The premises had been rebuilt after the Great Fire of London in 1666 and belonged to the Worshipful Company of Goldsmiths.

2     Peter Temin and Hans-Joachim Voth: 'Banking as an Emerging Technology: Hoare's Bank 1702-1742', MIT *Economics Department Working Paper* (2003).

3     On 17 March 1712 John Hoare was sworn in as a 'Common Measurer of all manner of Woollen Cloths, Friezes, Cottons, Bays, Stuffs and other things belonging to the Old and New draperies within the City of London'. This sinecure post was in the gift of the Lord Mayor, which his father was at the time.

4     See Peter Temin and Hans-Joachim Voth: 'The Speed of the Financial Revolution. Evidence from Hoare's Bank', MIT *Economics Department Working Paper* (2003).

5     On the flyleaf of a ledger in the Bank, dated 1690, which belonged to Sir William Benson, a close associate of Richard's and father-in-law to his son Henry, is a simple rhyme which could have been written as a tribute to his friend and banker:

> 'Thrice happy he who in middle state
>
> Feils neither want nor studies to be great
>
> Eats drinks and lives at home with ease
>
> Whilst warlike monarchs cross ye rorering seas.'

6     See entry for Richard Hoare in *History of Parliament: the House of Commons*, vol. 1690-1715, edited by Cruikshanks, Handley and Hayton.

## Chapter 2: Good Henry and the Charities 1718–1725

1     The house on the east side had been rebuilt after the Great Fire and was presumably two houses, as the property is referred to as 'Three Flower de Luce' and 'The Bell and Dragon'. Before the Fire the premises had also been two distinct properties one of which was called 'The Black Spread Eagle'. The first official grant of arms to the family of Sir Richard Hoare was to his grandson Henry 'The Magnificent' in 1776, and the shield in the coat of arms displayed a silver double-headed eagle on a black background within an 'engrailed' silver border. It is likely that this device had been used unofficially by the family long before this time in com-mon with another branch of the family who came from County Cork and from whom James Hoare, Comptroller of the Mint in Richard's day, was descended. (This branch also developed a strong banking tradition, quite independently of the Golden Bottle, and were in partnership in Lombard Street in the nineteenth century as Barnett, Hill and Hoare before their acquisi-tion by Lloyds Bank in 1884.) Although we cannot be precise about the date that the double-headed eagle was adopted by the Hoares, if it was not until after their removal to Fleet

Street, it is tempting to think that they were inspired by the old 'Black Spread Eagle' to take it as their device.

2    Hoare's trading position in South Sea Company stock has been extensively analysed by Peter Temin and Hans-Joachim Voth in 'Riding the South Sea Bubble', MIT *Economics Department Working Paper* (2003).

3    The other five bishops were George Smallridge, John Robinson, Thomas Sherlock, Robert Moss, William Dawes. Other lawyers included Francis Annesley, Henry Box, Whitlock Bulstrode and Edward Jennings, all members of the Inner Temple. John Cass and Thomas Crosse, both elected for the City and Westminster in 1710, contributed to the High Tory representation on Queen Anne's Commission.

4    In the first two decades of the eighteenth century a group of fewer than fifteen members attended the meetings, Sir Richard and Henry Hoare among them, accompanied by their colleagues from the Commission For Fifty New Churches: Robert Nelson, Edward Jennings, William Melmoth and a German Pietist priest Anton Boehme. He was a pupil of Dr August Hermann Francke, a professor of oriental languages at the University of Halle, near Leipzig.

One of Francke's greatest achievements was the sending of the first Protestant mission to India, known as the Mission to the Malabar Coast, with the support of the Lutheran King of Denmark and the SPG in England. Henry left a legacy of £50 in his will 'for the better support and furtherance of the charitable designs of the propagation of the Gospel in the east Indies'. The Mission to Malabar, which opened its account at the Bank in 1711 and remained on the books until 1875, made history by initiating and completing a translation of the Bible into Tamil, the first such translation into any Indian language.

5    The Stourtons had been a family of consequence in the neighbourhood since Saxon times. The decline in their fortunes began in the 16th century and as Catholics they were exposed to danger and discrimination over the next hundred years. The tenth baron was imprisoned for his supposed connection with the Gunpowder Plot in 1605, and the Royalist eleventh baron escaped from Stourton House when it was destroyed by the Parliamentarians in 1644. The twelfth baron lost his seat in the House of Lords under the Test Act of 1673, and his heir followed James II into exile leaving a heavily mortgaged estate and a ruined house. The arms of the Stourton family, 'sable, a bend or, between six fountains' refer to the springs in the valley below the house known as 'Six Wells Bottom' which had been identified as the source of the river Stour and gave to the new owner of the estate the idea for a suitable new name.

6    See Peter Temin and Hans-Joachim Voth: 'Banking as an Emerging Technology: Hoare's Bank 1702-1742', MIT *Economics Department Working Paper* (2003).

## Chapter 3: Henry the Magnificent and the Paradise of Stourhead 1725–1783

1    On his brother's death in 1725, Benjamin aged thirty-one, and his brother's son Henry ('The Magnificent') aged nineteen took equal shares of the main part of the profits while Christopher Arnold received a one-eighth share. When Good Henry's second son Richard entered the partnership in 1731 at the age of twenty-two, he too received one-eighth share. Two years later a new partnership agreement was drawn up and Henry, at twenty-seven became senior partner on half profits, while his uncle Benjamin took a quarter and Richard and Christopher Arnold received one-eighth each. For Benjamin this represented a sum of between £6500-£7500 per annum.

2    Woodbridge, Kenneth: *Landscape and Antiquity, Aspects of English Culture at Stourhead 1718-1838* (1970). 'In 1739 and 1740 [Henry] paid £3750 to agents through whom he bought works of art on a scale he never repeated … it is impossible to say for certain what the paintings were.' In Horace Walpole's 'Journal of Visits to Country Seats' 1751-84, (*Walpole Society Annual XVI*, 1927-28, ed: Paget Toynbee) Walpole 'later mentioned' pictures by Annibale Carracci, Domenichino, Dolci and Maratta, two by Poussin, and one by Gaspar, one by Claude and two by Rembrandt, two by Sebastiano Ricci: Italian scenes by Marco Ricci, Pannini, Canaletto, Anesi and 'various other paintings by seventeenth and eighteenth century masters …'.

3    Ibid., Woodbridge gives a full description and analysis of the creation of 'Henry Hoare's Paradise'. For a summary see his: *The Stourhead Landscape*, (1974).

4    Spence, Joseph: *Observations*, (ed: J M Osborn 1966), item 1105.

5    Letter from Henry Hoare to Lady Bruce 23 October 1762 in the possession of the Earl of Cardigan. Quoted in Woodbridge, op. cit. pp52-53.

6    Thacker, Christopher: *Building Towers, Forming Gardens. Landscaping by Hamilton, Hoare and Beckford* (2002) pp. 25-26.

7    Henry drew a substantial amount each year from the Bank although this varied enormously. On average, during the period 1750-85, following Benjamin's death, it was between £10,000 and £15,000 a year with lows of below £5000 in the 1750s and exceptional highs of £18,000 in the mid 1760s.

8    A large number of the goldsmith-bankers disappeared after the South Sea Bubble but overall, in the period 1725-1785, their numbers increased from twenty-four to fifty-two, although any precise figures have to be treated with caution since there were no reliable listings and individual bankers and their banking houses often appeared as separ-ate entries.

9    For discussion on private banking in the 18th century see: Joslin, D M, London Private Bankers 1720-1785, *Economic History Review*, 2nd series, vol. VII, No.2 1954 and Melton, Frank T : Deposit Banking in London 1700-1790, *EHR*, vol.XXV, No. 3 1986.

10    Kelch, Ray: *Newcastle, A Duke Without Money: Thomas Pelham Holles 1693-1768* (1974).

11    Letter from Henry Hoare to Lord Bruce, undated. Tottenham House Archive (Savernake), Wiltshire Record Office. Quoted in Woodbridge op. cit., p. 51.

12    Letter from Henry Hoare to Lord Bruce 13 Dec. 1765. Hoare of Stourhead Papers T36 Wiltshire Record Office. Quoted in Newby, Evelyn: *William Hoare of Bath 1707-92* (1990) p.14.

13    Henry's next-door neighbours, at No. 42, were, successively, the bankers Sir Robert, Sir Francis and Samuel Child whose premises in Fleet Street were only a stone's throw away from the Golden Bottle.

14    Smith, Eric E F: *Clapham* (1976) p.44.

15    Henry of Mitcham's entry into the Bank was triggered by the death of his cousin, Richard of Boreham, in 1777 whose 2000 shares were divided between young Henry and Richard of Barn Elms. Henry the Magnificent also gave Fat Harry 500 of his shares at that time to give him twice the amount of the new entrant.

16    See Clay C G A: Henry Hoare, Banker, his Family, and the Stourhead Estate. From: *Landowners, Capitalists and Entrepreneurs, Essays for Sir John Habakkuk* (1974).

## Chapter 4: Henry of Mitcham and the Napoleonic Wars 1778–1828

1    Under Harry's regime of maintaining strict order and regularity in the conduct of business at Fleet Street their duties were clearly set out. 'It is determined that Hugh Junior and Charles Junior shall examine the notes and the check ledgers and have the charge of the keys by rotation each alternate fortnight – Both to be in attendance during the hours of business unless leave of absence is granted by a senior partner. Hugh Junior is to continue to cast the ledgers and post the Ledgers of personal securities as heretofore and to have charge of checking and receiving interest on India Bonds – The Cash books during Charles Senior and Merrik's absence to be cast by Hugh Junior or Charles Junior according to the period of their several attendances which is likewise to mark the time for their several attendances in the City for the purpose of transferring stock etc Charles Junior to continue making entries from the Vouchers in the Cash Book, to receive monies from the Treasury and other Publick Offices and to receive the principal and interest of Exchequer Bills paid off.'

## Chapter 5: The Adelphi Hoares and the Red Lion 1828–1866

1    The journal, which he kept of his six-year sojourn on the continent, was written up in his later publication *Recollections Abroad: Journals of Tours on the Continent, 1785-91* (1815-18) and although he never went overseas again he continued the habit of travelling and recording in the British Isles, showing a particular fondness for Wales, where he bought a fishing lodge at Bala. His most ambitious works of scholarship were the illustrated folio volumes he researched, wrote and published on his own county. The first to appear was *The Ancient History of South Wiltshire*, which caused the *Quarterly Review* to comment in 1810: 'No antiquary had ever the same means or opportunities before Sir Richard Hoare, and no-one ever availed himself more entirely of the advantages which he possesses.' It was followed by *The Ancient History of North Wiltshire* and in 1822 by the first instalment of a part-work, *The History of Modern Wiltshire*, eventually bound in six volumes and completed after his death in 1844. Colt was assisted by a team of collaborators and they gathered together to work with him in his magnificent library at Stourhead.

2    Black, Iain: Private Banking in London's West End. *The London Journal* 28(1) pp. 25-59 (2003).

3    Haslam, Richard: Hoare's Bank, *Country Life* (27 January 1994).

4    Parker had only established his practice in 1826 but he was already engaged in what was to be the major work of his life: the adaptation of Italian villa forms for modern use in an English climate. His designs were published in 1832 under the (shortened) title of: *Villa Rustica*. In designing the Bank, Parker shifted his focus from rural to urban building but he retained his admiration for the Italian model which he used to great effect.

5    Repton submitted his proposed designs in one of his 'Red Books' in which, living up to his reputation for flattery, he chose to address his preface to Dorothea as if casting her in the role of muse: 'I venture to address this small volume to you as it is mor particularly for your accommodation and convenience that Mr Hoare has made the choice of the situation of Luscombe.'

6    It is possible Henry Ainslie had an illegitimate son, William Richard, born September 1857. He was sent out to Raincliff, New Zealand as a young man.

## Chapter 6: The Black Sheep: Henry Junior and Charlie Arthur 1866–1885

1       Henry junior wrote to Algernon Strickland, ' the seniors were very well off and the juniors had more than they wanted while the middle men if they were married were comparative paupers … many of our best clerks left and the others grumbled.'

2       In the absence of any formal agreement Henry's memorandum, which remained unsigned by Peter Richard, provided the basis for the Partnership Agreement which was written after Henry's death in 1866. This new agreement also remained unsigned by Peter Richard and, though its terms became effective, it remained in draft form until new articles were signed in 1874.

3       Agneta Bevan's father, Lord Kinnaird, was a partner in the Pall Mall bank, Messrs Bouverie, Ransom and Co.

4       As his son, Frederick, put it, in a letter to his elder brother, Harry, in 1951: 'what Leonard Harper [the agent] got out of Pips [Henry] what with Meadowbank and Raincliff is nobody's business.'

5       Butler to his friend Eliza Savage on 15 March 1874.

6       In the 'Observations' attached to the order for Henry's bankruptcy there appeared a brief statement summarizing the background to the case: ' The bankrupt states that since 1874 when he retired from a firm of bankers in which he had for some years been a partner, he has had no regular business or occupation, but has been engaged in connection with his estates and properties and also various Companies and undertakings in which he has been financially interested. He attributes his insolvency to losses by investments in Companies and undertakings which have proved unsuccessful; to the heavy outlay, interest and outgoings in respect of his landed property, particularly an estate in New Zealand, having largely exceeded the returns; and to depreciation in the value of his properties.'

7       On the day The Times reported the case of Kingscote v Sumner and Hoare, the artist William Dobson called at the Bank to withdraw his balance and collect his securities, which Henry Tilden handed over to him in person.

## Chapter 7: Recovery and War 1885–1918

1       After losing £21 million, through the failure of the Buenos Aires Water Supply and Drainage Company, Barings Bank was on the point of suspending payment when it was rescued by a concerted effort of support by the Bank of England in conjunction with leading joint stock and private banks. Hoare's stood guarantee for £50,000 which was subsequently cancelled by the Bank of England in March 1893.

2       Harry left a lasting memorial at Raincliff. During a short stay there before he joined the Bank, he worked on his father's ambitious scheme for a plantation of specimen trees on the land immediately around the homestead, including a magnificent avenue of lime trees leading to the house. Every evening was spent preparing cuttings to start a tree nursery. The planting was developed and continued after he left and has survived to this day as one of the most notable features of a much reduced estate.

3       The story of the 'Mercury' is told in Morris, Ronald: The Captain's Lady (1985).

## Chapter 8: Keeping Independent; Surviving the Blitz 1919–1945

1    Alfred, whose entire working career at the Bank had been overshadowed by the fall-out from Henry's speculations and Charlie Arthur's adulterous affair, wrote to Algy in February 1918 when survival was uppermost in everyone's minds. One way of ensuring continuity was to bring in sleeping partners to increase the capital in the Bank, 'preferably from the Hoare family but by no means excluding their relations by marriage.' He guessed that 'Stourhead Harry' ( Sir Henry Arthur Hoare 6th Bt ) would probably like to be one of them as well as 'the daughters both of Harry and yourself.' If they carried on as they were, all experience and recent history had shown, ' how readily a Partner once admitted may play the fool and if he has an important fraction of the capital of the institution so much the worse'. Algy's reply to this suggestion is not known and no record of the matter being discussed appears in the Partners' Memorandum Book at the time.

2    In 1939 Glyn Mills was in turn bought by the Royal Bank of Scotland, who thereby became the owners of three of the four banks from Vesey Holt's scheme of 1920.

3    A complete account of the strike appeared in the *London Strike Newspaper*, which was placed in the museum as a record.

4    In 1925 it was thought prudent to write out a set of rules for incoming 'Agents and Probationers' covering such issues as the dining arrangements, use of the Drawing Room when a Partner's wife was in residence, the entertainment of friends and other matters of etiquette. The 'new rules' perpetuated in every detail the arrangements already in force from the previous generation but any strain suffered from living by the 'rule book' for twenty-four hours a day was somewhat alleviated by the continued standard holiday en-titlement of eighty working days a year.

## Chapter 9: The Show Goes On 1945–2005

1    The 'Quintin School' is now called the Quintin Kynaston School.

2    Edward, Rennie's second son, is the only Agent in the Bank in 2005. He is the last member of the family to have been born in the house at Stourhead.

3    One of Derick's more popular stories concerned the case of the 'Cardinal's Jewels'. Elizabeth, Countess of Pembroke, distrusted her son, Robert, Earl of Pembroke, who was known as a 'rake and a profligate'. In 1829 she deposited a locked casket at Hoare's Bank which remained there, forgotten by the family, until 1911 when the Partners, in a review of the contents of their vaults, returned it to Wilton unopened. The key had been lost, so the lid was forced open and inside lay a fantastic gem collection which had once been the proper-ty of Cardinal Mazarin of France. The family were mystified as to the origin of these jewels but the motive behind the Countess's actions was clear. She kept the jewels a secret from her son, and in depositing them at the Bank she could rest assured that he would never know of their existence. If he had been able to lay his hands on them they would have been sold.

4    In 1974 the 'Big Four' clearing banks were Barclays, Lloyds, Midland and National Westminster. The term had been in use since 1969.

5    The establishment of a fully integrated computerized banking system has been swift. Hoare's were slow to start – in the 1970s they had no mainframe computer – but this has reduced the complications involved in the transfer of data from 'legacy systems'. The first Information Technology strategist was appointed in 1990 and the Information Technology Department is currently the biggest department in the Bank in terms of personnel.

# ACKNOWLEDGEMENTS

I would like to thank the Partners of Hoare's Bank, and members of the family, without whose constant support and encouragement this book would never have been written. I am enormously grateful to those numerous members of staff, past and present, who have provided me with essential material describing life outside the Partners' Room. Rennie Hoare's published and unpublished work has been an invaluable source for me as have the anecdotal memoirs of Sir Frederick Hoare. Caromy Hoare had the vision to see that a contemporary account of the extraordinary phenomenon that is Hoare's Bank might appeal to a more general readership. Over the years the Bank's archives have been a useful source of information for countless researchers and I would like to take this opportunity to express my appreciation of the work they have done which has given depth and breadth to our understanding of the Bank's history. Barbara Sands and Pamela Hunter have patiently dealt with my own enquiries and their presence at the Bank has enabled me to write a good deal of this, at home, in the country, and for that I am greatly indebted to them. Lastly I would like to thank Nick Robinson, Roger Hudson and Richard Haslam whose expertise has played such a necessary part in shaping this book.

Victoria Hutchings

## Picture Credits

**The Art Archive** 37, 56. **Jane Austen Memorial Trust** 108. **Bridgeman Art Library**/Ashmolean Museum, University of Oxford 98;/Coram Foundation, Foundling Hospital Museum, London 26, 43;/Courtauld Institute of Art Gallery 100;/Fitzwilliam Museum, University of Cambridge 175 top;/Guildhall Library, Corporation of London 38;/The Earl of Pembroke, Wilton House, Wilts 78-79;/Private Collections 28, 63;/Private Collection/Archives Charmet 174;/Private Collection/The Stapleton Collection 195 top;/Royal Academy of Arts 77 bottom left;/San Diego Museum of Art, USA 59;/Victoria Art Gallery, Bath and North East Somerset Council 62;/Wallace Collection, London 83;/Wimbledon Society Museum of Local History, London 95;/Yale Center for British Art, Paul Mellon Collection, USA 90-91. **Julian Calder** 218, 228-229. **Cromwell Museum, Huntingdon** 13. **Mary Evans Picture Library** 17. **The Fletcher Family** (on loan to Hoare's Bank)/ photo Philip de Bay 77 bottom right. **Getty Images**/Hulton 99. **Hoare's Bank** 2, 24, 41, 52-53, 55, 72, 73 top, 86, 87, 88, 92, 93, 111, 116, 117 top, 120, 127, 128, 136, 140, 142, 143, 145, 150, 151, 155, 157, 160-161, 163, 166, 171 top, 171 bottom, 173, 176, 186, 188, 192,193, 197 bottom, 200, 201, 202, 203, 205, 206, 207, 208, 209, 210, 211, 213, 214 left, 214 right, 215, 217, 220, 222/ photo Country Life 9, 112 top, 197 top, 219/photo Philip de Bay 11 top, 11 bottom, 12, 14, 18, 25, 27, 32, 34, 35, 40, 44, 45, 46, 50 top, 50 bottom, 58 top, 58 bottom, 67, 73 bottom, 74 top, 74 bottom, 78, 79, 80, 84, 97, 103, 106, 109, 112 bottom, 113, 114, 115, 117 bottom, 124, 134, 135, 138, 141, 158, 170, 175 bottom, 181 top, 181 bottom, 182, 183, 190, 204, 221, 224, 225/photo National Trust 33, 48, 71. **Sir David Hoare** 122-123;/photo Philip de Bay 118 top, 118 bottom, 119, 121. **The President and Fellows of Magdalen College, Oxford**/photo Nick Cistone 15. **The Mavor Family** (on loan to Hoare's Bank)/photo Hoare's Bank 10. **John Murray Collection** 102 bottom. **National Maritime Museum, London** 180 top, 180 bottom. **National Portrait Gallery, London** 16, 29, 51, 60, 64, 102 top, 130, 131, 152. **National Trust Photo Library**/Killerton House/photo John Hammond 132;/Stourhead House/photo Bill Batten 82,/photo John Bethell 75 left,/photo John Hammond 75 right, 110. **St Dunstan's in the West**/photo Philip de Bay 31. **Trustees of the Savernake Estate** 68, 69. **Stourhead House**/photo Richard Pink 76, 77 top. **Trinity Hospice**/photo Rob Moore 179. **Victoria Art Gallery, Bath and North East Somerset Council** 195 bottom.

# INDEX